Crossing Borders in University Learning and Teaching

Uncovering aspects of university culture which are often hidden or misunderstood, this book brings together international perspectives, showing the matches and mismatches between experience and expectation, as both staff and student face new academic cultures.

Drawing on the stories of students and members of staff in the higher education sector as starting points for analysis, this book considers aspects such as the dynamics and pragmatics of university settings, from tutorial to lecture; the assignment and multiple text types from reflective logs to essays; different interpretations of grades, grading and feedback. Topics are explored with examples from critical incidents and narratives in international contexts – both where staff or students cross cultures and borders, and where they are functioning within the university culture with which they are most familiar.

Ideal both for those new to learning and teaching in higher education, and those seeking to refresh their practice, this must-read book uses case studies and narratives to illustrate key challenges academics and students face. With consideration given to learning across cultures, the narratives and topics lead to enquiries which the reader can ask and research for themselves to find helpful answers to explain their own university experiences.

Jane Spiro is Professor in Education and TESOL at Oxford Brookes University, UK.

Crossing Borders in University Learning and Teaching
Navigating Hidden Cultures

Jane Spiro

LONDON AND NEW YORK

Cover image: © Getty Images

First published 2022
by Routledge
2 Park Square, Milton Park, Abingdon, Oxon OX14 4RN

and by Routledge
605 Third Avenue, New York, NY 10158

Routledge is an imprint of the Taylor & Francis Group, an informa business

© 2022 Jane Spiro

The right of Jane Spiro to be identified as author of this work has been asserted by her in accordance with sections 77 and 78 of the Copyright, Designs and Patents Act 1988.

All rights reserved. No part of this book may be reprinted or reproduced or utilised in any form or by any electronic, mechanical, or other means, now known or hereafter invented, including photocopying and recording, or in any information storage or retrieval system, without permission in writing from the publishers.

Trademark notice: Product or corporate names may be trademarks or registered trademarks, and are used only for identification and explanation without intent to infringe.

British Library Cataloguing-in-Publication Data
A catalogue record for this book is available from the British Library

Library of Congress Cataloging-in-Publication Data
Names: Spiro, Jane, author.
Title: Crossing borders in university learning and teaching : navigating hidden cultures / Jane Spiro.
Description: Abingdon, Oxon ; New York, NY : Routledge, 2022. | Includes bibliographical references and index.
Identifiers: LCCN 2021040875 (print) | LCCN 2021040876 (ebook) | ISBN 9781138387416 (hardback) | ISBN 9781138387430 (paperback) | ISBN 9780429426261 (ebook)
Subjects: LCSH: College environment. | College students--Social conditions. | Multicultural education. | College teaching. | Universities and colleges--Social aspects.
Classification: LCC LB2324 .S66 2022 (print) | LCC LB2324 (ebook) | DDC 370.117--dc23/eng/20211022
LC record available at https://lccn.loc.gov/2021040875
LC ebook record available at https://lccn.loc.gov/2021040876

ISBN: 978-1-138-38741-6 (hbk)
ISBN: 978-1-138-38743-0 (pbk)
ISBN: 978-0-429-42626-1 (ebk)

DOI: 10.4324/9780429426261

Typeset in Times New Roman
by Taylor & Francis Books

Contents

List of tables	vi
List of vignettes	viii
Acknowledgements	x

1	Crossing study borders: From discomfort to noticing	1
2	Being a student: Who am I as a learner?	15
3	Being a higher education teacher: Who am I as an educator?	37
4	Ways of learning: How do I learn?	58
5	Ways of knowing: What does it mean to know something?	81
6	Learning events: What happens in learning/teaching events?	103
7	Learning spaces: How do I experience campus and virtual spaces?	124
8	Kinds of assessment: What do learning and assessment activities mean?	144
9	Kinds of feedback: What does feedback mean?	169
10	Navigating study cultures: From noticing to learning maps	193

Index	212

Tables

2.1	Two approaches to intercultural transition	30
2.2	Becoming an ethnographer of your learning	33
3.1	University types and characteristics (based on Finkelstein et al., 2014, pp. 52–53)	51
3.2	Expectation gaps	56
4.1	Learning situation analysis	78
5.1	Analysing subject disciplines (derived from Becher and Trowler, 2001)	95
5.2	Hidden and explicit knowledge	98
5.3	Teaching sessions and learning tasks: analysing the match	98
6.1	Classroom modes of discourse (Walsh, 2011, p. 113)	114
6.2	Three kinds of talk (derived from Osborn et al., 2003, p. 215 and Walsh, 2011, p. 113)	115
6.3	Learning events and subject disciplines	118
6.4	Defining learning events	120
6.5	Defining the learning contract	120
6.6	Defining student talk	121
7.1	Three ways of looking at space (derived from Lefebvre in Brown, 2020)	131
7.2	The DEEP concept of spaces	134
7.3	Campus places	138
7.4	Optimal learning conditions	139
7.5	Optimal conditions in virtual learning	141
7.6	Making the transition from campus to virtual spaces	142
8.1.	The Cognitive Process Dimension – categories, cognitive processes (and alternative names) (CELT, 2021)	156
8.2	Six questions about task types: derived from assessment strategies in Scottish higher education (Hounsell et al., 1996) and from Gillett and Hammond (2009)	157
8.3	Five assessment purposes mapped against genres (derived from Nesi (2012), Gillett and Hammond (2009) and Bloom (1956))	159
8.4	Four discourse tools for analysing texts	161

8.5	Discourse question 1. How are the different parts (moves) indicated and what is their purpose?	162
8.6	Discourse question 2. Is there a reflective I and how does the author reveal or occlude her presence?	162
8.7	Discourse question 3. How and where are opinion/judgement/values revealed?	163
8.8	Discourse question 4. How are other authors/literature cited and referenced?	163
8.9	Using the four discourse questions	164
9.1	Kinds of feedback	188
9.2	Feedback preferences	189
9.3	Kinds of grades	189
10.1	Learning map 1: Prepare for differences	196
10.2	Learning map 2: Grice's cooperative principle and the pragmatics of asking questions (Grice, 1975; Murray, 2010)	197
10.3	Learning map 3: Questions and answers – teasing out tacit knowledge	199
10.4	Learning map 4: A noticing map (from Spiro, 2013, p.175)	201
10.5	Learning map 5: Help-seeking and help-giving	203
10.6	Learning map 6: Changing habits and Schon's moments of reflection (Schon, 1983)	205
10.7	Learning map 7: Growth mindset and learning independence	207
10.8	Learning map 8: Intercultural not international (Byram's savoirs, 1995 and Mader's intercultural abilities, 2010)	209

Vignettes

Induction and first encounter: Faisal	8
Changing university contexts: Cora	8
Changing university contexts: Cora	49
Teacher and student communication: Tara and Bashir	72
Changing subject disciplines: Mila	91
Interpreting learning events: Akio	113
Experiencing campus spaces: Carmella and Tanya	130
Navigating assessment types : Faisal	154
Interpreting feedback: Lihua	181

For Miecik Szpiro who crossed a border and became Martin Spiro 1922–2016.

Wherever I have lived,
walking out of the front door
every morning
means crossing over
to a foreign country.

Imtiaz Dharker

Acknowledgements

Many thanks to students who have provided inspiration and wisdom for this book in the following classes between 2011 and 2021: *Reflective Professional Development, Developing MA Literacies, Writing for Academic Practice, Language Learning and Creativity, ELT Changing Methodologies.* Their experiences and stories took me to almost every country in the world.

National and international networks have been helpful in introducing me to participants who have made rich contributions to this book: *National Teaching Fellowship network UK; Practitioner-Researchers network, the IATEFL Creative C-group.*

Brookes Teaching Fellowships have generously funded the following projects reported in this book: *Fostering Interculturality, Reflection in the Round.*

A National Teaching Fellowship funded the *Learning Interconnectedness* project and provided the support for researching schools with inspirational international policies, including Hawai'i.

Thanks to the British Council for giving me the opportunity to live, travel and work as a language educator in Hungary, Poland, India, Japan, Mexico, Egypt; and to Oxford University Press for giving me the chance to meet language educators in Malaysia, Sweden, Finland, Ireland, Croatia. These experiences planted the first seeds that resulted in this book.

The Westminster Trust funded a sabbatical during 2020 to gather insider stories for the *Crossing Study Borders* project. As this coincided with the covid year indoors, these interviews all took place online, so thanks to my 24 participants who generously gave time from their own homes to tell their stories.

Most of all thanks to the kindness of John who waited patiently for me to finish this book and nourished me in all ways on the journey.

1 Crossing study borders
From discomfort to noticing

The transition into higher education constitutes a learning leap, no matter how prepared a student might feel. Even if previous study has paved the way in terms of disciplinary content, and even if the higher education institution sits geographically around the corner, still there are new expectations for everyone: how one learns, what constitutes learning, what the required outcomes are, and what takes place inside and outside formal learning. How much more might there be to consider, then, when the transition is to a place that is entirely new, geographically, linguistically or culturally. In one context, questions in a lecture may be a sign of engagement whilst in another, of disrespect for the speaker. One institution might deem collaboration with peers to be developmental whilst another might regard it as a disciplinary offence. In one college a seminar may be a group of six and in another a theatre of a hundred students. Yet these may be just the visible face of much deeper differences which lie under the surface. These hidden hazards are often compared to an iceberg. What is seen is just the starting point, but to navigate these new waters safely, it is critical to appreciate what is hidden, and to have the tools of discovery to manage potential hazards.

Learning from new physical, linguistic and cultural places has been approached in several very different ways. The *'big C' approach* considers cultures as distinctive units of knowledge that can be easily packaged and taught. These are the aspects deemed typical to places, whether based on myth, stereotype or propaganda: flamenco in Spain, sushi in Japan or gondolas in Italy. Though visible and easy to illustrate, they are very far from a useful indicator of the place itself. These 'soundbites' of a culture lack nuance, give a single snapshot of reality, and are dismissive of different histories, complexities and multiplicities. Information is assumed to be fixed, rather than what one might learn from moment to moment, and from different people and interactions. Importantly too, this kind of knowledge is of very limited practical value in living day by day in a new culture.

A second approach focuses instead on the skills and strategies of interpreting a culture and being alert to the nuance of each situation. *Intercultural competence* involves the capacity to move sensitively and intelligently from one cultural context to another, interpreting clues in order to act appropriately on a

DOI: 10.4324/9780429426261-1

situation-by-situation basis. These competences have been categorised in several ways. Byram (1997) conceived of intercultural competence as five 'ways of knowing', which include the skills of critical awareness, discovery through interaction, interpreting and open-mindedness. Tests of intercultural competence have suggested eight conditions, to include: knowing, for example how institutions work; personal qualities such as tolerance of ambiguity and openness to difference; capacity to respond to situations; and specific communication skills such as awareness of politeness strategies and taboos (Camerer, 2014). These focus not only on the new culture to be negotiated, but on the learner themselves in this setting, and the openness and adaptability of their responses.

Pragmatics is one subset of this competence, which focuses on linguistic and non-linguistic interactions. Pragmatics involves seeking out the conventions and understandings which lie under the surface of language, such as noticing how the dynamics change when a more senior person in age or role joins the conversation, or how question and answer exchanges differ in a tutorial versus a lecture. A pragmatics approach teases out the qualities of well-functioning conversations and explores the sources of dysfunctional interactions to identify the building blocks of successful communication. Some teachers and researchers view these competences as enabling learners not only to use other languages competently, but to live and work adaptably in any part of the world.

This book aims to analyse real stories of students crossing learning and teaching cultures, through the lens of intercultural awareness and pragmatics. The stories represent a wide diversity of voices, both learners and teachers, first degree and postgraduate, first, second and third languages or cultures. However, they all have two things in common. Firstly, all the stories describe first encounters with a new learning situation, and benefit from seeing through fresh eyes. Secondly, all the stories describe moments of collision, when something shocked, surprised or discomforted. Being uncomfortable is a useful indicator that some new insight might be lurking under the surface. The two learning situations below are examples of mistakes being made which reveal both the assumptions of the first learning setting, and the different values of the second.

1   A student who is having problems completing her assignment and has missed several classes chooses another student in the class and asks if she can borrow his notes.
2   A new teacher meeting her class for the first time tells them to address her by her first name only, and without any title (e.g. Dr, Mrs, Professor).

What are the consequences of 'reading' these situations wrongly? The students here, Maurice and Shelley, represent the composite experience of several students who shared their stories in the Crossing Study Borders project: Maurice who lent his study notes, and Shelley who borrowed them.

Maurice was a supportive and kind student who helped a fellow student by lending her all his assignment notes. To his horror, he was accused of 'collusion' and involved in a disciplinary procedure for 'academic misconduct' when it emerged that his assignment and hers had identical passages and references.

> I was shocked that what I did was bad. I thought it was good to ask others for help and to choose a good student to help you. This was new for me and I did not have an idea of doing wrong.
>
> (Shelley)

In explaining the discomfort of these students, it is possible to see a mismatch in the social rules familiar to them, and in their new study situation. For Maurice, his former study situation had involved a great deal of group work and exchange of ideas, so he was accustomed to sharing and had been trained in the ground rules of acceptable collaboration from his former learning. Conversely, for Shelley, the idea of collaboration between students was entirely new. Her course leaders had encouraged the idea of learning from others and set up groups for peer-evaluation of written work. In addition, she had been encouraged to 'ask a native-speaker' to proofread her work. However, there had been no explicit explanation of the boundaries of sharing or collaboration, and the whole practice seemed to give her unlimited permission to receive support from others. Shelley was devastated to learn that what she had done constituted misconduct and placed Maurice as well as herself at risk.

In the second situation above, the student has come to 'notice' that forms of address are creating a block for her.

> When our programme leader told us to call her by her first name I couldn't believe it. It seemed so rude. So for a while I didn't call her anything. Then I realised that was perhaps even more rude so eventually I did do this but it never felt right.
>
> (Alessia)

For Alessia in her home setting in Brazil, the professor/teacher is marked for seniority through title. To address him/her in the same way as fellow students are addressed is not only a form of disrespect but does not properly differentiate the tutor from the students. This differentiation between roles was a significant factor in her former learning, as tutors were deemed to be the ones with knowledge, power and jurisdiction over success. Meanwhile, the tutor in this setting (Janet), aimed to create an atmosphere in which students and teachers were peers in the process of learning, both involved in the evaluation of success, and both equal participants in making the class sessions effective. She did not want to be named in a way that would set up distance and power between herself and her students.

Should these kinds of cultural differences be taught, or will any teacher or learner naturally transfer from the first to the second culture? This book takes the view that the values and attitudes that underlie these differences are rarely made explicit, partly because they may seem self-evident to those who live with them daily. When we move into a new landscape, we see it with fresh eyes; the surprises, collisions and failures of expectation highlight not only our new setting but throw a light on where we have travelled from as well. This book explores stories of fresh arrival in learning settings, and moments of surprise or discomfort. Through these stories we ask the questions: what underlying social 'rules' and assumptions are revealed? What attitudes to learning and teaching underlie these assumptions? As students or teachers, how might it be possible to navigate these differences successfully?

Ways of learning about higher education hidden cultures

This book aims to capture the distinctiveness of higher education settings by drawing on these moments of mismatch, discomfort, or surprise, as experienced by learners and teachers who have made transitions from one culture to another. Their stories are threaded throughout the book and illustrate critical moments of realisation or collision. Whilst we are in our comfort zone, or where our experience matches our assumptions, the ingredients that make up our comfort are difficult to recognise. It is when these assumptions are challenged and tested that we realise what they are.

The book derives its knowledge from 128 student and teacher stories gathered through learning diaries, field notes, interviews and focus groups between 2011 and 2021, and across four separate projects. These are:

- *Reflection in the Round* (RIR) with 38 student learning diaries and 10 annual focus groups of students on one-year postgraduate programmes between 2011 and 2020. In addition, teacher field notes track learning activities and learner responses during the same period. The project is published as Spiro (2013) and crystallised into teaching materials as Williams, Wooliams and Spiro (2020).
- *Fostering Interculturality* (FIC) with 16 participants, both staff and students, who identified as international, discussing their experience of crossing cultures in semi-structured interviews and focus groups. This project is published as Clifford et al., (2011) and Spiro et al., (2012).
- *Learning Interconnectedness* (LIC) with 50 international first degree students between 2010 and 2014 sharing weekly journals about their experiences of learning across cultures and languages. In addition, teacher field notes track cross-cultural learning activities and learner responses in the same period, 2010 to 2014 (Spiro, 2014).
- *Crossing Study Borders* (CSB) with 24 staff and students who identified as having crossed borders in learning and teaching, interviewed between 2020 and 2021 and published here for the first time.

The new participants in Crossing Study Borders were given pseudonyms, and their stories are threaded throughout the book; so these participants will be identified and differentiated. Other participants are named according to the study in which they participated.

A second source of knowledge are studies of higher education pedagogies, the student voice, and the cultural pragmatics of learning and teaching, published in international journals primarily between 1990 and 2021, but including earlier literature which is seminal and remains influential. This literature is a means by which the stories of learning transitions are contextualised, so each individual experience is recognised as a collective one, and becomes a means to corroborate, critique or expand on what is already in the literature.

Learning from insider voices

The insider voices of those who have studied, lived, taught and travelled between learning settings form the sources of knowledge in this book. Many do not identify with higher education learning, or the setting in which they study, and would not describe themselves as 'insiders' in any sense. We are using this term in the strictest sense, that the stories are first person accounts of lived experience, and not hearsay, nor learnt or taught knowledge. These insider voices are the vital bridge between research and practice. Scott et al. (2013) drew together multiple mini projects, each of which shed a new light on higher education experience through the voices of student insiders. Teachers, too, have told their stories with vivid clarity, from diaries of the agonies of an unruly secondary school language class (Appel, 1995) to inspirational accounts of outstanding school heads and the challenges of their daily lives (Laar and Holderness, 2018).

Czerniawski and Kidd (2011) remind us that insider voices in research are simply a reflection of the evolved 21st century world, with multiple platforms for people to be heard without anyone intervening, neither film producers, journalists, nor academics. Digital storytelling projects such as the one described by Anderson et al. (2018) show us what happens when children in a second culture are given the tools, they need to film stories of their lives in their first language, and are then left to their own devices to do so.

Of course, every source of knowledge can be contested, and there are questions that might be asked about the 'trustworthiness' of anecdote and story; and how this form of knowledge compares to numerical and performance indicators. The children's stories in the Anderson project, for example, were often allegorical, or fictionalised, and were not to be read as literal accounts. The primary heads whose stories are described in Laar and Holderness (2018) were all unique and distinctive, and there might be little applicability to others without their extraordinary grit. Yet providing finite answers is not the claim we make about the insider voice. Rather, these voices are indicators of the complexity of knowledge and the diversity of experience, and they act as caveats or complements to the knowledge provided by numerical data alone. Hamshire et al. (2017), for example, share four student narrative inquiries in Australia, United Kingdom, South Africa and New Zealand, and set their findings side by side with performance indicators. They found the student voice substantially complemented the numerical data and provided educators and policymakers with richly expanded information for making policy changes. At the same time, Laar and Holderness's stories of inspirational head teachers, or Appel's (1995) daily struggles with the secondary school class from hell, may not fit formulae for teacher or leadership development. The voices of students and teachers do not claim to offer definitive answers, nor to be representative, universal or generalisable; but they do claim to be communicating something about the complexity and diversity of the human condition, and its refusal to be prescribed or predictable.

Interview methodology

The stories newly gathered for the purpose of this book derive from the Crossing Study Borders project, in which learners and teachers described moments of discomfort or surprise as they crossed from one higher education context to another.

Participants were invited from eight national and international student networks, teaching networks and higher education hubs, including the Practitioner-Researcher network, National Teaching Fellowship network, and International Association of Teachers of English as a Foreign Language (IATEFL). The invitation asked:

Have you studied or taught at higher education level in any one of these:

- More than one country?
- More than one language?
- More than one culture?
- More than one kind of institution?

Do you have stories you would like to share, of crossing university cultures?
The criteria were further explained as follows:

- 'Culture' here can mean language, country, region or sector.
- 'Studied' means for a taught or researched award, at BA, MA, MPhil, EdD, PhD level or any professional qualification.
- 'Taught' means as a full or adjunct member of the faculty.

Volunteers who responded to this invitation, were asked five semi-structured questions designed to reveal significant moments in their study experience across cultures:

1 Were there any moments, as a student or as a university teacher, where you realised *things are done differently here*. Can you tell the story of what happened?

2   What did that moment reveal about your learning/teaching in these different settings? What was different/surprising/disappointing/pleasing/significant?
3   How far, and in what ways, did you need to do, change or respond differently as a result?
4   How did you feel about this?
5   What support, information or planning would have helped you prepare for this difference?

They were invited to respond either through online interview, face to face interview, or through email correspondence. The circumstances of Covid-19 in 2020 made face to face meetings non-viable, and of the other options, 21 selected online interview and three responded by email.

The participants

The participants in the five projects between 2009 and 2021 describe transitions between the following groups of cultures. Note that the groupings are geographical rather than political categories.

- Southern Europe: France, Spain, Italy, Turkey, Greece
- Northern Europe and Scandinavia: Finland, Sweden, Germany, Austria, United Kingdom, Ireland
- Central and Eastern Europe: Russia, Belarus, Poland, Hungary, Romania
- Asia: India, Pakistan
- South East Asia: Japan, China, Philippines, Taiwan
- Middle East: Jordan, Israel, Saudi Arabia
- Africa: Nigeria, Egypt, South Africa, Benin
- Americas: Hawaii, United States, Brazil, Canada
- Australia, New Zealand

Pseudonyms have been used to ensure confidentiality in line with ethical guidelines for qualitative research.

Vignettes

In addition to the direct reporting of participant voices, 'vignettes' have been constructed to highlight overarching issues and themes. 'Vignettes' can mean several things. They can be short stories designed by the researcher to act as interview prompts, or they can be a synthesis of research findings crystallised into a composite story. The first kind of 'vignette' is an informed invention of the researcher, used to trigger responses from participants that reveal their beliefs or values. In contrast, the second kind of vignette encapsulates the words of others, synthesising findings into composite sketches that become representative and illustrative of themes and patterns. These "stories offer an invitation for the reader to step into the space of vicarious experience, to assume a position in the world of the research – to live the lived experience along with the researcher" (Ely et al., 1997, p. 72).

It is in the latter sense that vignettes are used in this book. The interviews in each of the projects invited stories of moments where 'difference' is most acutely experienced and remembered, and thus the moments where the distinctive culture of one appears to be in collision with another. Each chapter synthesises these stories alongside knowledge gathered from the literature to arrive at 'composite sketches' or vignettes that highlight issues, themes and patterns. An example is the case of Faisal, whose story draws together themes that emerged in six of the interviews.

> **Faisal before arriving at a UK University**
>
> Faisal has recently arrived from Saudi Arabia to study psychology and business studies at a British university. At his high school in Saudi Arabia, he was a high-achieving student who had achieved excellent marks in the school-leaving exams and a high English language test score. He had focused on reading and writing skills, which matched the expectations and conventions of his study context at school. He was accustomed to studying in large classes following the procedures of the teacher carefully, and spending time at home reading widely and taking notes. Before travelling to the British university, he read all the books on the pre-university booklist, and felt confident, well-prepared and excited on arriving.

> **Faisal at his first class in the UK University**
>
> To his surprise, at the first class the teacher did not seem to expect the students to have done the pre-course reading: and in fact, most of the other students had not. Also, to his disappointment, the teacher did not spend much of the class time talking but put the students in groups to discuss questions they had about the course. Faisal was too shy to mention that he had done all the pre-course reading and felt he did not have many questions about the course. He also felt frustrated because the students did not seem to have any particular knowledge that was useful; and that he did not receive this knowledge from the teacher. He was also confused as to what he was meant to learn by talking in groups in this way.

In analysing Faisal's situation, a number of issues emerge. Faisal had spent some time focusing on the content of his course and was expecting this to entail a furthering of knowledge and information, carried over from the teacher and the course books to himself. He had no particular interest in fellow students as he did not expect to learn from them or with them. In contrast, what the teacher chose to emphasise at the first meeting was not the content of the course, but the importance of class cohesion and student dialogue. The teacher was also hoping to gather some ideas of the students' needs and expectations and to give students practice in exchanging information, solving problems and coming to team decisions. All of these skills, she felt, modelled those expected of psychology students.

This book considers the cultures of education which explain misunderstandings such as these. It also invites readers to review their own study settings in order to prepare for these differences. What constitutes 'good' learning in the new study environment? What clues are there that convey what this 'good learning' really means? What would help students make the transition from their first learning culture to the second? In this case, Faisal is discovering that the new study setting prioritises being confident amongst peers, sharing reading and knowledge with others, and using class discussion for developing ideas above 'pure' content knowledge. Whilst this book recognises that there are multiple and disparate pictures of learning experiences, what we focus on are ways of interpreting and understanding these experiences, navigating them successfully and being prepared for them either from a teaching or studying perspective.

Learning from the literature

Higher education literature

The 21st century has generated multiple studies in which the student voice is central: students describing their hopes and expectations, their learning experiences, their sense of belonging or misfit with their institutions. These studies could be classified into three types: those which position the students as customers in an increasingly 'marketised' view of education as 'value for money'; those which draw on student voice as part of a mission to make higher education learning and teaching meaningful, effective and fitting for the 21st century; and those which see learners as complex social beings whose learning is culturally and politically determined. These areas are, of course, all connected and even inextricable; but they have different starting points and see the student through different lenses: as a consumer, as a learner, or as a social being for whom studentship is just one of many identities. All these approaches, however, help us to contextualise the vignettes and voices we will be sharing, to recognise those issues which seem to be recurring and significant, and to interpret them from several angles.

INTERCULTURAL COMPETENCE AND THE RECENTRING OF 'INTERNATIONAL'

The notion of intercultural competence shifts attention from being different, other or strange in several important ways. Firstly, intercultural is a term that includes everyone: there is no distinction between home students and those who have travelled to their place of study, between those studying in a first, second or third language. What they all have in common is the experience of studying, thinking, reading, writing with individuals who come from many different starting places. Intercultural competence recentres the meaning of international to include everyone as equally responsible for traversing from their own starting place to appreciate the starting place of others. Secondly, what is needed to traverse successfully is not so much the accumulation of knowledge, as the building of personal competences, ways of thinking, seeing, understanding and empathising. The chapters that follow draw on the literature that expands this view and offers frames for understanding these competences such as Byram and Feng (2004), whilst literature that analyses higher education stories will be configured to ask the question: what can we learn from this? What ways of being, knowing, or thinking will help us to respond, as learners and educators?

CULTURAL PRAGMATICS

The cultural pragmatics of higher education is a missing link in the literature on academic literacies and higher education teacher development; but what is cultural pragmatics, and why does it matter? We could describe cultural pragmatics as a way of 'particularising' our understanding of human actions and interactions (Carbaugh and van Over, 2013), of defying the attempt to generalise from one situation to another, and of seeking out the hidden attitudes and beliefs which lie under the surface of what we say and do. Cultural pragmatists have formulated categories, which are useful tools for looking under the surface of interactions, such as principles, which make conversations cooperative (Grice, 1989) or rules of politeness which govern social etiquette (Lakoff, 1977). These categories offer ways of analysing: they are questions about interactions rather than answers. This is a paradigm shift from collective answers, which suggest that there is a 'typical' behaviour or response in each setting, or an expected set of interactions and relationships, or even that hidden systems and structures for each setting can be explained and generalised (Hofstede, 1994). The individual brings a cluster of other factors which make any collective analysis over-simplistic. The interesting aspect of cultural pragmatics is that it asks how the individual is embedded within the collective, or alternatively, how the collective informs the individual. The individual is likely to defy expectations, break conventions or experience collisions between one expectation and another. Carbaugh and van Over, (2013) suggest five 'discursive hubs' for thinking about this individual-collective dynamic: being or forms of identity; relating and social relationships; feeling or emotion; acting; and dwelling. These are useful 'lenses', through which to view the experience of the individual crossing borders in teaching and learning, and involve not only looking outwards at the institutions and structures of the place, but also inwards at how these encounters impact on who we are and what we know, understand and believe.

This book and discovering higher education cultures

Whichever position we take as a learner/teacher, our learning context is never culturally neutral, and we all position ourselves on the basis of values and expectations which may not be visible to us until they are tested. This book maps multiple transitions into higher education life – from one language, region, country, sector, or workplace into another. The discussions, activities and readings are designed to give readers the opportunity to be fully conscious and aware of their position, so they can take a principled approach to the possible challenges. Every participant in the higher education culture contributes to its construction. This makes it imperative for participants to be open to new information, comparison and analysis; to be ethnographers of the exchanges they engage in. This is a challenge for all engaged in higher education settings but one which offers rich opportunities to learn from one another.

What this book is not

This is not a book that contrasts cultures by stereotyping expectations of how each might function and behave. It rejects the big 'C' position described above, in that specific places and specific kinds of students are not the content of our learning. Whilst some stories identify place, there is never a suggestion that the story then becomes representative or even typical of one location. A student-centred study culture that matches our learning ideals can be found the other side of the world, whilst an authoritarian culture in direct opposition to our beliefs can be found on our doorstep; and meanwhile, these two opposite kinds of institution might be found side by side and differ as a result of multiple local factors. Thus, we will never claim that a particular vignette might happen only to one type of student and not another, or only in one place and not another. For anyone moving into higher education, even from one institution to another, something will be new, something unexpected and something experienced for the first time. Research such as the HEA project, Transitions (Scott et al, 2013), shows us that students make transitions to accommodate where they are, and differences between them are not so much connected with cultural 'set' attitudes, but to do with their own personal motivations. The introduction to a large learning transitions project tracking the experience of international students explains:

> the participants in this study did not correspond to the stereotypes of international students that feature in literature such as Hofstede (1994) and Cortazzi and Jin (1997). Some non-Western students embraced critical reading and writing practices, and some Western students found these challenging. A non-UK student found the critical practices on her course naïve and undeveloped in relation to what she was used to in her home country.
>
> (Scott et al., 2013, p. 152)

No prediction will come without exceptions; and none will be sufficiently nuanced to take account of the complexity of human response and experience. For example, there is much more in common between two students who both are highly engaged with their subject discipline than there is between two students who are perceived by an outsider as from the same 'culture'. Thus, this book starts with the stories of individuals, and analyses situations on a case-by-case basis, and in the light of studies that explore themes and issues, rather than specific locations.

Similarly, the idea of a dichotomy between 'international' and local students breaks down at the very first hurdle, in asking students with which group they identify. (Clifford et al., 2011). In a study at a UK higher education institution, teaching staff were asked to identify whether they were international, local with international experience, or local. Not only did most identify themselves as 'local with international experience', but many also found the split into these three groups irrelevant and meaningless in the real-world relationships between them. One of them says:

> I'm a bit struggling to see that the point is of – like I've talked to lots of staff who I work with and they are international and some are not international but I wouldn't like, discriminate, like as if I'm only going to go and talk to these or those or anything, but I find it useful to talk to people who are in my School or my discipline area, as the need arises according to whatever I'm working on at the time. But for me to go and talk to someone in Technology or Maths because they are foreign seems a really weird idea.
>
> (FIC)

What this book is

Instead, this book asks, not how one culture behaves as opposed to another, but rather how individuals experience situations from moment to moment, and what can be learnt from these collectively. The ten-year period during which these stories were gathered does reveal some changing trends, such as the normalising of online teaching and learning, much accelerated by the Covid-19 pandemic in 2020. However, the critical incidents themselves, and the kind of questions opened up, are timeless ones, and are those which are echoed too in the literature.

These questions can be clustered into eight main themes, which were those used to code and analyse the participant stories:

- How do students perceive themselves as learners?
- How do university teachers perceive themselves as educators?
- How do learners perceive learning?
- What does 'knowing' actually mean?

- How is learning conducted in different settings such as lecture, seminar, tutorial?
- How are physical and virtual spaces used in learning?
- What kind of learning and assessment activities are happening?
- How is work graded and marked, and how is feedback given and received?

Each of these questions form the basis for a chapter in this book, firstly from the perspective of participants themselves, and then through the lens of the literature. The final section of each chapter crystallises these insights into learning maps, for readers to review their own higher education situation and reshape them as opportunities for learning.

What this book aims to tease out, is the fact that, as travellers through higher education settings it is situations moment by moment we react to, with all the penumbra and subtexts that lie behind each of these. Moments of being uncomfortable in a new culture reveal not only where we are, but who we are and where we have come from. The book offers options for repairing this discomfort, whether it is to change, not to change, to accept or resist, or simply to understand a little better.

References

Anderson, J., Chung, Y.C. and Macleroy, V. (2018) 'Creative and critical approaches to language learning and digital technology: findings from a multilingual digital storytelling project', *Language and Education*, 32 (3), pp. 195–211.

Appel, Joachim (1995) *Diary of a language teacher.* Oxford: Heinemann.

Byram, M. (1997) *Teaching and assessing intercultural competence.* Clevedon: Multilingual Matters.

Camerer, Rudi (2014) 'Testing intercultural competence in (International) English: some basic questions and suggested answers' *Language Learning in Higher Education*, 4, (1), 2014, pp. 207-236. https://doi.org/10.1515/cercles-2014-0012.

Byram, M. and Feng, A. (2004) 'Culture and language learning: teaching, research and scholarship', *Language Teaching*, 37, pp. 149–168.

Carbaugh, D. and van Over, B. (2013) 'Interpersonal pragmatics and cultural discourse', *Journal of Pragmatics*, 58, pp. 142–145.

Clifford, V., Adeunji, H., Haigh, M., Henderson, J., Spiro, J. and Hudson, J. (2011) *Report on Brookes student learning experience project: fostering interculturality and global perspectives at Brookes through dialogue with staff.* Oxford Centre for Staff Learning and Development: Oxford Brookes University.

Cortazzi, M. and Jin, L. (1997) 'Communication for learning across cultures'. In D. McNamara and R. Harris (Eds), *Overseas students in higher education, issues in teaching and learning.* London: Routledge, pp. 76–90.

Czerniawski, G. and Kidd, W. (eds.) (2011) *The student voice handbook: bridging the academic/practitioner divide.* Bingley: Emerald Group Publishing.

Ely, M., Vinz, R., Downing, M. and Anzul, M. (1997) *On writing qualitative research: living by words.* London: Routledge.

Gebhard, J.G. (1996) *Teaching English as a foreign or second language.* Ann Arbor, MI: University of Michigan Press.

Grice, H.P. (ed.) (1989) *Studies in the ways of words.* Cambridge, MA: Harvard University Press.

Hamshire, C., Forsyth, R., Bell, A., Benton, M., Kelly-Laubscher, R., Paxton, M. and Wolfgramm-Foliaki, E. (2017) 'The potential of student narratives to enhance quality in higher education', *Quality in Higher Education*, 23 (1), pp. 50–64.

Hofstede, G. (1994) *Cultures and organisations.* London: HarperCollins.

Laar, B. and Holderness, J. (2018) *Reclaiming the curriculum: specialist and creative teaching in primary schools.* Carmarthen, Wales: Crown House Publishing.

Lakoff, J.P. (1977) '*What can you do with words: politeness, pragmatics and performatives*', in Proceedings of the Texas conference on performatives, presuppositions and implicatures. Rogers, R., Wall, R. and Murphy, J. (eds.). Arlington: Center for Applied Linguistics, pp. 79–106.

Murray, N. (2010) 'Pragmatics, awareness raising and the co-operative principle', *English Language Teaching Journal*, 64, pp. 283–301.

Scott, D., Hughes, G., Evans, C., Burke, P.J., Walter, C. and Watson, D. (2013). *Learning transitions in higher education.* London: Palgrave Macmillan.

Spiro, J. (2013) 'The reflective continuum: reflecting for change and student response to reflective tasks', *Brookes eJournal of Learning and Teaching*, 5 (2), [online]. Available at: http://ocsld.brookesblogs.net/2013/08/28/brookes-ejournal-of-learning-and-teaching-volume-5-issue-2/ (Accessed: 27th June 2021).

Spiro, J. (2014) 'Learning interconnectedness: internationalisation through engagement with one another', *Higher Education Quarterly*, 68 (1), pp. 65–84.

Spiro, J., Henderson, J. and Clifford, V. (2012) 'Independent learning crossing cultures: learning cultures and shifting meanings', *Compare: A Journal of Comparative and International Education*, 42 (4), pp. 607–619.

Williams, K., Wooliams, M. and Spiro, J. (2020) (2nd edition) *Reflective writing.* Basingstoke: Palgrave Macmillan.

2 Being a student
Who am I as a learner?

This chapter considers the surprises, confusions and conflicts as students travel from one study context into another. An encounter with the new can at best be exciting and refreshing, inviting us to look again at ourselves and our assumptions. One postgraduate student describes her move from Germany to the UK "like having a wardrobe with different clothes for different occasions" (CSB, Gerda). But with what degree of discomfort and conflict are these new clothes worn and others discarded? Are these changes superficial survival strategies, a form of role-playing and mask-wearing, or something that reaches deeper into who you are or want to be?

We might answer this question by theorising about collective versus individualistic cultures or thinking about power imbalance and inequities in each setting. This approach may well uncover deep structures that surround and underlie what we feel, but as an individual it is hard actually to *do* anything about them. In addition, these approaches risk implying that we are locked inside systems and will behave stereotypically within them. Philipsen (2010) suggests another approach to cultural encounters. For him 'culture' is not a place, country, or group but rather a historically and socially constructed set of rules, meanings and behaviours, which he calls a 'cultural code' (Philipsen, 2010 p. 162). This code might appear to be a locked system that reveals itself in moments of surprise and conflict. As this chapter aims to show, there are many ways in which this conflict is experienced; from imposter syndrome, to struggles with expectations about the student life, or pressures from peers to appear, or not to appear, serious about study. Yet knowing the code offers at least some options: to understand without changing, to change as one might play a role, or to internalise the new milieu and become someone different. Unlocking the code entails a process of observing: what people do to fit in, what they do to succeed, and how they come to belong. This process of observation, and the opening up of options, is both a more practical and a more hopeful route and is the one we explore throughout this book.

As with every chapter, the voices derive from more than 100 student and teacher stories gathered through learning diaries, field notes, interviews and focus groups between 2011 and 2021, and across four separate projects. These are:

16 *Being a student*

- *Reflection in the Round* (RIR) with 38 student learning diaries and 10 annual focus groups of students on one-year postgraduate progammes between 2011 and 2020. In addition, teacher field notes track learning activities and learner responses during the same period. The project is published as Spiro (2013) and crystallised into teaching materials as Williams, Wooliams and Spiro (2020).
- *Fostering Interculturality* (FIC) with 16 participants, both staff and students, who identified as international, discussing their experience of crossing cultures in semi-structured interviews and focus groups. This project is published as Clifford et al., (2011) and Spiro et al., (2012).
- *Learning Interconnectedness* (LIC) with 50 international first degree students between 2010 and 2014 sharing weekly journals about their experiences of learning across cultures and languages. In addition, teacher field notes track cross-cultural learning activities and learner responses in the same period, 2010 to 2014 (Spiro, 2014).
- *Crossing Study Borders* (CSB) with 24 staff and students who identified as having crossed borders in learning and teaching, interviewed between 2020 and 2021 and published here for the first time.

Listening to learner stories: who am I as a learner?

In the first chapter, we mentioned that there is a kind of literature about students which sees them as customers to be enticed to 'buy' higher education rather as they might buy a holiday from a travel agent. For example, Gottschal and Saltmarsh (2017) analysed the promotional websites of 39 Australian universities, and shared a case study of one university, in which education is marketed as a period of leisure and pleasure with scenes of happy students leaping into a swimming pool, cycling, running and boxing briefly interspersed with scenes of learning, such as in a library or dental lab. The promise of happiness is visualised in the language of an extended summer holiday.

We know, from studies into learner backgrounds, that students make the leap into study settings for reasons much more complex than this. The marketing literature tends to make the assumption that the 'customer' is white, incomed, middle class, unattached and young. There is also the assumption that higher education is an easily accessible life choice. This more than misses out the true diversity of student motivations; students moving across the world to study at great personal cost such as separation from family; part-time students keeping long hours into the night to study after a working day; BAME (Black, Asian, minority ethnic) who may feel there is no-one who looks like them in their new place of learning; or mature students struggling with poverty and juggling family commitments. These all constitute transitions from one culture or community to another and suggest there can be no composite that can possibly be representative. The only factor in common is that to study, for whatever reason, something needs to change. Are these changes surface ones, to do with behavioural 'tricks' and strategies, or deep-rooted ones that effect real transformations? Is a studying self in a separate box from other selves such as sibling, friend, colleague, carer or does it impact on everything you are? The stories in this section suggest a spectrum of responses to this question.

Katya moved from Poland to study in the UK and US. Here she describes the moment, in her new study setting, where she realised that her sense of what it was to be a student was painfully at odds with her professor's approach.

> In my culture, the private and public spheres were separate – two discrete identities with little cross-over. This had consequences in my new cultural environments on multiple levels, but two were particularly visible: sharing information about private life and dressing. I was a mature student with a little child in tow when I studied in the U.S. and the U.K., but it would never occur to me to talk about my family situation in class or use it as an excuse not to get things done (which is what I see a lot these days, and perhaps rightly so). When a professor once asked us for introductions and – knowing about my situation – mentioned my little girl and encouraged me to talk about her, I turned red and refused to continue the conversation. I just didn't know how to react to it; it felt too personal and intrusive, so I created a wall and I imagine that my response was probably seen as bizarre, if not impolite. (CSB, Katya)

One student studying for the first time in the UK, describes similar discomfort with her first 'welcome' to higher education life. Here she describes her invitation to a new students' reception in her new institution.

> I had this idea we would be introduced to our professors, it was quite important and formal and we needed to present ourselves as serious students. That was the idea I had with the word 'reception'. But when I got there everyone except me was wearing jeans like it was a uniform, everyone was drinking like you had to drink alcohol to fit in, and I couldn't tell who were the professors and who were the students. I just froze. Day one I thought, this isn't my place. (RIR)

This student is not alone in finding this first welcome to be symbolic of a bigger 'culture-blindness', and to fear that it might be an indicator of a further culture gulf to come. Schweisfurth and Gu (2009) discuss the difficulties that the undergraduate international students in their study had with aspects of British undergraduate culture such as how much value many first-year British students give to alcohol consumption and clubbing in their first year outside the parental home. Wei Wei, who travelled from China to the UK, tells of his social isolation in the first weeks at his new college.

> For me this was a big opportunity and all my family had helped for this big thing of coming to study in the UK. I learnt it was where I would get best education and I was ready and wanted to give all my thinking to this

study. All the others in my residence spent the first week in the student bar. I wanted to read the books but I was afraid then I wouldn't make friends if I wasn't doing the same as them. (CSB, Wei Wei)

Here are real tensions described from the very first entry, between the sense of self as a student whose "job it was" (Gerda's words) to take study seriously and to mark this in behaviour, dress and discourse; and the kind of settings and encounters which breached these boundaries. For Wei Wei, there has been much family and personal sacrifice to give him the opportunity to study; and being a student is a hard-earned and highly cherished role. Katya explains how dress was a way of representing self to the outside world, and separated her from others:

> Regarding dressing, school was a formal occasion to me so I would dress accordingly, and my peers in their shorts and t-shirts would often ask me if I was going out after class. It puzzled me every time, although I wasn't judging them on their sartorial choices. Funnily enough, I see the same thing in my exchange students from Europe – they dress formally and stand out from the class. As a result, they are often seen as 'stuck up' by English students, which is very unfortunate. (CSB, Katya)

The wearing of formal clothes suggests that learning is a serious enterprise marked from other roles for each of these storytellers (Gerda, Silvia and Katya). The collision of expectations which they describe is not so much that fellow students failed to take learning seriously. Rather, the learning role is signalled for them differently. They represent who they are as a learner in a different way.

These different notions can be characterised by the stories of Fabia, Chen and May. Fabia, a working-class single parent in a UK university describes her reasons for entering and staying at university:

> The whole reason for making this move was to be a qualified nurse, and give me and my daughter a better chance. I had no interest in anything else. No, I didn't go to any of the social events, didn't join any clubs or student networks. I don't know if I missed them – I had too much to do. (CSB, Fabia)

Fabia had a single focus as a student, and to make this sustainable needed to pare away any of the surrounding penumbra of student socialising and out-of-class activities. She resisted invitations to be on student committees and had no time to attend the evening socials.

> I was aware there was this other thing going on called 'being a student' but I just couldn't engage with it. For me, I was always a mother working flat out to make it work for me and my daughter. (CSB, Fabia)

Fabia's story is echoed in many narratives describing the challenges of the working mother, for example Julia, whose drive to study came from "determination that I wanted to change things and make a difference and be able to support us financially and move out of the neighbourhood that I was in, so that was on a very personal level" (Julia in Merrill, 2015, p. 1865).

For Julia and Fabia, there was complete clarity about what they were studying and why. We can also discern from their stories a high degree of discipline and focused attention. Fabia implies that she sees 'being a student' as a whole 'other thing', which has little to do with the hard work of studying and possibly even connotes its opposite. It could be that her construct of 'the student' does indeed come from the kind of marketing tools described by Gottschal and Saltmarsh (2017), and that somehow there is a buy-in to the notion that a student life is one of unlimited exploration and freedom.

Chen's story forms an interesting contrast. She describes a move from her school education in Japan to higher education in the United Kingdom. She tells the story of a very controlling family life and a disciplinarian father. For her "coming to the UK was a way I could become grown-up and do things for myself". She describes it, almost literally, as an 'escape' that was sanctioned by home and even awarded her status.

> It was so different that no-one said to do homework I thought it was OK then not to. The teachers were so kind and never said you must. I saw all this about freshers, join societies, go to welcome parties, meet new friends. I went wild a bit. Then when I got bad grades I was really shock (sic). (CSB, Chen)

For her, becoming a student constituted a leap to freedom from being a child controlled and directed by parents and at school by teachers. The problem, however, was that this new pathway seemed to be entirely unmapped and unclear, and teacher kindness was misunderstood as relaxed expectations and standards. Feedback was constructed positively so Chen was unable to 'read' that it was criticism. (We will say more about feedback in Chapters 8 and 9). Without the experience of being self-directed, Chen felt unsure what was expected of her. Somehow, she saw her peers engaging in this student life, and yet achieving high grades too. It was entirely unclear how they were doing this, or when exactly they were studying. For Chen's peers, studying seemed to take place around the edges of a busy multitasking social life, and was not necessarily visible to her. In fact, Chen's complaint was that her fellow students rarely admitted how hard they were working; and, indeed, there would be competition to show how little they had done.

Here we might meet May, who is in some ways the student that Chen is seeing, and interpreting. May is a multitasking student, working in the evenings in the student union bar to earn extra cash for her studies. She is connected through multiple social platforms with schoolfriends, friends in her running club, a gospel choir and an indie music group. These groups share information, images, events and news "I'd say at least 50 times a day – I am checking it always. It's like my brain". Studying is one of the tasks she splices into this busy life. In answer to the question, *how do you see yourself as a student*, she replies:

> I don't. I don't see myself as a student particularly, any more than I do as a person who sings, or lives in hall, or someone who likes walking, or someone with two sisters. It's just one of the things I do, and I don't expect to be doing it for long. (CSB, May)

For May, the cultural conflict in moving from a school in a small town to a large city university, is one of scale.

> What's overwhelming are the number of people, I never see the same people twice, there are different people in every class, the classes are too big and busy, the size of the campus is like a mini city. It was all too much at first so I just cling to the social groups I have and I am kind of with them virtually all the time and not really here at all. (CSB, May)

Though May might appear socially in tune with her setting, and to 'belong' to the mainstream, this is far from how she experienced it. On the contrary, she explains how her "body is sitting in the class" but her mind is almost always elsewhere. One higher education teacher explains how this looks from the outside:

> Students are juggling all sorts of things – it used to be that students' main activity was being a student and then we started to get students taking on part-time jobs – being a student is just one section of their lives that's competing with lots of other things – which aren't brought right into the university – as they are doing practical you are competing with their need to look at facebook and check their emails and run their social life. (FIC)

Working at the same time as studying is necessary for many students, as we see with Fabia who struggles to look after her little girl or with May, who needs to subsidise her studies by working in the student bar. The transition between settings, however, reveals very different study cultures in relation to working students. Winnie describes her experience moving from Canada to France:

> In France it was considered scandalous if you worked. My supervisor told me I couldn't finish if I worked. She said you can't reach the quality required and work at the same time – you needed to choose. We can't kick you out but you won't pass. If you were really serious you would quit work. (CSB, Winnie)

For Bridget, as with Winnie, working alongside study was absolutely critical, both financially and intellectually.

I believe self-reliance with self-confidence helped me achieve the subsequent two Masters level studies which were also completed while in full-time employment. The purpose was to progress through the various employments I had and the study programmes were pursued on a needs basis. I enjoyed the opportunity to apply the theory to practice which was enabled by being in full-time work. (CSB, Bridget)

Higher education settings thus vary hugely in their acceptance, or otherwise, of the student as concurrently in employment. Their approach is likely to connect with an idea of the stage of life when higher education learning takes place. Annabel describes her US learning as something one can opt into at any stage in life alongside work, family and life: "In north America it's quite usual to work and study at the same time. You can go back to study at any time" (CSB, Annabel). In contrast, Winnie explains the response in her French university:

It's because the European idea of studying straight after secondary school, you didn't have a career first or go back later. I was the oldest student by far at 27 – you are a student or a teacher but you can't be both. I was an anomaly because I was a teacher. (CSB, Winnie)

The expectation that higher education belongs in the brief life phase between school and employment might influence how the student is positioned: as a child to be protected and guided, or as an adult juggling work, family and financial demands. Aidan's account of moving from the UK to Japan maps this difference.

The main difference was a feeling I was going backwards in time. I was treated like a secondary school kid compared to the freedom of study in the UK. I was put in a bubble. It was double-edged; they were trying to accommodate you, but it feels like you are being protected, segregated. (CSB, Aidan)

When asked what this suggested to him about the contrast in study cultures, he explained:

It suggested to me that at university here students are treated more like children than adults (by the teachers, educators; although this may also be a highly cultural factor too), and they are considerably more innocent and reserved in their leisure choices (than in the UK). (CSB, Aidan)

For Chen, travelling in reverse from Japan to the UK, the sense of being catapulted from a highly supported to a highly autonomous setting was equally confusing. She felt at sea with the choices she was expected to make, and the juggling she perceived in others, between work and life. Around her in classes were mature students with extensive work experience, part-time students who she never saw outside class times, and retired students returning to study after a life of employment. Individual tutors might scaffold their subject discipline, but the overall expectation that students would manage their own learning was highly destabilising for her.

> I was very surprise (sic). I would prefer I did not have to make choices of which courses to study because I didn't know which was best. I needed a lot of help at first from my personal tutor. I was very afraid I would miss out something important I need to do. At home it was all clear and I just needed to study what I was told. (CSB, Chen)

What is interesting to note, is that over ten years of gathering stories of student reflections at the start and finish of a one-year programme (Reflection in the Round project), a large majority in each cohort believed that their peers were succeeding better in work-life balance than they and seemed to achieve study success more easily. Many of those studying in a second culture believed that there was a site of 'belonging' from which they were excluded. For Aidan, this was stark in that his group were actually separated from the locals in his Japanese university:

> The international students were very much placed in a 'bubble'. This causes a bit of a chicken or egg type situation – most Int'l Ss need the extra support when transitioning to a country like Japan, where getting by without strong JPN language skills is difficult to say the least – yet by placing them in such a bubble there develops this slight context of 'them' and 'us' (segregation), albeit not discriminatory. The different cultures plus segregation makes it difficult for some cross-cultural friendships, besides the overly confident Japanese who usually already have decent English ability who bravely venture into the 'Int'l crowd'. (CSB, Aidan)

The flashpoints that suddenly sweep away a sense of belonging can be both overt and subtle. Nine BAME students at a midlands university in the UK interviewed by Currant (2020) tell of moments when an academic discussion suddenly reveals attitudes which are exclusionist and racist. These moments reveal the extent of 'cultural oblivion' that may lie hidden under a veneer of good manners. Sometimes even gestures intended to be friendly and build rapport can become otherwise. For example: in one institution a teacher aimed to generate an atmosphere of camaraderie by exercising a one-to-one open-door tutorial policy without making this formal. Only students 'in the know', realised this. Emanuel, moving from France to the Netherlands, wrote,

> No-one told me till nearly the end of my programme that you could get help from the tutors. In my French college I could never have done that. I didn't get how everyone seemed to be saying, 'oh the prof says xyz' and I

would think, well when did he say that? Where? There were no sign-up sheets outside their doors, or booking arrangements, or anything I could make sense of, so I just didn't pick up you could do that. (CSB, Emanuel)

What Emanuel then did, was an illustration of the value of unlocking cultural codes. Recognising a system he had missed out on, he vowed to avail himself of this in the future, and to be on the alert for other such systems that might help him.

> In general I started to make much more use of office hours. This not only allowed me to get better grades but also helped in developing a more personal relationship with the TAs. This in turn made the course more fun and enabled me to learn more. I was also more on the lookout for how other students were approaching the courses. I wanted to make sure I wasn't missing out on other 'tricks'. (CSB, Emanuel)

The nine Midfordshire students interviewed by Currant (2020) also explain ways in which offers of help can be counter-productive, if they are unclear, too complex or time limited.

> there is so many people, so many advisors you can go to. You go to this person, they tell you no that is not me, you should go to this other person. So it should be so clear that this is this place for support if you need, you think you are struggling and you need help… it is like a big, very difficult maze to find out who can help me. In the end you just say why bother. (Janice in Currant, 2020, p. 98)

In the same focus group, another participant Salah explains help-seeking as loss of face, at odds with his sense of himself as a black male.

> There is support there but I kind of find it difficult sometimes to ask for help. – So, that's probably because of my background maybe. Whether it's ethnic or masculine? You want to be able to do things yourself. You're taught that you have to learn on the job and do it. (Salah in Currant, 2020, p. 10)

These testimonies recount the complexity of supposed 'friendly' offers of help or approaches that are intended to be welcoming but are culture blind. Such mismatches play themselves out most tangibly in the way language is used, and specifically in the differences between direct social approaches, and hedged ones. This is not simply a matter of linguistic difference. Katya in the account below, describes her deep discomfort towards polite 'hedging' and a culture of linguistic kindness.

> I was used to very straightforward, perhaps blunt style of communication, where you say what you mean and this includes positives and

> negatives. What I discovered in America, and even more so in the U.K., was people's absolute unwillingness to share any criticism or honest opinion, even within the safety of the classroom. Every opinion seemed to be veiled and I was frustrated with what I perceived as a wall I couldn't break through. Everyone seemed dishonest and untrustworthy to me – too kind, too understanding, too smiley, too interested in my well-being. It just didn't seem genuine – the smiles seemed fleeting, the interest superficial, the understanding short-lived. (CSB, Katya)

Katya's story shows she is highly skilled in recognising the cultural codes of her surroundings. Her strategy was to adjust her own behaviour to fit in, but at great personal cost.

> The problem that lived in my head was exacerbated by the fact that I came across to others as rude and uncouth, someone offering unsolicited advice, and critical when people sought praise. This aspect of my character took years to adjust, as I fought to remain 'real' until I felt I couldn't remain real anymore. (CSB, Katya)

This is a significant crisis in the process of transition and raises major questions about what it means to 'fit in'. Katya's experience is echoed by Gerda, as she offers a useful metaphor of 'translation' between cultures:

> As soon as I set foot outside the door it is like having a wardrobe with different clothes for different occasions – you put on with the language a different persona. There comes a time you suddenly come to realise you have to say, think things differently. The first year you get accustomed to the language – it's like academic speak I have to phrase things differently – you have to suggest, could you consider – it's all very nice, and if you take that literally as a German you'd be, well that's a bit wishy washy nothing – also in social occasions and lectures – I always feel too loud when I don't put on this very English persona, holding back. I constantly feel I have to hold back because I constantly have to in translating it to English speak so as not to offend anybody. (CSB, Gerda)

In her account, phrases such as 'suggest' or 'could you consider', typically used to hedge claims in the social sciences, are not simply a matter of a change in language. They require her to be a different kind of person and change to one that does not sit comfortably. This second person is constantly fearful of offending, and constantly holding back from her preferred way of interacting. More fundamentally, the academic language she is being taught suggests a different idea of what is valuable communication. For her, the language seems 'wishy washy', even 'nothingy', to convey no information or knowledge at all and to be dishonest, vague and even obfuscating.

Gerda identifies different approaches to the language of learning and what knowledge actually looks like. Chapters 4 and 5 ask what learning and knowing actually means; but for the purposes of this chapter, it is the effect on the student that interests us. Sally is a teacher who has made the shift from a college of further education to a university where she is doing a doctorate in education. For Sally, there is a profound gulf between her approach to language and knowledge and the one she has been asked to adopt.

> Before the EdD I felt like I could write, for the first 3 years I thought I could write, but by the end of the 3rd year I felt like I had lost all my specialist skills, I had lost education, it was like in the army where they bring you in, break you and build you up again. It felt like that. I still think I am going through that process now. It felt like a bootcamp. It felt horrible. I questioned whether I wanted to do it. I like writing but to read a journal article – this dreadfully written thing – agh! There's a style I can write in but I don't think that's the way the EdD wants me to write, or research papers want me to write. I am more of an everyday writer than an academic writer and that's the biggest challenge. (CSB, Sally)

For Sally, like Gerda and Katya, the language she is required to adopt represents another self that fits uncomfortably. Adopting this language is critical to success; and yet, it does not seem to be who she is, or even who she wishes to be.

We have seen in many of the stories above, that fitting in may entail behaviours that are alien and undesirable. How comfortable can Katya be at losing her sense of being real? Does May want to abandon her online social networks and instead engage with the networks physically surrounding her? What should Winnie actually do about working alongside study in her new college, which discourages it? Should Salah bite back his pride and seek help from tutors? And in the end, does Sally really want to change from the 'everyday writer' that represents her so well, to the academic writer that does not. If one were to adopt this new behaviour, for the sake of fitting in, how far would one need to go toward becoming someone different? Seeing the ingredients of success in the behaviour of others is not the same as either achieving it or desiring it. An overarching question is: how important is the final goal, and are these fundamental changes really needed in order to achieve it? If so, are they a change too far, and is the prize worth it in the end? We have noted the strong drive of students such as Julia and Fabia to support their families and improve their life opportunities; the sense of the dignity and purpose of education felt by Katya and Wei Wei; or the remarkable determination to become a doctor-practitioner demonstrated by Sally. What compromises were made, and what strategies used, to negotiate these cultural roadblocks and arrive at their goal? There may be some surface tricks which pave the way to a smoother connection, such as with Emanuel who simply came to recognise how he could sign up for tutorial support, and then was alert to other such tricks that might help him. More frequently, we have seen confusions and disappointments where a student arrives expecting one of these connections and meets an entirely different one: Aidan's experience of very controlled, formal socialising in Japan instead of the partying, clubbing life he had hoped for; Chen's difficulty in understanding how she is meant to balance the social whirl with academic study; Katya's frustration with bland politeness she felt to be untrustworthy and dishonest. We might ask whether there are ways to repair these mismatches, or whether a survival strategy that patches up the gaps is adequate. Our students in this chapter have described compromises, even a letting go of expectation. Knowing that these differences exist is perhaps less disturbing than the moment when the differences were revealed for the first time, and the firm ground you thought you were on was swept away.

Learner stories through the literature lens

This section views one of the students we met above, Katya, through the lens of recent research studies. Her account of study and teaching experiences in Poland, the US and the UK suggest five themes, which appear widely in the literature of student transitions: higher education as a hidden code; higher education as a site of belonging (or not); learning as adaptation to a new culture; higher education learning as impacting on identity and sense of self; and finally higher education as the threshold to independence and cosmopolitanism.

Here Katya describes more fully her experience of belonging, as she moved from Poland to study in the US and UK:

> Throughout my education in different cultural settings, I felt that I was in a constant state of 'catching up' – I had a lot of knowledge that impressed my teachers but my cultural ignorance left me clueless in many ways, and feeling like I didn't belong; it wasn't what I knew that seemed to count, but how I expressed that knowledge. But I kept striving to belong. Only years after and once I began to teach myself, I understood all these emotions and could properly reflect on them. I adapted to these different cultural circumstances, because adaptation is my superpower, but I sacrificed part of myself in the process. I was on a mission to fit in, to hide my accent, to change my ways, where I could have just been myself. At the time, however, I just didn't feel that 'being myself' was encouraged. At the same time, I learned so much in the process! I learned different ways to be in the world, I learned to be sensitive to others and not to be too precious about what 'being me' means. Change and adaptation are part of the process of personal and professional growth and – while they can be painful – they have real value and real-life consequences. I also learned how to be more empathetic and – ironically – also how to be tough with others. Knowing the value of change and adaptation can make you into a tank: if you can do it, everyone can do it ... (CSB, Alicia)

Hidden codes

I felt that I was in a constant state of catching up.

Katya is not alone in feeling that there is a hidden code which she is eternally trying to uncover. The UK Council for International Students (UKCISA) acknowledged, in 2015, that the social hurdles in making a transition into a second study culture presented the greatest challenge to international students and their institutions. Higher Education Academy data (HESA, 2018) show us that a students' sense of cultural connection with the study environment has a direct impact on their academic success, though these connections are not usually part of an explicit curriculum. The challenge of crossing study borders has been researched from the perspective of specific student groups: for example, Biemans and Van Mil (2008) studied the learning differences between Dutch and Chinese students, looking for culture-based generalisations; Campbell and Li (2008) researched the experiences of Asian students in New Zealand; Mcleod (2008), Korean students in the US. What emerges from these localised studies is not so much the specificity and distinctiveness of the challenges for each participant group, but their universality. Shared issues emerge, which are exactly those experienced by students we have met in this chapter. These studies report on communication issues, such as Carbaugh's (2007) study of empty friendship gestures in the Seattle area; educational systems and the transparency or otherwise of how these work (Ryan, 2013; Scott et al., 2013; UKCISA, 2015); and thirdly social systems such as "rituals, myths and stories" (Philipsen, 2010, p. 165) and the hidden structures lying under their surface. These three broad areas also arose in Adisa et al.'s study of student motivation, unpicking in his student group the sources of their discomfort in a new study setting (Adisa et al., 2019). Communicative, educational and social systems represent blocks to understanding wherever they are hidden, unfamiliar and unexplained, whether the student groups studied were Chinese, Dutch, Polish, Korean or self-identifying as local.

In Katya's sense of forever running behind, we see an apparently unbreachable gap between what is known and what is unfamiliar. Although we are reaching here into a different domain, service industry research has suggested the idea of gaps between hopes and delivered services, which are a very useful parallel (Parasuram et al., 1985; Marimuthu and Ismail, 2012). Borghi et al. (2016) use the first in Parasuram et al.'s list of five, the 'knowledge gap', to explore the mismatch in higher education students between what is known, and what is unknown. They suggested eight gaps based on a systematic literature search of the student voice. Amongst these, here are just three knowledge gaps reported both by students in their study, and by Katya and other students met in this chapter:

- The expectation that communication with the institution will be honest and authentic, and that student needs will be treated with respect, for example regarding issues of progression, academic conduct, handling of disputes (Marimuthu and Ismail, 2012).

- The expectation that bureaucratic processes be made transparent, such as registering (or not) for tests and exams; signing up (or not) for tutorials; enrolling (or not) for new programmes and modules.
- The expectation of accurate communication about courses, evaluation procedures and complaints processes, suggesting experiences of surprises, disappointments, mystification and grievance.

As we identify these, we can see that Katya is far from alone in finding that baseline knowledge has been withheld from her and she is therefore in a constant state of 'catching up'.

Belonging and identity

> *My cultural ignorance left me feeling like I didn't belong.*

We saw in many of our student stories in the last section that advisory, support and welcome initiatives often go astray because they assume the mainstream culture is representative. This is what Hawkins (2018) calls an 'oblivious culture' – the failure to make it transparent for those to whom it is not self-evident. Currant (2020) in his study of nine BAME students, recounts their acute sense of feeling 'outside', due to this cultural oblivion. His nine case study students in academic seminars, tell stories of peers revealing attitudes which suddenly 'other' them and which are not even recognised by their speakers as racist and exclusionist. Their experiences suggest that 'belonging' is far from an intangible state of being, but a state clearly built or damaged by words, behaviours and systems.

Yet an inclusive and welcoming learning community is worth striving for. Hawkins (2018) gathered recommendations from BAME students in a white university as to what could heal their sense of 'otherness'. Their recommendations include respectful and inclusive interactions, clear pathways towards support and advice, and seeing others like oneself, at all levels and into positions of leadership. These hopes must surely not be unique to one kind of collective voice. They emerge in Borghi et al.'s (2016) list of eight expectations, Mainardes et al. (2012) list of 33 expectations. In other words, the qualities of inclusivity most desired by those who feel excluded are the qualities of good learning communities in general and of best practice. The difficulty is where this best practice falls short. Very few of the students who told their stories in this chapter felt they were an insider to their new study culture. Even those who appeared from the outside to 'belong' and be successful within it, as Katya is, experienced conflicts of expectation, crises in self-esteem, and struggles with competing personae.

Feeling one does not belong, however, is not a static state of being. In all accounts of transitions into a second culture, a stage of alienation and separation is seen as typical. Adisa et al. (2019) calls the stage of struggle with the new culture, *storming;* Brown and Holloway (2008) call it *the shock of arrival.* There is wide acknowledgement that the feeling of not belonging described by Katya is part of a natural process, which changes, even if it does not ever entirely resolve.

Adaptation and acculturation

> *I adapted to these different cultural circumstances.*

Katya's story shows how she adjusted to the new culture in a series of painful steps, starting with the 'shock of arrival' (Brown and Holloway, 2008) at everything from the way her tutor addressed her, to dress and expressions of politeness. This is a stage described in the literature with multiple metaphors of turbulence, including 'storming' (Adisa, 2019), and 'disintegration' (Pedersen, 1995).

Yet feelings about a new culture are rarely static and, as with any relationship, there are peaks and troughs, periods of change and adjustment. Whilst the literature agrees these stages take place, there can be no definitive explanation as to when, what, how or how often. The only truth must be that individuals map their own journeys, at their own pace, with the literature suggesting certain likely stations en route. Table 2.1 suggests two interpretations of the journey, mapped 25 years apart and from two different studies into cross-cultural transitions. It will be seen at a glance, that Adisa et al. (2019) miss out the 'honeymoon' category, the stage of euphoria and excitement on first arrival. Indeed, amongst the students we met in this chapter, none actually identified these joyous first encounters as stories they wished to transmit. Perhaps this honeymoon period is so brief, or it transmutes so quickly into something more troubling that it is hard to recall without describing instead its transience.

Other differences between these two models are interesting. Adisa et al. (2019) are more hopeful in suggesting a stage they call 'functioning' in which the cultural tools are fully operational and work well for the student. Katya recounts this stage too, as a student who picks up the strategies she needs to succeed, whilst never fully believing in them, and in fact feeling she has left part of herself behind in the process. Her process more nearly maps over Pederson's model, as he describes 'adaptation' in terms of a nearer connection with the host culture, and the adoption of a new kind of emotional intelligence to accommodate it more empathetically.

Identity

> *I sacrificed part of myself in the process.*

Studies into language learning show us that the process of adopting a new language can be experienced as the adoption of a new self. Ehrman and Dornyei (1998, p. 184) tell us, after extensive research into learner motivation, that "language learning frequently entails new thought processes, identity and

Table 2.1 Two approaches to intercultural transition

Pederson (1995)	Adisa et al. (2019)
Honeymoon: first encounters which still carry the excitement of the new.	
Disintegration: phase of retreat, when the problems, embarrassments, frustrations and stress of dealing with the alien culture and unpredictable cultural encounters begin to weigh down – creating feelings of inadequacy, isolation and homesickness.	Storming: where the culture is experienced as new, discomforting, alien and where feelings such as failing to belong, running behind, not understanding are typical.
Re-integration/Reversion: In this phase, the sojourner becomes irritated by the ways of the host community and reconnects strongly with their home culture and its values that they now deem superior.	
'Adjustment': beginning to feel more at ease and more comfortable to operate autonomously. "During this phase, the sojourner constructs a new emotional intelligence that fits with their host culture and to escape from the empathic fog that has troubled their earlier dealings" (Haigh 2013: 198).	Acclimatisation: there is some reconciliation to the new culture, and a gradual understanding of cultural clues, what they mean and how to respond to them.
	Functioning: understanding, accepting and adopting the cultural tools needed for success.

values that can present a threat to learners". Such threats to self can be triggered by small events unseen to the outsider: Katya's discomfort with empty politeness, or awkwardness at being dressed formally. Yet Katya shows us these discomforts are far from merely surface. Pavlenko and Lantolf (2000) describe second culture learners reorganising "the plot of their life stories in line with the new set of conventions and social relationships sanctioned by the new community" (Pavlenko and Lantolf, 2000, p. 219). This is not only about new ways to speak and dress, but "new ways to mean" (ibid).

In making this leap, Katya describes adopting a new self. There is interesting literature that suggests life stories are a process of role-playing, taking on new selves without actually believing in them. Brissett and Edgley (2006) invite us to consider etymologies such as the ancient Greek term 'prosopon', which means both a ritual mask and a face; or 'persona' which is the ancient Roman term for a mask and a person. We have seen in our student stories above, some role-playing – for example Aidan joining in with socialising without really believing in the way this is happening. Whilst giving up something of their expectations, or even part of themselves as Katya describes it, there is an element of gain in the change. Brown and Holloway (2008) suggest other responses to the shock of arrival. One is to choose segregation: avoiding the host language, resisting change and blocking out the new culture. Another is to adapt to the new while staying strongly identified with the first culture and balancing the two. These are not necessarily fixed points, and they could be two stages in a life cycle, moving from resistance of the culture to an accommodation with it. Brown and Holloway see both of these responses as positive solutions to the struggle between first and new identities.

Cosmopolitan independence

> *Change and adaptation are part of the process of personal and professional growth and have real value and real-life consequences.*

Katya describes a journey with a destination in which she is aware of both gains in personal growth and loss in former self. This balancing of cultures has been widely researched amongst children who grow up, learn and relate in several cultures, and in so doing create a kind of third self that is neither one culture nor the other. These are called 'third-culture kids' but the validity of this experience for older adults is a subject of interest too (Barker 2018). In this third place, Katya recognises which specific ways of being she has lost or changed (such as her directness), and which she has gained (such as a new adaptability); yet she is still connected with who she was and has a sense of its value and authenticity. Haigh (2013) would describe what Katya has reached as cosmopolitan independence. He defines this as the point of arrival, when

> the sojourner feels at ease enough to be able to consider and cope with the potential, possibilities and differences between the two cultures, able to make their own decisions based on this cross-cultural awareness, and commonly even to become enthusiastic about the new culture.
> (Haigh 2013: 199)

His significant exemplum of cosmopolitan independence is Mahatma Gandhi as an Indian student studying in South Africa, reconfiguring his anger about apartheid into powerful influence and determination to effect change. So indeed, the process of cultural transition entails personal growth as assumptions, even comforts, are left behind and new challenges test and expand everything about who we are and what we believe.

Learning maps: who am I as a learner?

This chapter has shared the stories of Katya, Gerda, Aidan, Carmel and many others as they travel between study borders. The literature shows they are not alone in their experiences, and there are echoes with students in several parts of the world. However, we need still to ask how this might make a difference and what it is we can do with this knowledge. A suggestion is to become an ethnographer of your experience and notice what it is in your learning environment which you find strange, new, challenging or uncomfortable. This means:

> situate oneself wherever there is communicative conduct, and watch it and listen to it, with eyes and ears alert and open to the particularity of what one finds there.
>
> (Philipsen, 2010, p. 166)

To do so, in this section are six questions which can inform an ethnographer's notebook, whether your challenge is in communication, educational systems and practices or social systems and practices. Our students in the stories in this chapter had challenges in all these categories: what politeness means, how formal to be in class, how and when to access support, how to dress and present oneself, whether and when to play or study. We have also seen that there are choices: whether to understand without changing, to adopt a role, or to transform.

1. What cultural difference have you noticed that is significant to you for any reason?
2. Where/how is this cultural difference successfully negotiated?
3. What would you need to do/change to negotiate this difference successfully?
4. What would be gained by negotiating this successfully?
5. What would be lost by negotiating this successfully?
6. How would you best like to negotiate this difference (for example, notice without changing, adopt it yourself, find a compromise)?

Table 2.2 takes as an example the challenge noted by Katya, Gerda and Chen: indirectness in communication, excessive politeness and hedging such that messages appeared unclear and untrustworthy. Consider the example given for each question, and then add examples from your own experience.

Further topics for reflection and reading

Below are several studies of the crossing cultures experience of students in specific locations: Benin, Jordan, Syria, or with specific identities that make their experiences both distinct and also potentially marginalised.

We have mentioned several times thus far, that our discussions in this book do not focus on specific places or kinds of student. Here is an opportunity to explore some of those more specific contexts.

- How do these place- or student-specific studies expand our insights into the study culture?
- How far could the research strategies used for gathering and analysing information be applied to your own experience as a learner, teacher or researcher?

Table 2.2 Becoming an ethnographer of your learning

What cultural difference have you noticed that is significant to you for any reason?	Where/how do you see this cultural difference successfully negotiated?	What would you need to do/change to negotiate this difference successfully?	What would be gained by negotiating this successfully?	What would be lost by negotiating this successfully?	How would you best like to negotiate this difference?
Communication: indirectness and excess politeness.	Peers in class who understand the subtext: when a comment is in fact criticism or requires action.	Understand the subtext when used by others. Try making criticism myself using this 'hedged' approach.	Realising what people are really saying. Not being thought to be impolite.	My natural way of talking. I feel annoyed by the indirectness and find it untrustworthy.	In my own language, at home and with my own friends, I do not intend to change. I also will continue to check I have understood correctly by asking directly, e.g. "Do you mean I need to rewrite this essay?"
Your example					

About specific places

Al-Fattal, A. and Ayoubi, R., (2013) 'Student needs and motives when attending a university: exploring the Syrian case', *Journal of Marketing for Higher Education*, 23, pp. 204–225.

Al-Quhen, K.Y. (2012) 'Cultural diversity in university requirements and among international students at Al-bay university in Jordan', *European Journal of Social Science*, 28 (4), pp. 489–501.

Hessling O'Neil, M. (2012) 'You who have been to school, What have you become?: An ethnographic study of university life in Benin', PhD Dissertation, Michigan State University: East Lansing, MI.

About specific people

Caldwell, E.F. and Hyams-Ssekasi, D. (2016) 'Leaving home: the challenges of Black African international students prior to studying overseas', *Journal of International Students*, 6 (2) pp. 588–613.

Cole-Morton, G.S. (2013) 'Experiences and expectations of an African American male veteran student in higher education', EdD Dissertation, East Tennessee State University Johnson City, TN.

References

Adisa, T., Ajibade, M.B., Gbadamosi, G. and Mordi, C. (2019) 'Understanding the trajectory of the academic progress of international students in the UK', *Education and Training*, 61 (9), pp. 1100–1122.

Al-Fattal, A. and Ayoubi, R. (2013) 'Student needs and motives when attending a university: exploring the Syrian case', Journal of Marketing for Higher Education, 23, pp. 204–225.

Al-Quhen, K.Y. (2012) 'Cultural diversity in university requirements and among international students at Al-bay university in Jordan', *European Journal of Social Science*, 28 (4), pp. 489–501.

Barker, G. (2018) *Third-culture individuals*. Abingdon: Routledge.

Biemans, H. and Van Mil, M. (2008) 'Learning styles of Chinese and Dutch students compared within the context of Dutch higher education in life sciences', *The Journal of Agricultural Education and Extension*, 14 (3), p265–278.

Borghi, S., Mainardes, E. and Silva, E. (2016) 'Expectations of higher education students: a comparison between the perception of student and teachers', *Tertiary Education and Management*, 22 (2), p171–188.

Brissett, D. and Edgley, C. (2006) *Life as theater: a dramaturgical sourcebook*. 2nd edn. Brunswick, NJ: Transaction.

Brown, L. and Holloway, L. (2008) 'The initial stage of the international sojourn: excitement or culture shock?', *British Journal of Guidance and Counselling*, 36 (1), pp. 33–49.

Caldwell, E.F. and Hyams-Ssekasi, D. (2016) 'Leaving home: the challenges of Black African international students prior to studying overseas', *Journal of International Students*, 6 (2), pp. 588–613.

Campbell, J. and Li, M. (2008), 'Asian students' voices: an empirical study of Asian students' learning experiences at a New Zealand University', *Journal of Studies in International Education*, 12(4), pp. 375–396.

Carbaugh, D. (2007) 'Cultural discourse analysis: communication practices and intercultural encounters', *Journal of Intercultural Communication Research*, 36 (3), pp. 167–182.

Clifford, V., Adeunji, H., Haigh, M., Henderson, J., Spiro, J. and Hudson, J. (2011) *Report on Brookes Student Learning Experience Project: Fostering Interculturality and Global Perspectives at Brookes through Dialogue with Staff*. Oxford Centre for Staff Learning and Development: Oxford Brookes University.

Cole-Morton, G.S. (2013) 'Experiences and expectations of an African American male veteran student in higher education', EdD Dissertation, East Tennessee State University Johnson City, TN.

Currant, N. (2020) *"My stomach churns": belonging and strategies for belonging for BME students in a white university*. EdD Thesis, Oxford: Oxford Brookes University.

Ehrman, M.E. and Dornyei, Z. (1998) *Interpersonal dynamics in second language education: the visible and invisible classroom*. Thousand Oaks, CA: Sage.

Gottschall, K. and Saltmarsh, S. (2017) '"You're not just learning it, you're living it!" constructing the "good life" in Australian university online promotional videos'. *Discourse: Studies in the Cultural Politics of Education.* 38 (5), pp. 768–781.

Haigh, M. (2013) 'Toward the intercultural self: exploring the effects of Mahatma Gandhi's international education' in Ryan, J. (ed.) *Cross cultural teaching and learning for home and international students: internationalisation of pedagogy and curriculum in higher education.* London: Routledge, pp. 196–210.

Hawkins, G.L. (2018) '*White environments, Black students: a case study of dominant White realities' Higher Education.* PhD/HE Dissertation, Azusa, California: Azusa Pacific University.

Hessling O'Neil, M. (2012) 'You who have been to school, What have you become?: An ethnographic study of university life in Benin', PhD Dissertation, Michigan State University: East Lansing, MI.

Higher Education Statistical Agency (2018), 'Higher education student data' [online]. Available at: www.hesa.ac.uk/data-and-analysis/students (Accessed: 30 June 2018).

Mainardes, E., Raposo, M. and Alves, H. (2012) 'Public university students' expectations: an empirical study based on the stakeholders theory', *Transylvanian Review of Administrative Sciences*, 35, pp. 173–196.

Marimuthu, M. and Ismail, I. (2012) 'Service quality in higher education: comparing the perceptions of stakeholders'. Ninth AIMS International Conference on Management. Pune, India, 1–4 January.

Mcleod, K.D. (2008) *A qualitative examination of culture shock and the influential factors affecting newly arrived Korean students at Texas A&M University.* PhD Dissertation, College Station, TX: Texas A&M University.

Merrill, B. (2015) 'Determined to stay or determined to leave? A tale of learner identities, biographies and adult students in higher education', *Studies in Higher Education*, 40 (10), pp. 1859–1871.

Parasuram, S., Zeithami, V.A. and Berry, L.L. (1985) 'A conceptual model of service quality and its implications for future research', *Journal of Marketing*, 49 (4), pp. 41–50.

Pavlenko, A. and Lantolf, J.P. (2000) 'Second language learning as participation and the (re)-construction of selves' in J.P. Lantolf (ed.) *Sociocultural theory and second language learning.* Oxford: Oxford University Press, pp. 154–176.

Pedersen, P. (1995) *The five stages of culture shock: critical incidents around the world.* Westport, CT: Greenwood Press.

Philipsen, G. (2010) 'Some thoughts on how to approach finding one's feet in unfamiliar cultural terrain', *Communication Monographs*, 77 (2), pp. 160–168.

Ryan, J. (ed.) (2013) *Cross cultural teaching and learning for home and international students: internationalisation of pedagogy and curriculum in higher education.* London: Routledge.

Schweisfurth, M. and Gu, Q. (2009) 'Exploring the experiences of international students in UK higher education: possibilities and limits of interculturality in university life', *Intercultural Education*, 20 (5), pp. 463–473.

Scott, D., Hughes, G., Evans, C., Burke, P.J., Walter, C. and Watson, D. (2013). *Learning Transitions in Higher Education.* London: Palgrave Macmillan.

Spiro, J. (2013) 'The reflective continuum: Reflecting for change and student response to reflective tasks', *Brookes eJournal of Learning and Teaching*, 2013.

Spiro, J. (2014) 'Learning Interconnectedness: internationalisation through engagement with one another', *Higher Education Quarterly*, 68 (1), pp. 65–84.

Spiro, J., Henderson, J. and Clifford, V. (2012) 'Independent Learning Crossing Cultures: Learning Cultures and Shifting Meanings', *Compare: A Journal of Comparative and International Education*, 42 (4), pp. 607–619.

UKCISA (2015) 'International students in the UK: strengths, challenges and opportunities. A report on the UKCISA regional conferences 2014–2015' [online]. Available at: www.ukcisa.org.uk/uploads/media/221/17664.pdf (Accessed: 18 November 2018).

Williams, K., Wooliams, M. and Spiro, J. (2020) (2nd edition) *Reflective writing*. Basingstoke: Palgrave Macmillan.

3 Being a higher education teacher
Who am I as an educator?

This chapter explores the experiences of higher education teachers as they cross borders from one teaching context to another. We ask what it is they saw, learned, perceived when their familiar teaching culture collided with another. The stories reveal much about the hidden cultures within institutions, the qualities which foster belonging and self-esteem and the impact of this on growth and self-development as an academic. The moments of collision reveal the differences between rhetoric and practice in higher education missions, the subtle ways power and hierarchy manifest themselves, different ways higher education teachers and their workplaces define success and how higher education teachers decipher what is needed to belong. The concluding section of this chapter suggests learning maps for the educator to recognise the gap between personal positions and institutional ones and find ways of bridging them.

The chapter draws its examples from more than 100 student and teacher learning diaries, field notes, interviews and focus groups between 2011 and 2021, and across four separate projects. These are:

- *Reflection in the Round* (RIR) with 38 student learning diaries and 10 annual focus groups of students on one-year postgraduate progammes between 2011 and 2020. In addition, teacher field notes track learning activities and learner responses during the same period. The project is published as Spiro (2013) and crystallised into teaching materials as Williams, Wooliams and Spiro (2020).
- *Fostering Interculturality* (FIC) with 16 participants, both staff and students, who identified as international, discussing their experience of crossing cultures in semi-structured interviews and focus groups. This project is published as Clifford et al., (2011) and Spiro et al., (2012).
- *Learning Interconnectedness* (LIC) with 50 international first degree students between 2010 and 2014 sharing weekly journals about their experiences of learning across cultures and languages. In addition, teacher field notes track cross-cultural learning activities and learner responses in the same period, 2010 to 2014 (Spiro, 2014).

DOI: 10.4324/9780429426261-3

38 *Being a high education teacher*

- *Crossing Study Borders* (CSB) with 24 staff and students who identified as having crossed borders in learning and teaching, interviewed between 2020 and 2021 and published here for the first time.

Learning from higher education teacher stories: who am I as a university teacher?

The stories in this chapter derive from participants in three studies between 2009 and 2021. The first, *Fostering Interculturality* (FIC) focused specifically on 36 university teachers at a UK university who identified as having international experience. Participants were asked to share responses to two questions:

- What can we learn from approaches to education in other countries?
- How can we deploy this knowledge to become more cosmopolitan as a learning community?

Their responses were gathered in three focus group meetings over the space of an academic year; and followed up by interviews with fifteen volunteers. Participants in this study are identified by number rather than by pseudonym. The second study, *Crossing Study Borders* (CSB), invited students and teachers with international experience from a range of networks internationally. Twenty-four participants who volunteered to participate had experience as students, and 13 in addition had experience as university teachers and responded from both perspectives. These participants responded to the questions:

- Were there any moments, as a student or as a university teacher, where you realised things are done differently here?
- Can you tell the story of what happened?
- What did that moment reveal about your learning/teaching in these different settings?

There is more detail in Chapter 1 about this project, which is central to the knowledge in this book. The third study, *Reflection in the Round* (RIR), included 38 participants studying for a higher degree between 2009 and 2011, who were also university teachers concurrently with or prior to their studies. Over the course of an academic year, they were invited to explore:

> In crossing from one place of work to another, what was revealed about your beliefs and assumptions, and about the different hidden values in each of the settings experienced?

How do higher education teachers experience their university cultures?

The ethos of an institution is conveyed in both subtle and tangible ways, and its approach to teacher evaluation is one indicator of institutional culture. The participants in our studies tell us of higher education cultures where students being invited to evaluate their teachers would be unthinkable; through to others who describe a surveillance culture, with constant audits, supervisory observations and student anonymised feedback. The process of gathering feedback from students can also be widely different in kind and purpose: from a culture in which teachers gather and respond to student feedback as part of their teaching, to others where this feedback is heavily centralised and monitored. To expect one approach and find another raised issues for the higher education teachers in our studies, about self-esteem, sense of purpose, the meaning of professionalism and institutional values.

This section shares stories from those who moved from one sector to another, one profession to another, one country to another, and the differences they encountered as they made these transitions. Anna moved from a small private college with a collaborative ethos, to a state-funded university in a large city, pressured to be compliant with national regulations and competitive with rivals.

> In my first job in a small private college, every three weeks or so I would have a feedback session asking students what was going well in the module and what they needed next. We were encouraged to regularly gather feedback from students but were free to do this how we liked. When I came to this university, the student feedback was managed by a central administrator based on a national survey, they were answered anonymously, and the answers went straight to a central stats administrator who sent you your results with any negatives in red. The students were assured there would be no comeback for anything they said, and their name would never be revealed. I felt that it pitted the students against us, encouraging them to feel quite entitled. I felt none of this was about teaching better or understanding students better. It was all about delivering a good service and getting better 'marks' than competitors in the field. Whilst I had paid a lot of attention before to the feedback sessions I used to run, I just saw this feedback as a set of numbers being fed into a system that had nothing to do with me. (CSB, Anna)

Anna was fully committed to the idea of developing as a teacher in the light of student response and feedback. Her experience with this kind of feedback, however, gave her the impression the students were being treated as customers and her role was simply to please them and be compliant with their wishes. Danielle describes a similar ethos in a university in Spain. She also felt the approach to student evaluation of teachers diminished her and turned her skills into a service.

> Students give feedback like quality control in a supermarket. For teachers it's demoralising – they never get to assess their institutions, but they are squeezed into constant assessment by bosses and students. (CSB, Danielle)

Both Anna and Danielle describe a culture of constant surveillance and measurement of teacher practice, with teachers as cogs in a larger (and commercialised) machinery of which learning is the product and students the customers.

Sophie tells a different story, as she crossed borders as a teacher from Canada to central Europe. In her first university she regularly gathered feedback from students and did this as part of her class teaching. In her new place of work, no-one was doing this, nor did they expect her to do so. She found colleagues avoided discussion of what happened in their classes, or of any problems they might be experiencing.

> In my first institution we were always conferring on good practice, sharing materials, and troubleshooting problems with one another. In my new place, classrooms were sacred places and no-one else was allowed in. No-one had any idea what anyone else was doing or how. People were totally private about their materials or activities. If students didn't like a class they just dropped it and went to another one. There was no incentive to change and no learning from one another or the students. (CSB, Sophie)

In Anna and Danielle's examples, feedback was used as a mechanism for evaluating a service, and neither felt it had any useful 'washback' for their own practice, though it provided statistics about satisfaction. The culture they missed was not only one of rapport and direct dialogue with students, but also one in which they were able to respond to student evaluations directly, make changes in their teaching and think about their impact. Though Sophie's new institution was very different, she too missed this virtuous circle of gathering feedback and learning from it. A culture of cosy isolation in Sophie's example seemed to be as demotivating as a culture of constant surveillance. Sophie had the message from her context that higher education teachers were individuals trusted to "get on with things"; Danielle and Anna had the message that they were cogs in a larger corporation and their role was to keep its mechanisms working smoothly. Yet the outcome for each of them was the same: "there didn't seem to be any value attached to me as a teacher developing my practice" (CSB, Sophie).

Sally (CSB) travelled in the opposite direction: from an institution that had no interest in her as an educator or scholar, to another that gave her career development high exposure. Sally explains that, in her first college, she was "like a battery hen, on the run all day from class to class". Working, and earning your salary, meant being physically in the college, with long hours in the building and few breaks. When she changed to the new institution, "it was the first time anyone had ever asked what my own goals were and gave me time for them. Because I had never thought in terms of my own goals, I had no idea what they actually were". This focus on personal goals was both an inspiration and a problem for Sally. In her own interviews with fellow professionals, most felt that higher education "gave them space to grow. They wanted to be able to fail better". Attention to herself as a developing academic was an inspiring new dimension:

> it felt very individualistic, a place to be you, have your own agenda, to carve out your own career – there was a lot of interest in my interests, which I found really unusual, because I was from a place where you had a job to do, and suddenly I had a space to develop me, and that felt really peculiar. There had been no time for professional development in my previous job. It had been very prescriptive. But in HE it felt wonderful – when I worked in FE I felt like I was a battery chicken, cooped up, you produce as in the egg, do what you need to do, go back to your cage and don't grow – in HE it was like a suddenly became free range. (CSB, Sally)

Becoming a professional in her UK institution meant explicit programmes of development; qualifications such as a postgraduate certificate in higher education learning (PGCertHE) or a fellowship from the Higher Education Academy (FHEA) and forms of engagement such as peer observation, reflective diaries and self-evaluations, action research projects and peer learning sets. Another teacher, Kirsten, teaching in China for the first time, described the value of working alongside a local teacher in a spirit of mutual learning:

> she was a fantastic source of understanding and inspiration, and helped me to work through the challenges in ways that the students found acceptable. We approached this very much as a sort of peer-mentoring process – she learned from me about ways to teach interactively, which she said she would continue, and I learned from her a lot about the culture of Chinese education. (CSB, Kirsten)

More importantly, these cycles of learning draw attention away from outcomes and products, and towards process and self-development. They recognise the expertise of being a higher education teacher as additional to content scholarship and that this development is continuous and does not finish with a qualification or job title.

It is clear from stories of teachers whose experience straddles ten years or more, that the tendency towards professionalism has much accelerated in the past decade. Whilst there are some doubts about this burgeoning of formal development, as the section will later discuss, Tim finds this change fruitful: "Good things about now – in the past there was no training, you just mimicked what had happened before" (CSB, Tim). Dared writes of his move from Ireland to Australia in the 2000s:

> I remember peer observation schemes – they were always quite challenging for a lot of people, people always thought they were being judged. Now everyone wants to learn from each other, but even then peer observation was controversial. (CSB, Dared)

However, the university conveyed to Sally the message that skills derived from other sectors and professions were theoretically valued, but not practically so. They were not deemed to be transferable into the new context, nor were they conferred enough status to share with colleagues. Whilst she had many skills related to her teaching in the FE sector, which were valued at interview

> the minute I entered higher education that value was lowered, it had absolutely no symbolic capital. FE experience was seriously depleted in value. No-one tells you that overnight the value of your professional knowledge depletes. It's paradoxical, because that is why you were employed. (CSB, Sally)

Sally tells the story of a friend who moved from being co-partner in a small business, to lecturer in a higher education college. She, too, felt the 'self' she presented as a business professional was, not only undervalued, but taboo within her new institution. Her husband, an experienced higher education teacher, advised her

> not to take her briefcase, because the significance of a briefcase was business and she was now an academic. She found that really difficult, that she had embodied items such as a car, a briefcase, a suit, as the value of her impact in her professional career, items demonstrated her success, but they meant nought in HE, she could have dressed up as if she was doing the gardening, symbols such a briefcase, jewellery meant nothing. (CSB, Sally)

A participant in the Reflection in the Round project reflected on this same phenomenon, as she too began to 'dress down' for work, to fit in with the others, and explained it like this: "I think by dressing down I am saying – who I am at home is who I am at work. In other words, I *am* an academic, it's not something I become when I go to work" (RIR). Adopting a "change of wardrobe", in the way Gerda describes it in Chapter 2, or even a new 'mask', might at a deeper level suggest that the higher education teacher is separating teacher-academic self from other roles and is merely acting; so to dress "as if you are doing the gardening" (CSB, Sally) suggests congruity between who you are as a person and who you are as a teacher.

Whilst these higher education teachers described both the physical and emotional changes they needed to make in order to fit in, they also described alternative communities lying outside their actual place of work: national and international special interest groups, professional networks, subject disciplinary fora, journal editorial boards and conference meeting rooms. Within these virtual or outlying communities, they found like-minded peers and a more comfortable fit, whilst in their own workplaces they described collisions with opaque ground rules or hidden hierarchies. One point of difference is the capacity as a higher education teacher to influence change. Within their self-selected communities, they described their ability to influence "policy in the journal I was editing to include more qualitative research" (RIR), to create events "in my special interest group to look at new assessment guidelines" (RIR), or to champion new causes "in my professional network. We set up a petition for academics at risk (in Turkey)". Yet this capacity to influence seemed to be much diminished in 'home' institutions, where several teacher stories describe resistance to change. Katya described issues she notices crossing borders from Poland to the US and UK:

> The other issue in UK academia was the lack of tolerance for any change. When I came to the UK from the US, I was full of ideas and kept suggesting changes and improvements, but no one was really interested in these conversations. Change takes a long time here and you must be very patient and resilient if you want to implement any new approaches or solutions. (CSB, Katya)

She felt this resistance to change held her back and limited both herself and her institution. Dared compared Australia and the UK, describing the fragility of systems in the UK and their resistance to change even where this is actually part of their mission.

> The external examiner system, they don't have it in Australia and they don't need it. Here it's such a sacred cow, the whole approach to quality assurance, the systems themselves aren't properly tested. We had an external examiner who spoke the truth about the course, and the system suggests you have to do something about it. But the reality is you can't do anything about it because it comes back to bite. It shows that the systems themselves are fragile and exist in name only. (CSB, Dared)

For Dared too, the failure of the institution to respond actively to the external examiner's bid for change, led to his resignation. Systemic power manifests itself at the interpersonal level too. Carmel described her surprise at the overt nature of power between herself and her manager in a Saudi Arabian women's college:

> I was in the office one day and the CEO came in. She was very scary, never made eye contact, and didn't use English in front of us so very intimidating. One day, she came in and said something to the admin person in Arabic. After she left the admin person said she had said I should follow her. She walked very very fast to the office with me running behind her. I was shocked it was a huge office, beautiful view (whilst all

our classrooms had no view with frosted windows), piles of chocolates. She came out in perfect English. I had requested to work in a different office. There were three women's campuses and the one where I was was the furthest away from where I lived, 45 minutes or 1 hour's drive away every day on a bus that was sent to meet us. She said, "we got your request and no you can't." I don't think she knew how rude she was and how bad this whole meeting was – talking about me in Arabic so I couldn't understand, making me run after her. (CSB, Carmel)

Carmel's surprise comes from several bases: firstly, power in this institution was visibly marked by better working conditions and the symbols of luxury; secondly, the overt treatment of herself as an empoyee without agency to make changes. There appeared to be an assumption she would understand, as her rejection was not accompanied by explanation, or mitigation of any kind. Carmel's first culture was one with a strong discourse of politeness, hedging of bad news and minimising overt expressions of power in workplaces.

The cultural collision was experienced in reverse for those coming to UK institutions. A participant in Reflection in the Round (RIR) described the 'open door' policy with her head of department, and the ease of communication with her as line manager, including the formal milestones in the year where personal goals were reviewed.

> I didn't even know the word 'line manager' before, and it took me a while to realise that the annual meetings were for me and not for her. I don't think I'd ever spoken one word to my head of department where I worked before. (RIR)

Another participant in the Fostering Interculturality project told us: "I wanted to live in Britain and the academic system is less hierarchical, less inflexible" (FIC). One way that this flexibility demonstrated itself, was in attitudes to physical presence on campus. Sally described the very different cultures of judgement in her first further education sector, versus her new higher education sector.

> Working from home, at FE I needed to show I was really working through outputs – I needed to demonstrate I was doing something and earning my pay. In FE I was constantly on guard, there were constant demands from OfSTED, I was always being observed. You were constantly being prepared to be looked at, and having to explain yourself and show you were meeting standards. It was a waste of anxiety. In HE there is no-one looking over my shoulder all the time. (CSB, Sally)

The new HE sector Sally had entered suggests a structure in which university teachers are given agency and entrusted with doing their job well. This lack of surveillance suggests a flatter power structure at the interpersonal level, if not at the institutional level. Forms of address suggest hidden values in relation to power and status. One participant in the reflection project explains:

> over here (in the UK) it's just as taboo for colleagues to use each other's titles as the other way round at home. If you, say, called a colleague you work with Prof, it would be almost a joke – even if they actually are a Prof! (RIR)

This approach to naming was echoed by Andrea describing her first study place in Germany:

> In Germany it's much more formal, you would never use the tutor's first name, always the formal pronoun. They address you as Mr, Ms. You wouldn't use the academic title. Another thing, insisting on having your title used is considered very bad form, it's just showing off. (CSB, Andrea)

Student and teacher stories suggest a wide range of experiences with regards to levels of formality, forms of address and 'friendliness' as they cross from a familiar to an unfamiliar study culture. Here is Annabel's experience of how formality expectations changed as she moved from the US to the UK:

> In the US I would never call professors by their first name – even now when I am friends with one of them I am waiting for her to suggest I can call her by her first name. I would even look up their status to see whether to call them Doctor or Professor – it adds a degree of formality. It erases formality between teachers/students. The professors all dressed up in suits and ties. (CSB, Annabel)

These forms of address are far more than surface indicators of respect. Aidan describes his experience in Japan:

> one time a friend of mine in a Kanji class expressed to the teacher that he was cold 'Sensei, samui' (lit. Teacher, [I'm] cold), without the honorific politeness required by proficient speakers. Perhaps he should have known better, or perhaps he just didn't know how to say it properly, but the teacher was quite angry and she literally made him repeat word for word how to say it politely, which was incredibly awkward for everyone else in the class. It could have been done in many other more polite/less condescending ways, but it seemed the teacher wanted to make a point. More of a reflection on her personality than anything else, most probably, but still is a reaction which wouldn't happen in a UK university setting, where the students are all adults. (CSB, Aidan)

What, then, is the nature of a higher education teachers' connection with their students? Here there are a spectrum of expectations from: teacher as friend, peer, parent, mentor, authority. Of course, where the teacher is positioned is influenced by how the student is perceived. We saw at the start of the chapter, that teachers felt evaluation policies gave students the status of customers and teachers the status of service providers. We also learn a great deal by looking at the student perspective. Aidan, whom we met in Chapter 2 travelling to Japan, collides with his expectation that university students and their teachers might relate to one another as peers:

> Uni in Japan suddenly felt like I'd gone backwards to 6th form equivalent. It was okay to form friendly relationships with the teachers, but a certain power-respect was expected (as non-equals). Homework and attendance was diligently monitored. (CSB, Aidan)

Naming is part of this learning, acting as a signifier of power, seniority and distance. Here Aidan negotiates naming when a teacher is on the cusp of becoming a friend.

> I remember asking if I could address one of my favourite Japanese teachers by her first name, which she was quite surprised about and reluctantly agreed. In hindsight I think personally, being aware of my cultural background, she was fine with it, but perhaps was apprehensive because of how it reflected on her amongst her Japanese peers. (CSB, Aidan)

Whilst teacher as friend was crossing a boundary, teacher in a parental role was more acceptable in his setting: parental in that the relationship, though not 'friendly' in the sense Aidan had hoped above, would be informal and social, with some sense of the teacher's pastoral care of students.

> The Japanese students would exchange contact details with their teachers, texting them was a normal thing. There was a power relationship but in some ways also they were closer. For example with undergraduates they would go out for a drink with their lecturers. That would never happen here (in the UK). (CSB, Aidan)

Andrea described a transition between an ancient prestigious university, to a former polytechnic side by side in the same city. In the first the relationships were "much more personal"; in the latter students "see you as someone who doesn't have a life outside the office, you are a tutor you don't exist outside the university, then if they bump into you, they don't know what to say, they turn away, they don't actually speak to me in the street". What accounts for this kind of difference? Tim (CSB) compared cultures over time and described a shift within one institution from the 1980s to the present day.

> In the 80s students were real people – there has been a phased retreat from personal relations. Students sitting behind computers now. You had a sense then of who they really were – it was all about teaching. (CSB, Tim)

He mourned the 'centralisation' of the teacher-student relationship: for example, national surveys, central admission procedures and anonymised marking. "All these things used to be done by us in small teams and we followed every student right through from first application to graduation. Now that is all broken up into about ten different departments and people, and none of them within the subject team".

What, then, constitutes success for these higher education teachers? We saw in the stories of Anna and Danielle at the start of the chapter, that their universities were aiming for student satisfaction, whereas they themselves were seeking development of their own excellence as teachers. Sally, in contrast, found herself in a university which set up milestones such as certificates, fellowships and doctorates as indicators of success, whilst as an educator she preferred to put students, teams and teaching first:

> I can't really get used to the culture where you are there for your own career and development. I regard success as helping someone else to succeed and I am really most happy when someone has fulfilled something they wanted to do, been able to do something or succeeded and I could help them along. I have never been interested so much in just doing things for myself and can't get used to that. Even if there is success I would always consider it was the achievement of a team, or of the student I had worked with. In HE it's much more about me. (CSB, Sally)

In Sally's account, another spectrum of significant difference is revealed: between those university teachers for whom success lies in their empowerment of others and capacity to foster learning, in contrast to those for whom success lies in their contribution to scholarship and research in their discipline. For many of the teachers in these studies, the balance between these two is uneasy. Sally found research deskilling and contradictory to her professional priorities. In Chapter 2 we saw her beginning a doctorate programme and describing it as "breaking her confidence". Danielle, in contrast, was disappointed that there was no research expectation in her institution, and an expectation only that she would "deliver" classes to the satisfaction of students. For neither was the teaching-research balance right.

Other university teachers arrive from the entirely opposite perspective: committed to their subject discipline and successful scholars within it, having to think of themselves as educators seems a stretch too far. Andrea, whom we met earlier as experienced in two kinds of universities in two different countries, explained: "here is quite a lot of emphasis on qualifications, and more and more young academics are encouraged to do these, they are now a job requirement. However, they are still seen as an inconvenience" (CSB,

Andrea). She described the different approaches taken by the university lecturers, for them to engage with this:

> they do a portfolio, there were two really good submissions, one who had basically tried to do the bare minimum and get through, not reflective, just descriptive, from Classics. There is a general feeling in Classics that this is just educational talk and waffle, you just talk the talk and get it on your CV rather than opportunity to learn something about yourself as an educator. (CSB, Andrea)

Sophie described the clues within her university that suggested a research-oriented rather than teaching-oriented culture. Her colleagues listed staff publications at the end of every academic year, and staff had adopted the custom of pasting front pages of their books and articles on their office door. Colleagues were invisible sometimes for months during summer and sabbatical periods, with an expectation they were pursuing scholarly research; this absence would rarely be questioned, and especially so if there were clear outputs. Adrianna regretted the loss of a culture that provided space for academic research, as she moved from a research-oriented institution to one that was teaching-oriented.

> I was surprised there were meetings, development events, conferences we were expected to do in the holidays. The summer was when I was used to being on my own, that was sacred time. I needed it for my own writing. I really resented giving that up. (CSB, Adrianna)

Adrianna was clear, too, that in her first place of work, research was the activity that would ensure her tenure and value in the institution. She was in continual conflict in her new institution with peers who felt she wasn't "pulling her weight" and who expected her presence "for things that weren't helpful for my career at all". In the culture she was familiar with, the criteria for staff selection were publication record and the criteria for success and promotion were international research reputation. Danielle's institution in Spain, by contrast, selected teachers on the basis of teaching qualifications and references. Success was measured by student satisfaction, and promotion was based on the capacity to manage aspects of the higher education system such as recruitment or marketing. The institutions were based on very different economic models too: with Adrianna's first institution financed by world class research, and the second financed by student numbers. Andrea characterised the difference:

> in Germany it's much more first and foremost a teaching establishment versus here teaching is an inconvenience, it gets in the way of your research. (CSB, Andrea)

In the midst of this to-ing and fro-ing of surrounding cultures, the higher education teachers had their own notion of success and adapted to their new cultures, without losing this sense of their own purpose. Sally did complete her doctorate but found a niche in the university structure which played to her strengths developing and supporting colleagues. Anna did conform to the way feedback was gathered centrally but created feedback circles within her own teaching from which she could learn from her students. Andrea, who straddled one teaching-oriented and one research-oriented culture, brought into the former the skills of research rigour, and into the latter the attention to pedagogic excellence.

We have uncovered several polarities in this chapter, along which higher education teachers position themselves: professional or scholar, scholar or teacher, teacher or researcher, individual or member of a collective, compliant or creative; friend, mentor, parent, peer, co-creator or authority to their students.

Teacher stories through the literature lens

We shall explore the literature through a 'vignette' in which a culture clash placed a university teacher's career at risk.

Cora at her European university

Cora was a successful student at a European university, progressing smoothly from her first degree to a teaching fellowship that combined study for a doctorate and some undergraduate teaching. The teaching was strictly functional, helping to finance her research, and she just visited the department to teach. Her colleagues too spent minimal time in the department, as they often had second jobs private tutoring or in school. Her students did not complain about her teaching, and this seemed to fulfil her obligations to the department, alongside once termly department meetings.

Cora at her UK university

After her doctorate she moved to a university in the UK. The teaching started in early October, so she arrived a few days before, in good time for her first class. To her surprise, her 'line manager' told her she should have arrived three weeks earlier and had missed an induction workshop and several student welcome events. She was given a timetable of teaching development sessions, team meetings, and departmental meetings that extended well beyond what she regarded as Easter and summer breaks. In addition, her line manager explained a policy of formative assignments, office hours and online discussion sites, which seemed to triple the time attached to each taught programme. Cora assumed all these were optional, and that, as in her last institution, as long as students did not complain she

> was fine. She also assumed that, as a research-active lecturer, she was entitled to focus on research. After six months, her line manager called her in to say she was being given a first warning of disciplinary issues, for failing to comply with university teaching strategy, not engaging in development opportunities, and missing essential meetings that were integral to her academic responsibilities.

What went wrong with Cora in terms of her expectations, and those of her institution? Why did they fail to match so significantly? We can classify Cora's dilemma into several themes.

Kinds of institution: what is valued here?

One of Cora's dilemmas is that she has moved between two very different university structures. In his survey of young academics' career progression, Finkelstein et al. (2014) compared several kinds of institution. In some countries such as France and Cyprus, the lecturer in a state-controlled university is employed by the government rather than by the department or university. This means loyalties do not lie within the institution, as it is not the university that selects, promotes or develops them. Tenure and promotion depend, not on fitting well into the department at a local level, but on external judgements and paper assessment of national qualification and publications rather than through person-to-person interview. For Cora, in this kind of institution, it would have been folly *not* to have focused on her own research goals. Unfortunately, in crossing a study border she has moved into a very different kind of institution, one described by Finkelstein as 'institutionally anchored' (Finkelstein et al., 2014, p. 58). In this new setting, it is the university itself that chooses, employs and promotes its staff. Departments function as teams, at least ideally, and its members are expected to identify with and contribute to its life. Institutions of this kind, and teams within them, may vary in the way they balance individual research goals and active engagement with the collective; but still there is a significant paradigm shift from the institution Cora was used to, and the one she has arrived at. Another difference Finkelstein points towards, is the institution that founds itself on part-time professionals, or on academics who supplement their income with other employment. This may be an economic necessity, and the system is flexible enough to allow for it, whether covertly or overtly. In contrast, contractual agreements in Cora's new workplace include exclusion of other paid regular employment, and full professional identification with the new institution; an identification carried into all other external roles, such as consultancies, committee, examining or publishing roles. In other words, in her first institution Cora felt she was acting for herself; whilst in her new workplace she was expected to act in the name of her new institution, and to represent it in all her professional roles. Table 3.1 summarises these various universities.

Table 3.1 University types and characteristics (based on Finkelstein et al., 2014, pp. 52–53)

Academic type	Characteristics	Example of settings
National/government-anchored State-controlled	Employed by the government Recruitment by government Promotion not predictable Faculties are not organised as collegiate units but as hierarchies of authority Promotion is through the subject discipline	France – teaching and research separated Germany – teaching and research integrated
Institutionally anchored	Employed by the institution Promotion more predictable Faculties function collegially rather than hierarchically Academics are colleagues rather than in competition	UK
Part-time professional	'cadre of professionals who teach part-time'	Mexico/Latin America
Community-anchored	'danwei' – university as a place of residence, including family life; academic as engaging in the conventions, lifestyle and aspirations of and within the community	China
Hybrid	Combining aspects of several of these, such as: part-time professional/part-time employed by an institution	

In a review of 248 mission statements from universities globally (Cortés-Sánchez, 2018) trends were revealed specific to different types of university. Publicly funded universities emphasised their mission to the community; privately funded universities emphasised the value of education for the individual. Another tendency was for smaller universities to focus on the value of life skills, whilst larger universities focused on the value of world-leading research excellence.

Being an educator: is research enough?

We also saw, in Cora's story and in several of those in the section above, that higher education lecturers had very different attitudes to teaching from an inconvenience that "gets in the way of research" (CSB, Andrea), to a "reason why I am here" (CSB, Sally). Cora's first institution was a government-driven institution, promotion depended on single-minded attention to her own career and neither she nor her colleagues were encouraged to view teaching as an expertise distinct from scholarship. Yet the growth in educational qualifications for higher education worldwide suggests that Cora's experience is rapidly becoming out of date. National organisations worldwide have formalised qualifications for the higher education educator, for example: Qualifications Framework in the European Higher Education Area (QF-EHEA); the Australian Qualifications Framework; the New Zealand Qualification Framework and Higher Education Academy framework in the UK (Quality Assurance Agency, 2014). These aim to provide standards of teaching excellence in universities, theorised by its transformational potential (Kreber, 2005 and 2013). They also provide a developmental structure for growing as an educator. To become a fellow of the Higher Education Academy, the educator needs to evidence a number of competences such as: keeping up to date with the scholarship of their subject and of higher education teaching; being responsive to feedback from peers, students and appraisal processes; and actively engaging in professional development to maintain standards of excellence in teaching and subject knowledge (Quality Assurance Agency, 2014).

These include the very skills and areas of development Cora has been reprimanded for lacking. Vasudeva et al. (2020), sampling 36 African universities, found that they too marketed and strategically prioritised "educational excellence" (Vasudeva et al. 2020). This mission is not empty rhetoric. Higher education academics strongly align themselves with this goal too. Nabaho et al. (2019) conducted a study at Makerere University in Uganda, researching academics' perceptions of good teaching. A thematic analysis suggests that their views are widely shared. Educators engaged in the HEA fellowship development process (Aktar and Oxley, 2019), mission statements from Harvard (2020), Wisconsin, Cambridge universities (2021), studies of Hong Kong university students (Morrison and Evans, 2018) suggest that these are the qualities they value and aim for in their teaching role:

- being knowledgeable
- being student-centred
- demonstrating good communication skills
- undertaking research-based teaching
- demonstrating professionalism
- being approachable
- being organised
- teaching skills that supported student learning and encouraged critical thinking
- the teacher's ability to give clear explanations.

Even if these qualities are not overt, they may be implied in messages made known to staff and students. Harvard University's mission statement to students sends a message to academic staff to be philosophically principled educators as well as subject specialists:

Education at Harvard should liberate students to explore, to create, to challenge, and to lead. The support the College provides to students is a foundation upon which self-reliance and habits of lifelong learning are built. (Harvard mission statement, 2020)

Forming an identity: who am I as a university teacher?

Cora's sense of identity as a university teacher has been shaped by the university context she first experienced, and in this she is entirely typical. 59 studies of teacher identity were reviewed by van Lankveld et al. (2017), and they found five factors shaped teacher identity:

- a sense of appreciation
- a sense of connectedness
- a sense of competence
- a sense of commitment
- imagining a future career trajectory.

Cora's first university had a part-time culture, created partly by economic necessity and partly by focus on personal career goals. Academic posts were precarious, competitive and unpredictable. These structures were not designed to foster appreciation or connectedness, but rather a necessary focus on individual survival. This came to be her expectation and shape her sense of the academic's role. It is therefore unsurprising that she might collide with a changing university culture that had other expectations. Lankveld et al.'s study (2017) suggests that universities convey underlying culture through 'implicit messages'. As Cora's story shows, in being 'implicit' these messages may not be clearly received, especially if they are couched as options, hedged or mitigated, or even assumed and never made explicit.

It is interesting to ask whether a changing institutional setting might change Cora's sense of who she is as an academic; and if so, what might be lost or gained by this change. Scartezini and Monereo (2018) followed the development of four university teachers to track the impact of an educational programme on their sense of self. The study found that teaching development did indeed change these teachers' sense of themselves as academics, in relation to three features:

- representations and perceptions of their own academic roles
- concepts of what it means to teach, learn and assess the courses they teach
- the feelings they associate with their duties.

Strategies suggested in the study include analysis of critical incidents such as the one in this section, when Cora is made aware that her view of her role is fundamentally at odds with the university's; and that change is necessary if she wishes to remain there.

54 Being a high education teacher

Learning maps: who am I as a university teacher?

The sets of quotations in this section represent several opposing views that emerged from stories in this chapter. Use the questions below to help you map and analyse your views and context for each polarity. The chapter closes with a table for you to explore your own experiences in relation to one or more of the issues.

- Where do you sit personally/ideally between the positions in each category?
- Where does your institution sit?
- What is the gap between these two positions?
- How significant is this gap to you/to the institution?
- What would you be prepared to do/change in order to bridge the gap?
- What would you *not* be prepared to do/change to bridge the gap?

Navigating polarities

Polarity 1: Your institutional culture (open classroom or closed?)

Classrooms are sacred places and no-one else is allowed in.

◄─────────────►

I am constantly being prepared to be looked at, having to explain myself and show I am meeting standards. I am used to being observed at any time.

Polarity 2: Your identity (educator or scholar?)

I am first of all a scholar and academic, and secondly a university teacher.

◄─────────────►

I am first of all an educator. I never get time to do research because I always put students first.

Polarity 3: Your loyalties (to yourself or to your institution?)

First and foremost I need to develop my career as a researcher and scholar.

◄─────────────►

First and foremost I want to be a supportive member of my team and make a difference to the institution and to my students.

Polarity 4: Who am I with my colleagues?

What do you talk about with your colleagues? How true are these quotations in your own situation?
   We don't talk. We just do our teaching and then go home.
   TRUE ◄─────────────► FALSE

Being a higher education teacher 55

University politics. The chat about college politics is interminable. It's all we talk about.

TRUE ←——————————————→ FALSE

Social, personal, private and family. I keep my private and public lives completely separate.

TRUE ←——————————————→ FALSE

Teaching issues. It's completely taboo to admit you have any problems in your classes.

TRUE ←——————————————→ FALSE

Your discipline. I really expected that higher education teaching would be a meeting of scholars, but we never actually talk about our subject.

TRUE ←——————————————→ FALSE

Polarity 5: Who am I with my students?

Which of these describe your relationship with students? Which of these describe the relationship you are **expected to have** in your institution? Is there a gap between these two positions?

I regard my students as **peers and friends**. We socialise and spend time together outside formal teaching, and I know about who and where they are in life.

TRUE ←——————————————→ FALSE

I feel **parental** about my students: I am concerned for their personal welfare as well as guiding them academically, though there is some degree of formality as with an older relative.

TRUE ←——————————————→ FALSE

I regard my relationship with students as **mentor** to mentee: I am there to provide support and guidance where it is needed, not to control and direct their learning.

TRUE ←——————————————→ FALSE

I am a **facilitator** of student learning. It is they that must do the learning, but I provide the opportunities and resources.

TRUE ←——————————————→ FALSE

I have spent 20 years acquiring expertise in my subject, so I expect students to appreciate and respect that I am **an authority** and follow my guidance.

TRUE ←——————————————→ FALSE

The students have paid for learning and I am there to provide it.

TRUE ←——————————————→ FALSE

I regard them as **apprentices** coming alongside me to learn my skills.

TRUE ←——————————————→ FALSE

Table 3.2 maps Cora's story but also invites you to map one 'expectation gap' of your own.

Table 3.2 Expectation gaps

	Cora's example	Your example
Your position in relation to one of the polarities.	I am first of all a scholar and an academic.	
Your institution's position.	You are first of all an educator.	
What is the gap between these two positions?	I find all my time is given to teaching and I do not have time to prioritise my own research.	
How significant is this gap to you/to the institution?	Very significant to me as I am falling behind with my own research goals. Very significant to the university as they say I am failing to meet my responsibilities as a member of staff.	
What would you be prepared to do/change in order to bridge the gap?	I agree I need to give more time to my own development as an educator. However, I am going to apply for a sabbatical and apply for research awards.	
What would you *not* be prepared to do/change to bridge the gap?	I am not prepared to sacrifice my research times to do this though – specifically summer holidays and breaks.	

Further topics for reflection and reading

The article below explores the specific identity experiences of Japanese university teachers.

- How far do these insights shed light on identity experiences for university teachers in other parts of the world?
- How far could you replicate these research strategies in your own setting?
- If you were to ask the same questions of university teachers in your own setting, how would their answers differ or compare to these?

Nagatomo, D.H. (2012) *Exploring Japanese university English teachers' professional identity: new perspectives on language and education.* Clevedon, UK: Multilingual Matters.

References

Aktar, T. and Oxley, L. (2019) 'Promoting student engagement by strengthening the link between research and teaching in higher education: an early career researcher perspective', *Higher Education Pedagogies*, 4 (1), pp. 167–179.

Cambridge University 'The university's mission and core values'. Available at: www.cam.ac.uk/about-the-university/how-the-university-and-colleges-work/the-universitys-mission-and-core-values (Accessed: 26 June 2021).

Clifford, V., Adeunji, H., Haigh, M., Henderson, J., Spiro, J. and Hudson, J. (2011) 'Report on Brookes Student Learning Experience Project: Fostering Interculturality and Global Perspectives at Brookes through Dialogue with Staff'. Oxford Centre for Staff Learning and Development: Oxford Brookes University.

Cortés-Sánchez, J.D. (2018) 'Mission statements of universities worldwide – text mining and visualization', *Intangible Capital*, 14 (4) [online]. Available at: www.intangiblecapital.org/index.php/ic/article/view/1258/738 (Accessed: 26 June 2021).

Finkelstein, M., Iglesias, K., Panova, A. and Yudkevich, M. (2014) 'Prospects of young professionals in the academic labor market: global comparison and assessment', *Educational Studies*, Higher School of Economics, 2, pp. 20–43.

Harvard University (2020) 'Mission statement'. Available at: www.harvard.edu/faqs/mission-statement (Accessed: 6 June 2020).

Kreber, C. (2005) 'Charting a critical course on the scholarship of university teaching movement', *Studies in Higher Education*, 30 (4), pp. 389–405.

Kreber, C. (2013) *Authenticity in and through teaching in higher education: the transformative potential of the scholarship of teaching*. London: Routledge.

Morrison, B. and Evans, S. (2018) 'University students' conceptions of the good teacher: a Hong Kong perspective', *Journal of Further & Higher Education*, 42 (3) pp. 352–365.

Nabaho, L., Oonyu, J. and Aguti, J.N. (2019) 'Academics' perceptions of good teaching: assessing the degree of parity with student evaluation of teaching questionnaires', *Africa Education Review*, 16 (4), pp. 95–111.

Nagatomo, D.H. (2012) *Exploring Japanese university English teachers' professional identity: new perspectives on language and education*. Clevedon, UK: Multilingual Matters.

Quality Assurance Agency (2014) 'UK quality code for higher education, part A: setting and maintaining academic standards'. Frameworks for higher education qualifications of UK degree-awarding bodies.

Scartezini, R.A. and Monereo, C. (2018) 'The development of university teachers' professional identity: a dialogical study', *Research Papers in Education*, 33 (1) pp. 42–58.

Spiro, J., Henderson, J. and Clifford, V. (2012) 'Independent Learning Crossing Cultures: Learning Cultures and Shifting Meanings', *Compare: A Journal of Comparative and International Education*, 42 (4), pp. 607–619.

Spiro, J. (2013) 'The reflective continuum: Reflecting for change and student response to reflective tasks', *Brookes eJournal of Learning and Teaching*, 2013.

Spiro, J. (2014) 'Learning Interconnectedness: internationalisation through engagement with one another', *Higher Education Quarterly*, 68 (1), pp. 65–84.

van Lankveld, T., Schoonenboom, J. and Volman, M. (2017) 'Developing a teacher identity in the university context: a systematic review of the literature', *Higher Education Research and Development*, 36 (2) pp. 325–342.

Vasudeva, S. and Mogaji, E. (2020) 'Paving the way for world domination: analysis of African universities' mission statement', in Mogaji, E., Maringe, F. and Hinson, R. (eds.) *Routledge studies in marketing: understanding the higher education market in Africa*. Oxfordshire, UK: Routledge.

Williams, K., Wooliams, M. and Spiro, J. (2020) (2nd edition) *Reflective writing*. Basingstoke: Palgrave Macmillan.

4 Ways of learning
How do I learn?

Stories about learning

The stories of learning in this chapter come from three projects we have met in earlier chapters: *Crossing Study Borders* (CSB) as the voice of teachers and students with experience of learning across more than one culture, language or region; *Fostering Interculturality* (FIC), including focus groups and interviews with university staff and students who identify as 'international'; and *Reflection in the Round*, (RIR), a long-term project (2011–2021) in which higher education students track their views of learning at the beginning, middle and end of their programmes, in shared diary reflections and focus groups. The participants in the last two studies are identified by number rather than pseudonym, and will be labelled TT for teacher voices, and S for student voices in order to differentiate these two groups.

Students and teachers: learning and interacting

It is easy to assume that learners whose earlier schooling was teacher-centred will transfer that expectation into subsequent learning experiences. It is certainly possible that modes of learning develop as a habit, simply because this is what is consistently experienced. These habits are not necessarily either fixed or preferred as an approach or ideology – it is just that this is what is known. Exposure to something different can change what is seen as typical, and revise what is known, expected and preferred. It is interesting to ask how far we can travel from our first learning experiences to an approach that is new and different. Every learner will make this transition uniquely, but importantly, it will also depend on how the transition to new approaches or pedagogies are prepared and scaffolded by the teacher, and the kind of learning environment in which this is experienced. Here we meet Carmel, whose story was introduced in earlier chapters, as she describes the mismatch between her expectations and those of her learners in a Saudi Arabian girls' college.

> The pressure is on the teacher to make students learn. No-one expected the students to work. Everything was spoonfed. In a test, they just want

DOI: 10.4324/9780429426261-4

answers given to them to memorise, they don't want to know why an answer is right or how to get there for themselves. They expect teachers to make you learn as if it's a magic trick. They can't bear it when the answer isn't just right or wrong. They ask what's the answer, and are frustrated if it's not just one correct thing. Doing anything independently or individually is not done, they all want to be the same, one answer for the whole group. They don't get when you ask for an opinion that everyone can have a different opinion. The older women expected to learn if they just turned up. They didn't realise practising, doing homework would help. They had never been told that. (CSB, Carmel)

Carmel's observation is that "*they had never been told*" anything different, and that they were acting with an expectation that had never been questioned. The pressure as a teacher to meet this view of classroom interaction was strong, and Carmel struggled between several options: to conform to the idea of classroom as a social meeting place, to work with the few students in the class who genuinely wanted to learn or gradually to change attitudes to learning. She chose the third, remaining congruent with her own beliefs about the value of education and the facilitating role of teaching:

We had to explain why we were doing things, for example, role-play or circling particular words. They didn't expect the activities to be about them learning for themselves. (CSB, Carmel)

Carmel's learners, whether consciously or not, seem to regard learning as a body of knowledge to be communicated by the teacher: a transmissive view, which has the danger of rendering the learner passive, and bypassing learner responsibility to change and develop their own thinking. Given this view, activities such as role-play lack clear validity as ways of learning, and Carmel described her struggles explaining why these are useful. Danielle has a similar story as her views of active learning collided with those of students in her college in Spain. In her case, the students whose views of learning differed from hers, were not prepared to compromise or change:

I had one student who presented a complaint – they believed in transmissive teaching. The Head of Admin supported the students, though they were 8 out of 25 and the others were all quite happy. They took it into their heads they wanted me to stand and teach at them, not with them – that's the way the schools work and what they expected. (CSB, Danielle)

Danielle's story suggests not only the expectation that learning can be 'done' by the teacher, rather than by the learner, but also that knowledge is finite, uncontested and easily transferrable. To suggest alternatives, or imply there are no 'right answers', is disrupting the smooth transfer of knowledge. This internalisation of teacher as responsible for learning is a route towards rendering the learner passive. Our learner stories suggest it also leads to demotivation and boredom. Jake writes of his crossing borders from a UK to a US university: "*Students were rarely excited or fired up by their subject. It was just something the university demanded which they had to pass in their first or second year*" (CSB, Jake).

In contrast, Tim describes his experience of teaching students (in India) eager to show their engagement with learning. By encouraging class discussion and questions, he hoped to generate a spirit of exchange and mutual learning. However, he found that the comments and questions were being used competitively as a form of display. Questions to the teacher seemed to be "*stage-managed to put the teacher on the spot. They were showing off their question but didn't really want a reply, it was all bravado*" (CSB, Tim). His experience was echoed by Karen in her postgraduate seminar settings in the UK. She felt disappointed that discussion was not collaborative but rather self-seeking and points-scoring; she had expected

> postgraduate learning would be different, in that we would learn *with* each other. But it wasn't like that at all, everyone wanted to show how much they knew and I felt embarrassed to admit when I didn't understand something. (RIR)

In reflective notes, this peer group shared the following anonymised views: they describe "*fear of failure*", "*not keeping up with other people*" and "*worry that I have missed the point*" (RIR). This group seem to have responded to these fears, either by 'displaying' knowledge as 'points-scoring', or alternatively, sitting in silence. Some in the RIR focus groups describe situations where "*the whole class sat in silence even when the lecturer told us to ask questions*". When asked to suggest reasons for this, they expand on the anxieties mentioned above: "*well for me I was afraid to ask a question in case it was really dumb*" (RIR).

These stories, though illustrating different kinds of teacher-student mismatch, do suggest that interaction, its purpose and value, and its contribution to learning, cannot be assumed if it has not been clearly explained or experienced as an approach, or its benefits have not been clearly demonstrated. Luke, team-teaching in Romania, describes his transformation from a teacher-centred to a learner-centred teacher, why and how that happened and with what benefits:

> I began much more conservatively and cautiously, I was much more controlling of the classroom – or at least attempting to. In particular I had a colleague who looked like King Lear and he was, in terms of admin a total shambles, but he really loosened me up, much more student focused, bringing students in, using their expertise, their knowledge. A lot of these were part time students who were practitioners in their field with wisdom to share – this colleague introduced me to the joys of much more

> interactive, much more student-centred, more based around questions rather than answers – that has been all to the good for students. It was just another of these lovely bits of happenstance that I was thrown into team teaching with my colleague. (CSB, Luke)

Thus, to transform from one kind of learning to another depends on the building of bridges. For Luke, his colleague had modelled an interactive student-centred approach, and its benefits were evident both to himself as teacher and to the students. Kirsten, describing her own multicultural classroom, suggests the importance of building trust between learners and teacher before change can happen.

> I realised that I take for granted that students know how to interact in class, and that they expect to make mistakes, because that's how they learn. I teach them that – and over time, they learn to believe and trust that they can learn by trial and error in a safe classroom. For UK students, there are challenges in interaction, but I always build in safety nets, and they quickly learn to get the most out of these interactions. This made me realise that for international students studying in my classes, that safety and scaffolding towards interactivity may have been missing, especially with this perception of an 'authoritative' teacher, and that they may actually be missing out even back at my home university. It made me realise how much of what I consider 'normal' in the classroom is actually socially constructed. (CSB, Kirsten)

From the student perspective, making this shift from one expectation to another is bumpier than the route suggested by Luke and Kirsten. Gerda, whom we met in former chapters, describes the shift from being in a teacher-centred classroom as an undergraduate in Germany, to a learner-centred one as a postgraduate in the UK:

> I would find it much easier if someone said just do this but that would be counter to being a masters' students but you can see a red thread leading to the dissertation. It wouldn't work if you prescribed it you find out how to define your own topic.
>
> The programme was more controlled, less open as an undergrad in Germany. It is more hierarchical even in education. The lecturers are the great authority. (CSB, Gerda)

Though the more open-ended route was mapped and scaffolded in the way Kirsten describes above, still she found the transition from one to the other to be a struggle:

> at the beginning I read an academic book and couldn't understand what it said. That is a really big thing. When I learnt about multilingual

62 *Ways of learning*

> learners that was exactly what I experienced and I thought thanks God it is normal. When you ask how can you prepare I think that would be so helpful – explaining to students that this might happen because you have the interference, you do have to learn vocab and you have to learn content. At the beginning I had to sit there and make my own vocabulary book – it takes forever. (CSB, Gerda)

What helped for Gerda, over and above teaching guidelines, was theorising and contextualising her own struggles and realising they were 'normal'. She then created strategies of her own, learning new vocabulary alongside new content. Gerda was teasing out one aspect of her learning, which was not adequately scaffolded by her teachers:

> even though I always considered my language quite good, I constantly, and even now with my third essay, German intervened, it interfered very actively, I was there, I wanted to write something and I couldn't find the English word which is really annoying, fascinating but also annoying and is a disadvantage. (CSB, Gerda)

Many of the student stories draw attention to the challenge of language, and the leap to academic writing. For very few was this a natural way of expressing learning or conveying knowledge, whether in the first language or a second language. Amongst the Reflection in the Round diaries gathered over 12 years, academic writing is the most frequently mentioned anxiety in the first weeks of higher education study. These range from Gerda's example of interference between a first and second language, to "*how much should I cite others*", "*when do I give my own opinion?*", and myths such as: "*I was told never to use I*"; and "*academic writing uses longer sentences*" (RIR focus groups). Academic writing, for many, was a way of 'showing what you know' and as something you could either 'do' or 'not do' (RIR diaries and focus groups) and not part of what was being learnt. Katya describes her frustration with this as a university teacher crossing borders between Poland, the US and the UK:

> The greatest difference in terms of *teaching* in the U.K., in comparison to the U.S., was that I was given no space to help the students with their writing skills (which was just part of the curriculum in the U.S.). There seemed to be this expectation that students would learn how to write academically 'by osmosis'. After the first batch of essays I marked here, I was so distressed with their quality that I started 'smuggling' into my seminars instruction on how to write, although not all students were happy with that, I must say. Despite the evidence otherwise, they thought they knew how to write already, bless them. This is why I eventually morphed into a learning developer, in fact. (CSB, Katya)

Whilst later chapters will consider student-supervisor relationships as a further kind of interaction, this section has teased out several potential areas of collision between teacher-student views of learning. Who is responsible for learning, the teacher or the student? How is learning to be achieved, through the transmission of knowledge, or through process, challenge, exchange and experimentation? Is there an endpoint to learning, which I can display, or is this continuous and ongoing? Are there hidden challenges in my learning, which the teaching does not take account of, such as language and academic writing?

What do I feel about learning with other students?

The stories in our three research studies suggest that students in learning settings find that support groups of likeminded and kindred-spirited others make the difference. But these groups may have nothing to do with the new place of learning. Often the places of support were those built long before university, and outside of it: home, family, religious, political, sports, social or cultural groups. May, who we met in Chapter 2, felt little connection with those around her where she studied, being well joined up with the world she had shared before becoming a student. For busy working parents and students such as Fabia or Julia, there is little room in a busy life to become involved with other students, and making friends is far from being the goal of higher education learning. Andrea describes the difference in her experiences of two settings, one in Germany and one in the UK:

> German uni isn't a social space, because so many people study in the city they grew up in they have friends from school, less of a need with the syndrome we have in British universities of finding your friends for the rest of your degree as soon as possible, they feel that very strongly. They need to find a new social bubble.
>
> In Germany universities are education establishments rather than places which are meant to grow you up. It's culturally not done that you go to uni as a stage in life: you go to study a subject and enter a profession. (CSB, Andrea)

The potential for disappointment is great where a student hoping for new friendships and networks encounters a culture of stay-at-home peers who already have their social life established elsewhere. Aidan, for example, went to Japan in the hope of making Japanese friends, and was disappointed to find the local students had a very different idea of socialising.

> Lots of Japanese uni students engaged in 'Circles' (societies) as their main form of leisure outside of class – similar to the UK perhaps, but there seemed to be far less of a focus on socialising OUTSIDE of uni – which for my experience at uni in the UK was the main focus. Exploring bars, pubs, drinking culture was not the same. (CSB, Aidan)

The learning settings themselves will subtly indicate what is the intended nature of interactions between students: whether these are to be actively encouraged, with spaces and opportunities for socialising, or the reverse. For example, we saw earlier that Aidan was placed in a bubble of students also recently arrived in the country, sending the message to him that integration with local Japanese students was not an expectation. Chen, in parallel, arrived in the UK from Japan to find a whirlwind of opportunities to mingle, so many in fact that she felt overwhelmed and unclear where academic study was meant to fit in. Both had high hopes of university being a social scene as much as one where learning happened, and both were confused as to how this was meant to be negotiated.

This does not mean, however, that in the study settings students may not work together and value the support of others. Luke described as a lifeline in his transition from Sweden to Morocco, the support of other students in his class and recent graduates. For him, this latter was the most powerful ally in helping him to decipher what was expected of him.

> I did an introductory Spanish class I found that really interesting. When I got confused, not sure what the lecturer was on about, working with other students.
>
> recent graduates – deliberately tapped to talk to the students, they are only a few steps away, they are incredibly powerful – because they are able at one and the same time identify with the students, and students see the graduate as themselves in one or two years time. (CSB, Luke)

Luke describes here a process of individual study in which he draws on the support of others as a form of self-help. Yet our stories suggest multiple mismatches in expectation as to whether students support one another, compete with one another, or quietly get on with their work independently. Walter in Scott et al. (2013) shares narratives of international students at a postgraduate institution in London. In this study, a participant, Joanna, explained her disappointment that, in discussion groups, people were "*showing off*" rather than using this as an opportunity to learn from one another. Her home experience was of students working with one another collaboratively "*constructing together*" but in her new setting, "*people are not sharing ideas – and that makes me feel a bit bad*" (Scott et al., 2013, p. 19). An educator, too, describes her hope that students will work together cooperatively and constructively, and the disappointment when this is not their preference or expectation.

> Group work they hate it, they hate working together, they'd much rather be independent and do their own thing. For instance, one of the things they love doing is an independent study module here it's just them on their own working on a little project. So – to me the independent nature of how they see themselves within the university is more of a problem. (FIC)

Andrea, having crossed study borders from student to teacher in an elite UK university and then a former polytechnic, suggests the fragile conditions, which make a group cohere or not. In the elite university, students living together in college continued a seamless flow of collaborative study in and outside class:

> They do more collaborative work outside class than (the former poly) students. Out of class they discuss things that we were talking about in class, but it's less frequent with (the former poly) students – they just go home and forget. (CSB, Andrea)

She tells us that from year to year the cohesion of the groups changes, perhaps depending on the multiple factors we have suggested: living locally, in college or at home; studying part-time or full-time; juggling study alongside work or family. Groups which share characteristics seem to bond together well and support each other better. For example:

> The (English Language undergraduate degree) lot this third year were incredibly tightly knit group, especially certain chunks, 4 of them lived together, there was a really big group of 5–8 met in the library, talked about the dissertation, hung out together, there was a lot of stuff there. But it's different from year to year how they gel but there are always some who just come to class and don't socialise with anyone, maybe they don't live locally. (CSB, Andrea)

One key feature of kinship is attitude to learning. Where students share motivation, or approach to study, strong bonds are formed; and in reverse, antipathies can be built for those who disrupt or threaten that approach. The groups described by Andrea who 'gel well' both socialise and study well together. Our stories show that highly engaged students such as Julia, Wei Wei and Fabia, who prepare studiously, can become annoyed by and resentful of others who fail to do their own work, similarly to Faisal in Chapter 1. Students who regard learning as collaborative such as Joanna and Gerda, can become disappointed by those who regard it as competitive and an opportunity for display. Carmel described her experience moving from student life in the UK to teaching in a Saudi Arabian college for girls. Here, her expectation of what happens in a classroom was at extreme odds with her students whose culture she had entered:

> They came to class to socialise, it was freedom from school and even from home. They had 4 hours in class with 4 different teachers, reading, writing, speaking, grammar taught separately. They would come in with coffee, food, it was their new independent life, 4 hours out of the home. Teaching wasn't really why they were there. Their parents were paying, most were there to have a chinwag. At first it was shocking – hard to not

> see it as rude, 'not now girls'. In the end I had to make space for it, trying to put any ideology about work into them just wouldn't work. 5/10 minutes at the beginning and end of class I would let them chat and also had to let them eat in class too though we weren't meant to. They would have this food order app called 'hunger station'. They would start calling up their order in class and sometimes someone would have to leave the class to collect the order for all 20 of them. That meant they would then have to get fully dressed again in hijab, bring in food for the whole class. It was very disturbing, annoying even if you did make space for it. (CSB, Carmel)

Even within this group, where the dominant culture was strongly oriented away from serious study, there were clashes and collisions in hopes and expectations. Carmel describes the occasional students at odds with the mainstream:

> Occasionally one student would want to learn – would get annoyed if the teacher got to stop, would tell each other off, snap at each other if one wanted to learn. They were so passionate about it. 1 in 10 was really keen and would ask 'how do I learn teacher?' (CSB, Carmel)

Carmel, like Emanuel in the examples earlier in this chapter, developed 'tricks' to cope with the mismatch in expectations. She created the space for the girls in her class to order food and socialise and began to harness this towards learning; but in the end, and again like Emanuel, she found herself compromising and changing her expectations of what she hoped to teach and hoped her learners would achieve.

In contrast, Gerda describes a class where everyone shares a view of learning, both amongst themselves and with the teacher.

> What I really enjoyed was that it was all so multicultural that was really brilliant, especially as I am taking the TESOL courses, that was brilliant just hearing how it is in different cultures, how language works in different cultures, in Japan, people have worked in Thailand, the cultural difference of learners, that was what I really enjoyed that it wasn't just British, Africa – there was one girl in the class, she said we don't read stories we listen to them. (CSB, Gerda)

There seemed, in this case, to be multiple features which enabled the group to cohere; all were adults studying mid-career and highly motivated to do so; and all shared the view that the class was a place for mutual exchange. There was no sense of separation between a group that 'belonged' and a group that did not, but rather this class community was a place where everyone had an equal share. There were clearly learning conditions which enabled this, as well as the demography of the group, and it does provide us with clues for what learning might look like when 'cultural codes' are being unlocked. The implications of this for the educator is discussed in the next chapter.

This section serves to show the role of interactions between other students as part of the shaping of who one is in the study setting. We have seen a range of ways students position themselves, from participation in a closely knit study group, learning, socialising and studying together; to students whose support lies outside the place of study entirely and who only minimally connect within it. We have noticed that the groups which work well share a view of learning or share an approach to leisure and socialising or have some other possibly long-term kindred connection.

What do I feel about learning independently?

Learning independently is both an overt and covert expectation for many students as they enter higher education: overt in that this may be explicitly included in higher education mission statements, spelt out at a general programme level, or criteria for success within specific courses. However, for many students in our studies, the expectation is covert in that learning independently is another hidden challenge, not always scaffolded or explained, with students expected to arrive 'ready-formed' with a shared view of learning on arrival in higher education. In addition, there may be scepticism or even confusion about the value of independent learning, if a learner experiences this as unregulated and disorganised teaching. Conversely, the student expecting to be independent, may experience regulated and controlled learning as coercive and infantilising.

Aidan describes moving from flexible, self-directed undergraduate learning in the UK to very regulated study in college in Japan. While he very much appreciated the extraordinary efficiency and ordered nature of this learning, and the many skills he developed as a result, yet he struggled to find a balance with his wish for independence too.

> The pedagogy was more serious, much less laid back. I had to attend every class, do daily homework, daily tests, and weekly kanji tests with up to 50 vocab items. I learnt I couldn't half-ass this. Classes were only in the morning, then as soon as I got back I would spend a few hours doing the work and only went out when it was finished, the only way I could get through it. I was told off if I missed classes or missed homework. It taught me lots about study strategy. I had always got off with minimum effort. It taught me time management, focus, planning. My grades when I got back in the 4th year you could see they were much higher than the earlier years before Japan.
>
> I liked the conformity. I have always been split about compliance or individuality. With the compliance, it's efficient, safe, people are polite and respectful, but it is a loss of independence. I have always wanted efficiency, things just run well and there is no judgement, they accept who you are despite the conformity. It's a paradox – the efficiency is fantastic, but you can't really be who you want to be. I think it will always be my

dilemma, conforming or being individual and I will never quite work out which is best. (CSB, Aidan)

Aidan's final words, *"conforming or being individual and I will never quite work out which is best"* speak for many students in these studies. Students describe the importance of teachers *"letting go"* and giving them the chance to choose topics, projects and ways of studying. They valued *"having a lot of options"*, *"choosing what you really want to do"*, *"you want to sort of spread your wings a bit, to look a bit further out"* (RIR). Another student describes the importance of taking risks by studying abroad as opposed to the easy option of staying at home and felt this kind of courage transferred into other parts of life and *"prepares you for other things as well"* (FIC).

The spreading of wings has taken place geographically and physically for these students, in studying in a second educational culture; and their expectation is that this will be matched by intellectual expansion too. This latter was a crucial factor in their choice of study away from home. Exploring what this expansion might entail included the capacity to think critically, and to question both the teacher and the literature. Three student teachers from China and Taiwan describe this in distinct contrast to their experience at home: *"the teacher says in Tai Wan just follow me, children will just believe the teacher – memorise the content of the coursebook. Different here is critical thinking – always critical thinking"* (FIC). The Chinese teachers expressed a similar view: *"in China we just sit together to listen to one teacher. Here we should think why?"* (FIC) and *"Here in UK we learn more about how to think and reflect but in China we just follow teacher – teacher says we should read more and more – they never say we should challenge author's ideals"* (FIC).

Students also mentioned the extent to which they learnt from one another and understood their own culture better as a result. Here, student teachers noted the ways in which a teacher-centred classroom prohibited opportunities to learn from one another and to resolve individual learning blocks as a result: *"The group discussion is the most important thing – the way we share ideas. Sometimes you are blocked, but if you talk to others, I have some clues"* (FIC). One student explained how studying about current issues and problems relating to the built environment in England would prepare her to anticipate and address these issues in a 'new way' in her own developing country, Morocco (FIC).

Embedded in these statements is student awareness of something being learnt over and above content and subject matter, in terms of their own self-confidence or capacity to initiate learning. Where they record this virtuous cycle breaking down, however, is where the freedoms, options and expansions implied are not matched by knowledge and resources. The learner experience is continually changing within the cycle of study. During this cycle there may be a gradation from dependence to independence, which needs to be carefully managed. When mismanaged, this process can be experienced as bewildering and unhelpful by the learner. In the data derived from training teachers, 'independent learning' was perceived by some as generating the opposite of its claims. Some student teachers experienced, rather than a notion of independent learning, a culture of informal support that expanded, rather than reduced, the role of the teacher. Ecclestone et al. (2008) suggests that this pastoral role, embedded into the British school system, in fact infantilises the learner and induces dependence, rather than its reverse. The student teachers noted the heavy burden of pastoral support in schools: "*Yes, what surprised me is you are not just a teacher, you have to do all this pastoral help. It's not just your subject*" (FIC). The expectations of formal as well as informal support appeared to change boundaries between learner/teacher, rendering the teacher more vulnerable. In this culture of 'freedom to learn', the burden of responsibility (and blame) lies with the teacher. One student teacher from Morocco noted, "*Here it's the teacher's fault if pupils do badly whereas in Morocco you need to study more – it's not the teacher's fault*" (FIC). They noted the challenge to the status of the teacher, and the fact that this status needed to be negotiated continually. A student teacher from Italy noted: "*Teachers don't have the power. You have to negotiate. They can't use punishment*" (FIC). Many of the sanctions these teachers had been accustomed to in their own cultures, were not exercised in the UK: (in Italy) "*behaviour is a subject, as important as anything else. You can fail the year if your behaviour isn't good*" (FIC).

Thus, independent learning emerges as somewhat problematic, both in its practice and in its conceptual framing. 'Student-centredness' may be seen, through this data, as actually threatening the authority and positioning of the teacher; as potentially drawing attention away from the subject and from the challenges inherent within it; and as potentially encouraging a sense of 'entitlement' in the learner, which replaces 'independence' with 'lack of discipline'.

The students suggest that learning independently meant at best freedom, opportunity and expansion and at its worst, it meant lack of discipline, failure to take responsibility for learning, or confusion about expectations. The most valued learning relationship was not with the teacher but with fellow learners. The actual term 'independent' was rarely the one chosen by the informants. Phrases used more frequently were 'autonomy' (FIC), 'doing it for yourself' (FIC), 'working on your own' (FIC); or simply, 'learning without a teacher'.

The university staff, in contrast, focused on two issues not significant in the student findings: the learner/teacher relationship as a key factor in 'independent learning' and the quality of the learning outcomes. Their own responsibilities of setting new parameters for students' engagement with learning emerged as critical. For example, several staff spoke of the importance of setting high expectations of students as soon as they entered university. One described it as the 'unfrozen moment' (FIC) where students are open to change in their learning and are responsive to greater intellectual challenge. This is the moment when they could be introduced to the complexity and contestable nature of knowledge. They saw students as having become 'strategic learners' (FIC), focusing on learning that was assessed rather than valuing the full learning opportunity. Amongst strategies they suggested for engaging students, was embedding research in the undergraduate curriculum. Another strategy was making modules relevant to careers/employability, ensuring that students had 'products' relevant to their future job profiles, such as portfolios of work, publications, conference presentations, prizes. The connecting characteristic of these was the possibility of 'independent projects', 'learning for themselves': *"one thing they love doing is an independent study module here it's just them on their own working on a little project"* (FIC). However, one potential block to independent learning described by staff, was lack of self-confidence: *"some students come against these barriers and (say I can't) either because of a lack of self-confidence or unwillingness to try or to take risks"* (FIC). This might be ascribed to low levels of success in school leading in turn to low expectations. Staff felt it was the role of higher education to break this cycle of failure by both expecting and demanding high standards and by designing learning to be achievable so students would experience success. They were concerned that too often first year studies confirmed students' high school understanding of learning – *"getting filled up with wisdom and knowledge"* (FIC). *"So many of them, you know, sit back and watch, when in fact they're not going to learn anything that way"* (FIC).

A further aspect of staff discussion, which was not reflected in the student discussion, was the quality of the outcomes that emerged from 'independent learning'. Staff felt that the independent learner was one able to take a critical stance towards authority and knowledge. Some felt this was a factor that differentiated the British university from their own, *"Analytical and critical, questioning authority – I think these are all attributes of the British education system"* (FIC). A further characteristic of 'successful learning' expressed by staff was the capacity to be 'original', again identified as a cultural difference within the British system: *"[In British education] there's an emphasis on originality ... There's an emphasis on creativity so the student actually creates things instead of copying"* (FIC). Staff also saw independent learning as fostered in the informal staff-student relationships in the UK education system: *"a happy relationship between students and lecturers; there is no relationship of master and servant, it's a collaboration and friendly relationship"* (FIC).

Transitional independence: support or self-direction?

It emerged for both groups, however, that the issue of when, if and how much support to give was problematic: that too much support was perceived by both groups as stifling, and too little was perceived (largely by the student group) as confusing and neglectful. The data illustrates the conflict between support for learning and student self-direction. On the one hand staff and students report the importance of stepped support, a *"step-by-step approach [which] will help the weaker students to get through, to pass"*. For example: *"I had some students, they said someone should have made us work harder in our first year and second year. And we didn't learn enough ... they felt, they didn't read enough, they weren't pushed hard enough"* (FIC). On the other hand, they report the problems of excessive guidance: "*but ... that it (step-by-step guidance) is demotivating for the very talented and capable students*" (FIC).

Conversely, students found autonomy too early was confusing and unhelpful: "*I was shocked we had to do this ourselves – at home we would have been told exactly what to do. I didn't know how to begin at first, but I understand it now*" (FIC). This view is echoed by staff, aware of the mutability of the student relationship with independent learning. They mention the need for "*building [self-directed learning], you would scaffold this through a programme, so students can be given far more support in the first year, but this would diminish over time*" (FIC). Providing this degree of scaffolding in the early stages of study, however, was recognised as potentially problematic. Simplifying ideas at first, and then gradually "*looking at the complex forms and its contestability*" appeared pedagogically sound. However, one staff informant continues by saying, "*I think that sometimes students find that really difficult because we [have] confirmed their understanding of what learning is about – that it is not self-directed, it is not contestable*" (FIC).

What emerges from the data to inform the higher education teacher?

Educators in higher education have looked at learner independence from many angles. These include: the importance of time management, effective reading strategies and working in teams as a specifically learnt behaviour (Bradbeer, 2000); the importance of clarity in learning outcomes and assessment criteria and clear identification of learning resources (Gibbs, 1999); the development of problem-solving and decision-making skills and a staff-student interaction that allows students to "*develop skills in planning, interpersonal communication, team work*" (Jacques, 1989, p. 21).

The groups of informants mention several of these points in their own account of effective learning and teaching. The key ways in which 'independent learning' was actually described and experienced as a benefit included: learning as student-centred, participatory, collaborative, flexible, developing criticality, encouraging originality and creativity. This latter was explained further by one of the staff informants: "*students actually create instead of copying*". The actual practices valued by staff and students included: students as researchers; the collaborative relationships between staff and students; open interaction and group discussion.

However, all informant groups suggest that without mutual responsibility from learner and teacher, 'independent learning' can mean lack of discipline, lack of rigour, lack of structure, and lead to bafflement and isolation. Both staff and students mention that a learning situation that is too directed and supported can lead to passivity and instrumental learning for assessment only. All suggest the challenge of finding the balance between too much support – leading to dependence; or too little – leading to confusion. In addition, what emerges from the data is the understanding that the learner's preparedness for autonomy is actually in a state of flux, and the learner-teacher collaboration needs to change during the cycle of study. This is described by one of the staff informants as 'phased scaffolding'. This might be achieved in a number of ways suggested by the informants. Tasks need to be constructed so students are clear how and why these are learning opportunities; group work needs to be principled to maximise student involvement; key values such as criticality need to be modelled and made transparent for students to understand what this really means in practice; learning from and through one another might need to be explicitly 'taught' and framed. The apparent polarities that emerge in the data need to be continually balanced and fine-tuned: for example, the teacher's desire for learning objectives to 'emerge' implicitly versus the student's tendency to be instrumental and study for assessment; the teacher's wish to lead, facilitate and guide, in contrast to a student's preference (at times) for knowledge to be made explicit: "*why doesn't the teacher just give the answer?*"

While independent learning is held up as an ideal within higher education, the realities of students' demanding lives and the diversity of their backgrounds and preparedness for tertiary study may make its practice problematic. Although we have as an academy explored both the principles and the tools for independent learning, new and more questions remain to be asked: what happens when there is a mismatch between our understanding of independent learning as educators, and our students' experience of this? Are we really fine-tuning our strategies to take account of the varied demography of the classroom and the change in student needs over the cycle of their study? Is there a danger that, as educators, we are over-supporting, generating dependency rather than its opposite? While the studies being shared here do not claim to offer definitive or generalisable principles, they do open a window into the multiplicity of experiences and responses to this core ideal in our educational philosophy; and they do invite us to question when, and how, and if, and for whom, it can really work in practice.

Learner stories through the literature lens

The vignette below is a composite derived from the many stories described in this chapter. The communication disrepair in this situation sheds light on all three ways of learning we have considered: learning through teaching; learning independently; and learning with other students. What has gone wrong, and how can the literature corroborate and inform the stories shared in this chapter in general, and Tara and Bashir's situation in particular?

> **Tara (teacher) and Bashir (student)**
>
> Tara set up a task in her Business Ethics class, which involved students working in groups of three researching a choice of one amongst several topics provided. She asked students to identify the topic that interested them and find two other students who had made the same choice. They were then to share

out specific research roles, prepare their topic, and present in class three weeks later.

Three weeks later Bashir comes to see Tara to tell her he is not in a group because he had been waiting for her to allocate him to a group. He hasn't finished the activity because he has been trying to do all the research roles himself, and as a result he is putting in a formal complaint for her neglect of his interests.

Learning through teaching

In a survey of the qualities that university admissions officers look for in the good student, conducted by International Schools (Lewis, 2021), 'a positive attitude to learning' comes top of the collective list. But what does a positive attitude actually mean, and what happens if it is interpreted by teacher and learner in entirely different ways?

Tara has set up an activity in which 'a positive attitude' includes the capacity to make choices between a range of topics, find others with shared interests, and divide up research roles. Implied here is a belief in learning as of 'growth mindset' (Dweck, 2016), the belief that one perseveres through challenges, learning from setbacks and failure. Dweck defines the person with a 'growth mindset' as someone who has the belief they can progress through their own efforts and by learning from others (Dweck, 2016). In other words, they are not defeated by the task being difficult, and are aware hard work is the necessary route to achievement. Yet what do these capacities mean in practice? Is hard work the capacity to mirror what the teacher has said and prescribed, or to internalise this into one's own thinking processes? If Bashir's experience of learning is the former, by what route does he come to understand that in fact his teacher is expecting the latter interpretation of learning and hard work? In their study of 55 Hong Kong undergraduates, Kember and Wong (2000) found beliefs about learning straddled a complete spectrum from learning as active to learning as passive. What the study was searching for, however, was how these beliefs correlated to student evaluation of their teachers. As might be expected, students valued their teachers more highly when teaching style mirrored student beliefs: students who believed in a transmissive model of teaching valued more highly their teachers who delivered this expectation. Whilst this might not be a surprising finding, it leads us to ask: how might a student shift their perception of good teaching, and thus of their own approach to learning? What kind of scaffolding or support would be needed for this to happen?

We know that many students arrive expecting the kind of learning that served them well in their first study situation. Dukhan (2020) conducted an interesting study into the learning expectations of first year students that were the first generation to study at a higher education level in post-apartheid South Africa. The survey showed that a high percentage of the new arrivals expected rote learning to be sufficient for university study, as matching their earlier schooling. The challenge for first generation students might be not so much learning at higher education level but changing assumptions about what learning entails. In the case of Bashir in our vignette, if his earlier learning experience entailed memorising what the teacher said or what was read, how is he to interpret the leap towards self-directed research skills and self-selected topics and groups?

These more developmental skills are deemed missing for many students in accounts of their study experience. Mauro et al. (2020) canvassed the views of 2572 Italian undergraduates through web surveys, asking them about the way their study met their learning expectations. The findings from this survey data, were that students found the university met functional and extrinsic needs but was much less effective in supporting them emotionally and personally. They found their learning focused on concepts and theories, rather than on experiencing or building soft skills such as those needed in the group activity set up by Tara: the experience of problem-solving and collaborative research, the soft skills of working in a team, negotiating and cooperating with others.

We cannot, however, separate students' evaluation of their higher education teachers from the students' own engagement and motivation. Gisjelaers (1995) study in Maastricht of the correlation between students' self-esteem in relation to their subject, and their evaluation of their tutors found that "*the more students were afraid to fail, the less a tutor did what the student thought he/she ought to do and the more the student depended on the tutor's supportive role.*" Clearly the student-teacher relationship will be enhanced if the student is perceived as succeeding and engaging with the subject, but what constitutes success, and what constitutes engagement? In addition, what is the perception of where the responsibility lies in ensuring these take place?

Many studies show that a student's sense of wellbeing is highly connected with a sense of support and rapport with their higher education teachers. De Souza et al. (2019) studied the acclimatisation of 680 Brazilian and Portuguese university students to a new university culture. They found that those who perceived their university teachers to be supportive also had a greater sense of wellbeing and a greater sense of their university's preparedness for them. Students in Hong Kong (Morrison and Evans, 2018), asked to evaluate the effectiveness of their university teachers, arrived at similar criteria: students most valued teachers who helped them think critically, who gave clear explanations and who gave concrete and practical examples. These teaching skills suggest closer interactions and more dialogue than are likely in large settings such as lectures, but are most workable in seminar, tutorial and small group settings.

Connecting this, then, to our story of Tara and Bashir, we have an example of Bashir valuing his teacher according to his former experiences and finding her wanting. His expectation is to learn from her example, whilst her expectation is that he makes his own decisions and navigates choices. In experiencing this failure of expectation, Bashir's self-esteem and sense of wellbeing in this class has plummeted, and his only frame of reference is that it must be the teacher's fault, since he is doing everything he believes to be good learning: committed to his subject discipline, trying hard to understand his task. What Tara has taken for granted is that Bashir might be able to understand the three chosen topics and have the self-confidence to find others to form a group; what has in fact happened is that all the tasks and topics for Bashir represent obligations, and to choose might mean losing aspects of study, which could be crucial. In addition, he is less interested in what he can learn from others in a group and expects knowledge to come from direct interaction with the teacher, so in not being offered the latter he feels she has been negligent. Meanwhile, Tara regards team learning as something she is actively developing; by encouraging problem solving in teams, she is simulating the practices they will follow in the business and working world. She aims to build these skills indirectly through the activities she sets up and has not therefore made them explicit. Here lie the foundations for their communication breakdown.

Learning independently

The UK has evolved a questionnaire which interrogates nationally the student experience of higher education study. Students are invited to evaluate their access to resources, advice, community and feedback as critical ingredients in their learning (Office of Students, 2020).

Whilst this is not explicitly spelled out, it is hoped these multiple sources will become the learner's tools for self-development. Rather than being guided along a single path under the direction of a lecturer, they are invitations for the students to take their own journeys, and to open the doors that interest them. However, this cornucopia of opportunity can have the reverse effect; information at every turn can appear to direct, pressurise and confuse.

In the international schools survey, 2017, 80% of university educators described newly arrived students *"inability to think and learn independently"* and 75% felt their students lacked *"social skills and, even more worryingly, common sense."* (Lewis, 2017, online). Are these 'social skills' to be learnt by osmosis through the environment of independent learning? Or to be scaffolded and planned through tasks and teacher intervention? A study by Uiboleht et al. (2019) with 33 undergraduates, showed that a credo of independent learning is all very well, but for learners actually to acquire this independence, *"it is also crucial to design elements which guide and structure **students**' learning"* (Uiboleht et al., 2019, p. 1456). In their study, where teachers depart sharply from this approach, students felt their learning was actually hindered. Their study is corroborated by several others. Jankowska (2011), for example, interviewed Central and Eastern European (CEE) students at the University of Bedfordshire, and found that the student relationship with their HE teachers was critical to their experience. She describes her own experience of 'distancing' from her teachers, requiring her to 'find my own way' too early in the study process, before she felt she had the resources she needed to do so (Jankowska,

2011, p. 811). The students in her data group comment on the value they experience in developing their own creativity and formulating their own projects. What is interesting in this data is the balance experienced by students, between 'asking for help' and freedom to pursue their own creative direction (student data from Jankowska, 2011). Winch (2002) identifies three necessary conditions for the exercise of autonomy or independence: permission to do things for yourself, knowledge of what needs to be done and the power to do it. In the case of Bashir, being asked to select his own topic without having the full knowledge of what they mean is disempowering. Being asked to select a group without feeling he has the permission to intervene into other preformed friendship groups, is equally disempowering; and seeing his peers forming natural friendship groups that exclude him also drains him of power and agency.

Learning with other students

Of the admissions officers surveyed in the International Schools study (Lewis, 2017), 91% cited experience in teams as an indicator of capacity to succeed at university: sports teams, committees or school councils. As they select students, they explicitly value the ability to work as a team member, to lead and to cooperate with others, to solve problems together and to work with others consultatively and supportively. If these are not skills developed in earlier learning stages, can they simply be 'acquired' through osmosis, or do they need to be explicitly taught and scaffolded? A mirror image of university admission tutors' expectations are those of students, surveyed in 2020 and 2021 on their experience of learning and teaching during the Covid-19 pandemic (Jackson, 2020, 2021). The survey found that a majority of students:

> want more personal attention from lecturers and tutors, with more one to one support. They want help with accessing technologies and learning resources, and they want their universities to be clear in communications both about what the corporate university is planning and what's happening on their course. (Jackson, 2020, online)

Although Bashir's experience was prior to the pandemic, we can see that his needs in relation to teacher support would be accentuated in a pandemic situation. The conclusions to the 2020 study are those which relate to his experience too:

> Though students are clearly struggling with accessibility of technology and learning resources, facilitating online interaction, developing connections between students and lecturers, and delivering consistent and friendly communications seem to be their biggest priority. (Jackson, 2020, online)

Forming these connections, however, is not straightforward. The skills of forming and functioning well within a group are likely to be affected by both language proficiency and self-confidence in relation to peers. In his study of the flipped classroom, Butt (2014) found that undergraduates studying in a second language had concerns about learning from other students in groups, as opposed to from the lecturer; for example, they didn't consider the notes to be as comprehensive when acquired through group interaction, and they considered their peers to be less organised and systematic. However, those more confident with their language, or operating in their first language, by contrast preferred group study to other teaching modes, with individual study next, and the large lecture as the least preferred. So, group interaction is not language-neutral and an assumption that it might be is something that has perhaps failed Bashir in this instance. How do you join a group if others do not initiate an invitation and how do you form one for yourself if you do not have the language or protocol for taking this initiative yourself? If this cultural gap combines a fear of being rejected, you then have a negative mix very likely to lead to the outcome we have seen for Bashir.

As we have suggested throughout, the issue is not so much that Bashir's earlier learning was founded on different principles as the fact that the expected approach to learning has not been adequately explained and prepared. Research studies of students crossing cultures corroborate this view. A Turkish participant in Busher's research says: *"you've got different styles of teaching rather than there is an English style and a Turkish style. It's down to individuals"* (student data in Busher, 2011, p. 396). Apfelthaler et al. (2007) describe the different 'myths and stereotypes' connected with different types of learners and deconstruct them. Whilst students focus on 'doing it for yourself', staff focused on the ways in which they might scaffold and prepare students. Whilst students felt the key outcomes of independent learning were autonomy, the spreading of wings and the opening of life opportunities, staff focused on more specific learning qualities such as the capacity to critique authority, and to respond creatively and originally to tasks.

Precisely what Bashir needs in order to make sense of group-forming is some kind of scaffolding that gives him an equal footing with his peers. Uiboleht et al. (2019) studied 33 undergraduate student responses to different kinds of learning environment. They found that, even where teachers claimed to have a student-centred approach to learning, the actual learning environments they created were widely variable; and only those which genuinely engaged the students in learning activities, and focused on learning rather than delivery of content, were experienced as positive. What is interesting in this study, is that university teachers varied in their actual adoption of a learning-centred approach, even where they claimed to be espousing it. According to the students' evaluations 'student-activating teacher-learning activities' was the critical difference between an effective learning environment and a 'dissonant' one, yet within one institution there appeared to be a spectrum of approach, from top-down teacher-centred learning environments, to student-empowered learning environments, with students overwhelmingly preferring the latter.

Learning maps: how do I learn?

Using Table 4.1, prepare your own critical incident analysis of a learning situation that went wrong and required repair.

Plot your critical incident by finding two points along each spectrum:

1 What I expected.
2 What I experienced.

Learning as transmission of knowledge ←——————→ learning as learner transformation
Teacher as responsible for learning ←——————→ student as responsible for learning
Group interaction as display ←——————→ group interaction as co-operative learning
Learning for compliance ←——————→ learning for independence
Learning as memorisation ←——————→ learning as innovation
Group-forming as trigger to confidence ←——————→ group-forming as trigger to fear of rejection

In considering these mismatches, what strategies would bridge the gap from the perspective of the learner? From the perspective of the teacher?

Making values and assumptions explicit ←——————→ demonstrating values as implicit
values through actions/examples ←——————→ values as implicit
Opening choices and options ←——————→ limiting choices
Breaking down activities into sub-skills ←——————→ focus on the 'big picture' of the task
Controlling the activity ←——————→ 'freeing' the activity

Table 4.1 Learning situation analysis

	Learning interaction with teacher	*Learning with others*	*Learning independently*
What was your expectation?			
What was your experience?			
What was the mismatch?			
What was revealed by this mismatch?			

Further topics for reading and reflection

These two autobiographies offer richly fascinating accounts of what it is to change from one culture to another. These writers describe their forced migration as children, rebuilding their lives and ways of learning in a new place and language. Dina Nyeri travelled from Iran to the US and UK, Eva Hoffman from Poland to Canada.

Hoffman, E. (1990) *Lost in Translation: A Life in a New Language.* London: Penguin.

Nyeri, D. (2019) *The Ungrateful Refugee.* Edinburgh: Canongate Books.

You might use their stories as inspiration to build your own learning autobiography as you progress from school to college, from college to the working world. These are already many borders to cross, but where there are new cultures in addition to this, there are many ways a view of learning might be challenged and tested. The two autobiographies select moments and milestones in this journey.

- Which moments and milestones in these two life stories are most meaningful to you?
- Why, and which aspects of your own life do they connect with?
- If you were to select your own moments and milestones in your learning, what would they be?

References

Apfelthaler, G., Hansen, K., Keuchel, S., Mueller, C., Neubauer, M., Ong, S.H. and Tapachai, N. (2007) 'Cross-cultural differences in learning and education: stereotypes, myths and realities' in Palfreyman, D. and McBride, D.L. (eds.) *Learning and teaching across cultures in higher education.* New York, NY: Palgrave Macmillan, pp. 15–35.

Bradbeer, J. (2000) 'Supporting student independent learning: guide for tutors', *Miscellaneous Papers No. 3*, Department of Geography: University of Portsmouth.

Busher, H., Lawson, T., Wilkins, C. and Acun, I. (2011) 'Pedagogy, empowerment and discipline: comparative perspectives of novice teachers in England and Turkey reflecting on the "other"', *Compare* 41 (3) pp. 387–400.

Butt, A. (2014) 'Student views on the use of a flipped classroom approach: evidence from Australia', *Business Education Accreditation*, 6 (1), pp. 33–44.

de Souza, S.B., Veiga Simão, A.M., da Costa Ferreira, P. (2019) 'Campus climate: the role of teacher support and cultural issues', *Journal of Further & Higher Education*, 43 (9), pp. 1196–1211.

Dukhan, S. (2020) 'Value for learning during this time of transformation: the first-year students' perspective', *Higher Education Research and Development*, 39 (1), pp. 39–52.

Dweck, C. (2016) 'What having a "growth mindset" actually means', *Harvard Business Review*, 13 January2016 [online]. Available at: https://hbr.org/2016/01/what-having-a-growth-mindset-actually-means (Accessed: 26 June 2021).

Ecclestone, K. and Hayes, D. (2008) *The dangerous rise of therapeutic education.* Oxford: Routledge.

Gibbs, G. (1999) *Teaching more students: independent learning with more students.* Oxford: The Polytechnics and Colleges Funding Council.

Gijselaers, Wim H., Nuy, Herman (1995) *Effects of motivation on students' ratings of tutor behavior.* Paper presented at the Annual Meeting of the American Educational Research Association (San Francisco, CA, April 18-22, 1995) https://files.eric.ed.gov/fulltext/ED383668.pdf (Accessed: 10 October 2021).

Hoffman, E. (1990) *Lost in translation: a life in a new language.* London: Penguin.

Jackson, A. (2020). 'The expectation gap: students' experience of learning during Covid-19 and their expectations for next year' [Blog] *WONKHE Research.* Available at: https://wonkhe.com/blogs/the-expectation-gap-students-experience-of-learning-during-covid-19-and-their-expectations-for-next-year/ (Accessed: 26 May 2021).

Jackson, A. (2021) *The expectation gap II – students' hopes for learning and teaching in the new normal [Blog] WONKHE Research.* Available at: https://wonkhe.com/blogs/the-expectation-gap-ii-students-hopes-for-learning-and-teaching-in-the-next-normal/ (Accessed: 26 May 2021).

Jankowska, M. (2011) 'A reflection on adaptability, achievement motivation and success of Central and Eastern European students in one English university', *Compare*, 41 (6) pp. 801–818.

Jacques, D. (1989) Independent learning and project work. Certificate in Teaching in Higher Education by Open Learning. Oxford: Oxford Centre for Staff Learning and Development.

Kember, D. and Wong, A. (2000) 'Implications for evaluation from a study of students' perceptions of good and poor teaching', *Higher Education*, 40 (1), pp. 69–97.

Lewis, J. (2021) 'Top 7 qualities universities look for in student applicants', *The Student (part of Times Higher Education)*, Available at: www.timeshighereducation.com/student/advice/top-7-qualities-universities-look-student-applicants (Accessed: 26 June 2021).

Mauro, C., Manna, R. and Palumbo, R. (2020) 'Filling in the gaps in higher education quality: an analysis of Italian students' value expectations and perceptions', *International Journal of Educational Management*, 34 (1), pp. 203–216.

Morrison, B. and Evans, S. (2018) 'University students' conceptions of the good teacher: a Hong Kong perspective', *Journal of Further & Higher Education*, 42 (3), pp. 352–365.

Nyeri, D. (2019) *The ungrateful refugee.* Edinburgh: Canongate Books.

Office for Students (2020) 'National Student Survey Core Questionnaire' [online] www.officeforstudents.org.uk/media/d462a46b-0eba-42fd-84a1-c8b6dc883c99/nss-2020-core-questionnaire-and-optional-banks.pdf (Accessed: 26 June 2021).

Scott, D., Hughes, G., Evans, C., Burke, P.-J., Walter, C. and Watson, D. (2013) *Learning Transitions in Higher Education.* London: Palgrave Macmillan.

Uiboleht, K., Karm, M. and Postareff, L. (2019) 'Relations between students' perceptions of the teaching-learning environment and teachers' approaches to teaching: a qualitative study', *Journal of Further & Higher Education*, 43 (10), pp. 1456–1475.

Winch, C. (2002) 'The economic aims of education', *Journal of Philosophy of Education*, 36 (1) pp. 101–117.

5 Ways of knowing
What does it mean to know something?

This chapter explores what it means to *know* something, from the perspective of both learners and teachers. We ask what higher education is actually aiming to achieve and what is the desired end-goal of study? Is it about knowing your subject deeply for sheer love of it, or developing a honed knowledge base that prepares you for a specific profession? Is it to develop the self-discipline and competences that will be useful in any employment or subject discipline, or is it simply to nourish intellectual, spiritual and personal potential? Is it possible for study to be all of these? How explicit are these end-goals and how clearly communicated from institution to teacher to student?

The chapter considers misunderstandings when student, teacher and higher education institution fail to have shared understanding of the answers. It asks what different participants in the higher education experience believe knowledge actually to be: knowing oneself, knowing a finite body of learning, knowing as infinite and ever-changing, knowing as the process of recognising what you do not know. Whilst these questions may seem metaphysical and abstract, yet they lie under the surface of every discipline, manifesting themselves in the way learning, teaching and assessment take place. The stories shared in this chapter indicate the consequences of these hidden beliefs about knowing and suggest the deep sub-structure behind the study of subject disciplines in higher education.

The chapter derives its knowledge from more than 100 student and teacher stories gathered through learning diaries, field notes, interviews and focus groups between 2011 and 2021, and across four separate projects. These are:

- *Reflection in the Round* (RIR) 38 student learning diaries and 10 annual focus groups of students on one-year postgraduate progammes between 2011 and 2020. In addition, teacher field notes track learning activities and learner responses during the same period. The project is published as Spiro (2013) and crystallised into teaching materials as Williams, Wooliams and Spiro (2020).
- *Fostering Interculturality* (FIC) with 16 participants, both staff and students, who identified as international, discussing their experience of crossing cultures in semi-structured interviews and focus groups. This project is published as Clifford et al., (2011) and Spiro et al., (2012).

DOI: 10.4324/9780429426261-5

- *Learning Interconnectedness* (LIC) with 50 international first degree students between 2010 and 2014 sharing weekly journals about their experiences of learning across cultures and languages. In addition, teacher field notes track cross-cultural learning activities and learner responses in the same period, 2010 to 2014 (Spiro, 2014).
- *Crossing Study Borders* (CSB) with 24 staff and students who identified as having crossed borders in learning and teaching, interviewed between 2020 and 2021 and published here for the first time.

Learning about knowing from insider stories

To say that higher education is about learning a subject discipline is far from a straightforward, or even uniformly accurate, statement. Rather, both the literature, and learner stories suggest multiple interpretations of what it means to 'know your subject'.

Two thousand years of knowledge or co-construction?

Andrew's story below suggests two opposing views of what knowledge means. At one end of the spectrum is Andrew's story of a teacher who believes he represents *"two thousand years of learning"*, and his students should respectfully listen to him imparting that knowledge. Meanwhile Andrew's version of knowledge entails teacher and learners learning side by side, each of them bringing something new to the classroom:

> I was invited by the British Council to work with teachers in Pakistan on language teaching methodology. What a compliment to be taken to such a distant country and culture!
>
> At the first coffee break I sat with the local teacher trainer. He lit a new cigarette; I was conscious of how it gleamed so whitely and how tightly the slim cylinder of paper enveloped the tobacco. He was not smiling. I did not try to interpret this.
>
> 'What is your methodology?'
>
> Problem. I don't think of methodologies. I think of relationships and what we might share and what we might do to achieve something of our hopes and aims.
>
> 'I do not see myself in the classroom as the reservoir of knowledge and skills which I must teach mainly by explaining and drilling. I see myself as lucky enough to be in a room with lots of other, albeit, much younger people. And I am so aware that our experiences of life and our talents are all so different. I see English teaching as a way of enjoying the company of other people and doing interesting things with them ... through English ...'
>
> His back had stiffened. He drove his new cigarette into the ash tray. It buckled. It was irretrievably unusable. It smouldered.

Ways of knowing   83

>He stood up, pushing his chair back, suddenly, it tottered but didn't fall.
>'When I walk into a classroom, I represent 2000 years of study and I expect total respect!' He strode away.
>I had the prospect of one more week with him and the teachers.
>My humanistic approach was born out of the evolving history centred on the West. The humanistic movement, for me, began in 1968 with the revolutions in Western universities and more individually, the hippie movement. I had a week with the trainer and teachers to reflect (in my own mind) on the extraordinary assumption that someone with such a different individual and social narrative should be able to contribute to individuals and societies founded on such different narratives.
>My colleague may have heard about the unrest in the universities in the West but he did not live in the experiences of it, nor indeed why it happened ... and what happened next. So why should my 'approach' and his 'methodology' find compatibility? (CSB, Andrew)

Andrew's story illustrates the fact that our view of 'knowing' might seem so self-evident it hardly needs explaining; and yet it is far from being so, differing not only from subject discipline to discipline, but within it as is the case here, with two teachers of language and literature. We might characterise Andrew's Pakistani educator friend's position as this: he, as teacher, 'knows' his subject, acquired through decades of tireless study and millennia of scholarly predecessors. His 'knowing' entails lifelong immersion in his subject. The goal of education is that his learners might come to mirror him, his level of expertise, the depth and historical grounding of his knowledge; and to do so they need to give way to his expertise and be exposed to it in all its depth and erudition. Andrew's position, however, is entirely the opposite. For him, everyone brings into the learning their own unique knowledge, and the classroom is a place of mutual development, a co-construction of knowledge.

Paradigm wars: quantifiable or unquantifiable?

Another way we could characterise the difference between Andrew's view of knowledge and his colleague's is that Andrew's knowledge is not finitely defined and cannot be easily measured. It is continuous, evolving, co-constructed and beyond easy definition. His colleague's, however, could be defined by the two thousand years that preceded him, by a scholarship or form of knowing that can be measured, replicated and defined. The struggle between these forms of knowledge is often far from abstract. It affects what learners choose to learn, what teachers choose to teach, as Otto illustrates in his story of teaching in a recently post-apartheid South Africa:

>One issue that we had to overcome was my expectations about what the students knew already and that they were expected to build on knowledge

that they had covered in earlier years and on other modules on their course. There seemed to be a student culture of knowledge only being needed to pass the module that they were studying at the time and not applying an holistic approach to their studies. (CSB, Otto)

If students believe the only meaningful knowledge is that which is measured and assessed, why would they engage with other areas of learning covered in previous years, already measured and accounted for? If this is the teacher's view too, how will this affect teaching? Andrew tells a story that illustrates this:

> I sat in on a colleague's lesson. He is a very experienced teacher and a good and empathetic human being.
> 'What did you do last weekend?' he asked a student in the class, clearly practising the past tense form and clearly linking the activity to the student's actual experience. So far so good.
> 'I swim across Lake Balaton doing butterfly.'
> 'Swam!'
> And he asked the same question of the next student ... and so on.
> At the end of the lesson I said to my colleague, 'Did you hear that first student tell you that he swam across the biggest lake in Central Europe using the most difficult of all the swimming styles?'
> My colleague is a good man and he was ashamed.
> How easily he could have said, 'Gosh! That's amazing! You swam across Lake Balaton!' (CSB, Andrew)

For the teacher, the purpose was for students to demonstrate knowledge of the measurable skill of using correct language forms; other kinds of 'knowing' were overlooked in the fulfilment of this central goal.

This kind of knowledge is also easier to assess, being measurable by multiple choice, memory tests, yes/no questions and checklists of knowledge areas. Participant ID 4 in the Fostering Interculturality study describes the shock of moving from one kind of assessment to another more open-ended kind:

> the exams we had in the States are pretty much directive – when I saw an open-ended exam I was amazed and thought – wowo how do you answer this? You are not meant to write yes or no to an answer but marshall all the information and knowledge and views and things and then describe them in an essay. (FIC)

The first assessment asked 'what do you know?' whilst the second required 'soft' skills such as criticality, synthesis of sources, formulation of an argument and creativity. Measurable or beyond measure also represents a paradigm struggle. Every aspect of learning, research and teaching falls across this divide. Alison (CSB) describes what creativity 'looked like' within these two different paradigms. In her definition, creativity entailed "*different perspectives*" and thinking

Ways of knowing 85

"*outside the box*", and creative work was assessed through student exhibitions, installations, and artist statements about their work, influences and processes. Travelling to a conference in China, she found creativity at this conference was assessed with "*an established activity*" such as drawing, "*people would be asked to complete the drawing and then assessed for creativity. It was didactic and narrow in its range*". In many ways, it could be suggested that measurable knowledge comprises compliance, uniformity and convergence, whilst less measurable knowledge entails innovation, individualism and divergence. Danielle's example illustrates this contrast, as she moved from a private college in Spain to a public university in the UK. She explains that, in Spain the approach was "*very transmissive – here's the info, reproduce it in an essay*", whilst in the UK college:

> it's much more interactive, required deeper understanding, you couldn't just reproduce what other people thought, had to understand it. Spanish style is much more literature based, a compilation of other people's thoughts. Here (in the UK) we are interested in what students bring to it, whilst in Spain it's how much you know about existing knowledge. (CSB, Danielle)

The paradigm struggle also plays itself out in the approach to research, and the value attached to data that is open-ended and non-numerical, versus data that can be evaluated statistically and quantitatively. These two approaches to knowledge draw on very different sources of information. The first may include transcripts of interviews, diary notes, reflective journals, drafts of work in progress, observations, with the aim of revealing the human condition in all its diversity and complexity; whilst the second might include surveys, questionnaires, tests in sufficient quantities to carry statistical significance and suggest generalisations and comparisons. Both have their place and purpose, both yield richly important information, and both offer different kinds of answers to problems, yet there can be scepticism and even antagonism between proponents of each position. Alison describes her experience in China:

> My paper was the only one that was qualitative – all the others were quants. People were heckling me and shouting me down though I explained ethnographic and narrative but they kept shouting this is not research where are your statistics. One woman stood up to defend me. (CSB, Alison)

She encountered the same antagonism at a conference in St Petersburg, Russia:

> My research was looking at the idea Creative pedagogies for empowerment. I sent off the abstract they said they were interested but were over subscribed for speakers but would I do this as a poster presentation. I did do that and they started with that – walked round and saw I was the only

86 *Ways of knowing*

> qualitative researchers in the posters and at the whole conference. Everyone else had hardline quants. I had unequivocally negative responses and like China they were quite angry and hostile. How dare you call this research even though I had a strong literature base. (CSB, Alison)

Alison's dilemma was not that she had travelled from one region to another, or even one language to another; but rather, that she had moved from a qualitative culture into a quantitative one, and the two do not always comfortably mix – although research would be much enhanced and deeply enriched if they did.

Knowing your profession or knowing yourself?

Andrea, whom we met in previous chapters, describes the way in which three different institutions represented three different approaches to subject knowledge. Her university in Germany focused on subject discipline as a route to a career; in the elite university she moved to in the UK, the focus was on the scholarship of the subject; whilst in the 'new' university and former polytechnic, there was a focus on transferable skills. Each of these approaches led to a different way of teaching too:

> in Germany the study is a targeted means to get to a specific career. Unspecific skills are potentially less important there as you are in a discipline-specific setting for a specific job. Whereas in UK unis we have to concentrate on the transferable skills to show them what comes beyond the degree. They could go into public relations, business, anything. They go straight into work so they need to be really aware of what their transferrable skills are. (CSB, Andrea)

Jake perceived his undergraduate programme as intellectual growth with generalised goals such as developing deep and critical responses to his reading:

> At Cambridge the unspoken sub-text was that we were literary gentlemen capable of penning a literary appreciation and only seeking to widen our horizons and discuss the whole scope of English literature. (CSB, Jake)

Moving to the US, his MA in literature was approached as a professional training to become a teacher. The assessments were precise and instrumental, and he was expected to 'know' his subject in breadth rather than depth. His experience of shift in culture highlights differences between a scholarship approach to 'knowing' and one that we might call 'praxis' or practical apprenticeship. This approach to 'knowing' determines, not only why something is studied, but also what is studied. Andrea explains her attitude to subject choice in a German university, where the purpose of higher education study is to become qualified for a career:

you study engineering to do engineering. The value of humanities MAs was always much much lower – an MA in Philosophy people would go why? Why would you do that unless it's part of a teaching degree? People would be very suspicious why you are wasting time at university wasting your time with no end goal. Those subjects live off the teaching degrees because those subjects are taught in school and people need teachers, but if you did the subject without the teaching degree people would wonder what you were up to. (CSB, Andrea)

The *praxis* approach to knowing brings the values and culture of the profession into the classroom. Dared, whom we met in earlier chapters, crossing borders between Australia, Ireland and the US, describes crossing disciplinary borders between humanities and business. Whilst humanities were taught in a spirit of mutual learning and debate, business was taught to simulate the tough working world.

You have these micro-cultures and I think the approach to studying Business is rooted in trying to recreate authentic business type contexts of studying and learning. Business is quite competitive. Whenever we did assignments they did something that would be very threatening in humanities, they would publish your results and show you how you performed in relation to everyone else in the class, they used to circulate the three best essays so everyone got to read the three best essays, and that whole dynamic was very interesting and created all kinds of tensions, was antagonistic to learning but it was part of the Business culture. (CSB, Dared)

Dealing with unhedged judgement and loss of face were conceptualised as part of a fast and ruthless business world. Problem-solving situations that require hard decisions in a fixed space of time; or 'dragon's den' simulations, where only one project passes the post and the others fail, all reflect the way knowledge is conceptualised, and the way the working world is being mirrored. Sally too talks about the fast decisions and actions expected in her first qualification-oriented department, in contrast to another department where knowledge is slowly acquired and problematised:

At higher education everything you did was theorised, talked about, rationalised – everything moved much more slowly. In further education (skills-oriented towards qualifications) they just cared about action, but in HE the action was always the last thing at the end of a long process. For example, applying for a research grant the team asked for three years: we said, we can do this in three months, but they said no let's ask for three years. (CSB, Sally)

We might have expected the stories of knowledge as professionalisation to describe audits, standardisation, competences and regulations. Certainly, this is implied in many of the stories: of medical students, trainee teachers, trainee nurses, apprenticed engineers. But what emerges more significantly is the difference in learning culture: where knowledge is demonstrated by clear decision-making, appropriate behaviours and conclusive judgements. Professional knowledge is judged not only by fine gradations but by a resounding yes or no, membership or not, qualified status or not.

Whilst the professional learning approach ensures the knowledge base of every graduate is the same, knowledge as a personal learning journey could be characterised as the reverse. For every graduate, it means something different, finely tuned to their unique life trajectory. Sally describes the transition from one culture to the other, as she moves from her training college to higher education:

> The demand to articulate your own argument and find a voice: no-one had ever asked for those things before. FE was all about the collective, and knowledge was a commodity. It wasn't your idea of success but OfSTED and inspections – unthinkable to have worked out your own criteria for what was and wasn't working. In HE knowledge is something to create, and take control of. You could work out what knowledge was valid and it was work for yourself too and your own improvement. (CSB, Sally)

Luke describes his doctorate process as finding a thread that connects all the stages of his life and articulating this as knowledge.

> I am discovering that my life does seem to make sense in terms of a strong thread, not least around student centred learning and authentic teaching.
> ... it means I am making what was implicit, explicit. For example, I stumbled into work by Rick Steiner about hope theory. I do see myself as very hopeful person, and it strikes me as hope is a driver for change – and hopeful thought produces pathways to practical change and progression. Those are definitely things that mean a lot to me and also drive my teaching. In our teaching, with our students, we are both staff and students are hopeful players. Why would be a student or a lecturer if we didn't think there was a way of making a change. (CSB, Luke)

The difference between a profession approach to knowledge and a personal development approach can be transformative. Luke suggests this in his description above, as does Sally whom we have met several times in this chapter. So, what does that personal development really mean in practical terms? What is the knowledge being reached for and how is that demonstrated? Katya, in Chapter 2, described the gulf between her own cultural expectations and the ones she met in the US and UK. Although adaptation felt like a tearing away from her authentic self, she also describes new forms of knowledge acquired through this process:

> I learned so much in the process! I learned different ways to be in the world, I learned to be sensitive to others and not to be too precious about what 'being me' means. Change and adaptation are part of the process of personal and professional growth and – while they can be painful – they have real value and real-life consequences. I also learned how to be more empathetic and – ironically – also how to be tough with others. Knowing the value of change and adaptation can make you into a tank: if you can do it, everyone can do it ... (CSB, Katya)

This new kind of knowing is a huge leap from the place Katya first describes, "*on a mission to fit in, to hide my accent, to change my ways*". For Gerda, this personal learning entailed precise ways of internalising academic skills and recognising that her challenges were not unique to second culture students but felt by all students.

> One example, we had to read a book by O for SLA and her style of language was killing me, because everything was in the passive voice, she replaces every normal word with another word she must use a Thesaurus, but even A as an American and H as English said I can't understand what she is saying, I don't understand a word, I thought oh thank God it's not just me. But also, then you get to the point you can understand the majority of the article that is such a victory when your brain goes into English academic language and reads content rather than just seeing the language.
>
> Having this automatic reading now, I can read and understand the content, what is interesting the progress made – first I thought I can never write a 1000 words. My last assignment I ended up with 7000 words and I had to cut, my heart was bleeding, I had to keep to the word count – so all those experiences together are really helpful. (CSB, Gerda)

Many of the struggles in adaptation to a second culture study are language based, as Gerda and Katya describe. Chris describes teaching the sociology of law in Pakistan and China. Here, individual words are entry points into the professional culture:

> One example was the Pakistani students who asked me 'What is this "rule of law" that you keep mentioning? We have never heard this phrase.' As it happened, lawyers in Pakistan were that very week demonstrating against their government's over-riding of court decisions, so I had a ready example to show them. On another occasion a Chinese student came to me and asked 'This word *institution* that you use. Is it a normal English word? They never taught it to us.' 'Then you are very fortunate,' I told her, 'as you are learning only the way the word is used in sociology, not the variety of other meanings that will be confusing British students.' (CSB, Chris)

Luke describes a similar failure of transfer from one language culture to another, as he teaches community developer officers in Romania:

> a presentation to a group of community development officers but also to local activists and of course it's always fatal when you think you are being clever – so I knew the continental term to talk about 'animateur' and 'animateuse' and there were these sniggers and so I stopped – OK what is so funny – and they explained, 'animateuse' is a woman of the night. It was salutary because it was something I had taken for granted. (CSB, Luke)

For him, some of the differences between expectations were literally untranslatable. He describes teaching rural development specialists in Romania, with a translator mediating his world view with those of his participants:

> Working in a rural area of Romania – quite soon after Ceacescu – dealing with people, citizens, professionals who had lived under a communist system. It seemed that people expected the state to provide. The ideas we were coming up with that citizens could exert agency, contribute to decision making, contribute ideas – seemed very alien.
>
> A lovely translator called D – she was translating with this group of rural development specialists – with one particular man she looked me in the eye and said, the gentleman is saying but in my opinion he is a pompous oaf. So you are standing there and you are trying not to laugh – she was saying he is a party member. (CSB, Luke)

Our stories show that different views of knowing can lead to misunderstanding, confusion, even direct anger and antagonism. In these stories, personal assumptions about knowing are sometimes only fully felt and known when they find themselves in conflict with another. Some of these oppositions may appear irreconcilable, as in the case of Andrew and his colleague that started this section, or as Luke's translator realised. These differences are difficult to acknowledge and even harder to bridge. Katya, whom we have met several times, tells us of this struggle from her perspective both as a student and as an educator crossing borders:

> I can also see that many of my colleagues struggle to be inclusive in terms of different worldviews and attitudes. They get offended if a student expresses themselves in unusual ways and don't take into account their cultural background. Instead, they have the unrealistic expectation that students will understand how to behave in the academic context and what values academia has, and that they will instantly subscribe to these values and participate in their perpetuation. It's easily done; I'm guilty too. (CSB, Katya)

A starting point, however, is recognition of these different positions, and an appreciation of where they come from intellectually.

Learning about knowing through the literature lens

Mila's story below is an example of the fact that differing views of knowledge are not abstract but lead to real and critical breakdowns in understanding. Mila's story entails several transitions or border crossings, also identified in the Higher Academy study edited by Scott et al. (2013): from pure to applied subject knowledge, from first degree to postgraduate, from home to international and from one discipline (science) to another (social science). It is a composite story echoed by several of our project participants, who describe this kind of knowledge clash variously as devastating and tortuous. How can the literature help to contextualise Mila's story and elucidate its causes and consequences?

> I loved my subject, physiology and anatomy. In my first degree I was assessed through quizzes and short tests, lab reports, class presentations and knowledge checks and I always did well in these and knew exactly what to do. When I moved to medical law tasks were clear, or at least I thought so. I read the cases, thought about the problems, and listed my solutions with reference to the literature. I was shocked with my results and the negative comments. I hadn't explained my reasoning, theorised which position I had taken, been critical of the literature or recognised my own bias, etc. etc. But these kinds of skills had never even been mentioned.
>
> I realised that there seemed to be an assumption that the mature students knew or understood or were able to write academically in the discipline. Knowing the subject wasn't enough, there seemed to be a whole other knowledge which I couldn't grasp, I didn't even know the questions I was meant to ask. Even though the subject teachers never mentioned this, they seemed to evaluate not what we knew but what we did with what we knew. In other words, I thought I was learning a subject but found I was learning to become a different person – maybe my future professional self. Until I grasped this difference, I continued to get borderline grades and nearly failed the programme.
>
> (Based on stories of Gerda, Bridget, Katya, Pattie, Anna)

Knowing as higher education mission

a whole other knowledge

Mila suggests that there is a *"whole other knowledge"* beyond the subject, which she is expected to demonstrate. Is this kind of knowing in the curriculum or not? Barnett (2004), in his account of the university, suggests that the curriculum *"comes down to answering two crude questions: 'What should we teach?' and 'how should we teach?'"* (Barnett, 2004, p.62). His view of 21st century higher education is that its diversity is so wide and its approaches so heterogeneous, that it is impossible to talk of a shared philosophy, or even a shared definition of what higher education learning is. Instead, we might need to interrogate each higher education setting and each programme for the clues they give about *"what to teach"*. For Mila to carry her expectations from one setting to another is likely to present surprises, even were she to stay within the same discipline and same city.

One place to start are higher education mission statements. It is here where universities make explicit their views of knowledge and how this might impact the lives and behaviour of their graduates. Arcimaviciene (2015) interrogated 20 European university mission statements through the lens of metaphors chosen to illustrate their purpose. She found that the surface statements were couched in the rhetoric of sustainability, freedom of speech and transformational learning, but their metaphors revealed a different subtext:

> evoking traditional dogmas of the conservative ideology grounded in the concepts of the transactional approach to relationship, competitiveness for superiority, the importance of self-interest and strength, and quantifiable quality.
> (Arcimavicience, 2015, p. 1)

For example, quality of the staff, their research and their teaching excellence were often couched in terms of quantity, using business terminology such as 'asset', 'investment', 'global appeal' (Oxford) or competitive terminology such as 'foremost university' (Compultense University Madrid), 'special status' (Lomonosov), 'ground-breaking' (Utrecht), leading or world-leading (Edinburgh, Utrecht, Heidelberg, Zurich) (Arcimavicience, 2015, p. 6). What is claimed, and what is truly demanded, may be different things. Mila felt at first her task was to know her subject well; she then adjusted to the awareness that her task was to become a different, more critical professional. Yet, at another level, a subliminal message from her institution was that she be a participant in ground-breaking research and teaching excellence and do justice to this through her results. These are many transitions to negotiate, not only for herself but for her lecturers. What are *they* to convey to their learners: subject disciplinary knowledge, professional knowledge, or competitive edge alongside other parallel programmes? Even more tangled is the web, if all these layers are not acknowledged or made explicit.

How institutions articulate their core goals is likely to percolate through the system and find itself in the kind of teaching, which is valued, and the kind of learning outcomes which are promoted. Here, for example, are the mission and purpose of two US universities, where students will learn to:

> learn, discover, heal, create – and make the world even better (Rochester, OIRA, 2017).
>
> Discover, examine critically, preserve and transmit knowledge, wisdom and values (Wisconsin, OIRA, 2017).

These exalted purposes all suggest that there is 'a whole other knowledge' beyond the subject discipline, which the student is expected to absorb through the higher education culture. As they stand, these purposes are too broad to be teachable and too generic to be meaningful as learning goals. They are qualities of personal transformation which take time, months, even years, and are beyond what can be clearly articulated in one assignment. So, whilst Mila might see in these statements and missions a 'whole other knowledge', in themselves they will not help her to understand what is expected of her.

Knowing as praxis

my future professional self

Another kind of 'knowing' is oriented towards 'doing' in the world, and the goal outcomes are expressed as achievable and teachable units. Describing qualities and skills in this way has been variously labelled: graduate attributes, competencies, qualities or outcomes; generic attributes; transferable, employability or soft skills; and core capabilities (Hill et al., 2016, p. 155). But whatever the name for them, they are units which are clearer to grasp, and which are designed to make sense in the working world as well as in an educational setting. Examples of these generic qualities are:

- curiosity for learning that makes a positive difference
- courage to expand and fulfil their potential
- passion to engage locally and globally (The University of Edinburgh, 2020)

University of Edinburgh graduates are:

- creative problem solvers and researchers
- critical and reflective thinkers
- effective and influential contributors
- skilled communicators

(The University of Edinburgh, 2020)

Graduate attributes described in this way are not oriented towards a specific career or workplace. Whilst this gives them wide applicability, there is a danger they may fail to answer two burning questions that lie behind Mila's story, and many others like her: *what I am expected to do?* and *why, in terms of my future?* Dicker et al.'s study (2019) of 340 students, 17 employers and 32 staff, found that "higher education institutions and academic staff must articulate the value of the academic offer more clearly to their students" as these were simply not self-evident and especially so when their connection to a future professional self was unclear. (Dicker et al., 2019, p. 1425). Other studies, such as Cavallone et al.'s (2020) research into Italian student views, bear out this conclusion: students are often less engaged when no links are made with vocations and careers, even when concepts and ideas were well taught.

Yet it is possible for graduate attributes to be finely tuned to specific 'future professional selves'. The University of Edinburgh expands their definition of graduate attributes to suggest they have the capacity to be discipline-sensitive and unique to each student:

> we might identify some common areas that we want our students to develop, but students will have their own starting points, progress and experiences in these areas while at the University which will shape them as individuals
>
> (University of Edinburgh, 2020)

Surveys suggest that graduate attributes which relate explicitly to the workplace are valued by both students and their future employers. Engineering students at Dublin City University (Beagon et al., 2019), for example, found that problem solving in teams developed both their skills as engineers and more generic ones of value in any work context, such as "teamwork, communication skills, understanding of the design process and self-directed learning" (Beagon et al., 2019, p. 850). Simulation of 'real-world' tasks gave their learning face validity and purpose.

There is another issue that emerges in both Mila's story and the literature: the skills and attributes expected by educators are not always those received by students. For example, 640 science undergraduates and 40 of their teachers at Queensland University, Australia, were asked about their perception of what were they learning and why (Matthews and Mercer-Mapstone, 2018). Their findings showed a mismatch in perceptions, and an urgent need for academics and students to establish 'shared perspectives' about expected learning outcomes (Matthews and Mercer-Mapstone, 2018, p. 644). Their suggested way of achieving this was through a curriculum model with three steps: planned – enacted – experienced, leading a student from knowing about, to knowing from within and acting on the basis of this.

Transferable skills also represent the kind of 'knowing' which leads to 'praxis', or professional application in the working world. The subject discipline is oriented towards applied ways of knowing, or what Kratochwil (2018) calls "acting and knowing". In some praxis-oriented disciplines, such as engineering, medicine and law, standards of knowledge are regulated by national boards such as the General Medical Council (gmc.org.uk) or the Law Society (www.lawsociety.org.uk/), and the end-goal is the conferment of professionalism by these core gatekeepers. This kind of knowing is specialised, discipline-specific, and focused on precise and standardised competences.

Yet within professional settings, knowledge itself is slippery to define. Appreciating that knowledge is uncertain and continually subject to new emerging information, has been part of the thinking in many professional disciplines; in management (for example Rindova and Courtney, 2020), medical science (for example Laugesen and Østergaard, 2015 on diabetes onset), even response to disaster (for example Button, 2016 on response to environmental catastrophe). Atherton (2003) invites us to think about the case of small businesses, where "knowledge is contingent upon unpredictable internal and external factors" (Atherton, 2003, p. 1379). He describes knowledge-as-knowing in this context, multiple ways of reconsidering what we know as situations change.

Here we see Mila's dilemma as she enters her studies with a sense that knowledge is fixed and capable of duplication. As she transforms into an aspiring professional, she is now being asked to rethink knowledge as if it is capable of revision and interpretation. Her border crossing is from knowledge as fixed, to knowing as the continued interrogation of uncertainty.

Knowing disciplinary cultures

knowing my subject was not enough

Entry into a new subject discipline has been compared to immigration into an unfamiliar tribe (Becher and Trowler, 2001; Trowler, 2008) with all its hidden values and tacit knowledge (Jalongo et al., 2014). Each of these 'tribes' have their own conventions, rules and forms of belonging, which are rarely made explicit and may not be recognised until they are actually breached. There are no explicit mission statements but, rather, subtle clues that are both at the surface and in the deep structure of the discipline. We can characterise these disciplines across two polarities: pure or applied, hard or soft. Combinations of these determine where the researcher is positioned and how the discipline describes its knowledge. These are best explained through examples of the disciplines themselves, as seen in Table 5.1.

Table 5.1 Analysing subject disciplines (derived from Becher and Trowler, 2001)

	Hard	Soft
Pure	**Pure sciences** (e.g. physics, biochemistry): **'hard-pure'** *concerned with universals such as the qualities of gravity or components of carbon monoxide research is often based on quantities and result in discoveries that change our view of the natural world* Success depends on a high rate of publication	**Humanities** (history) and pure social sciences (anthropology): **'soft-pure'** *concerned with particular places, times, people research is often based on what people say, think, how they behave research expands our understanding of the human condition and its specificity* Individuals carve out their own life careers and success can come from a few high-quality publications
Applied	**Technologies** (mechanical engineering): **'hard-applied'** *Purposive, pragmatic, mastery of environment, resulting in products* Entrepreneurial, professional values, patents and publications, role oriented	**Applied social sciences** (education): **'soft-applied'** *Functional, utilitarian, professional practice, resulting in procedures* Outward-looking, uncertain in status, intellectual fashions, publication rates reduced by consultancies, power-oriented

For example, a hard-pure subject such as physics might make claims to generalisability, using verbs such as *shows, evidences, reveals*; whilst a soft-applied subject such as education might be far more tentative in its claims, using verbs such as *suggests* and modals that 'hedge' claims such as *might, may, could* (see hedging in science writing Salager-Mayer (2011), and the use of modals in hedging (Hardjanto 2016). In soft-pure disciplines, others in the field might be regarded as rivals and competitors, 'straw dogs' to be torn down; whilst in soft-applied disciplines such as education they are often seen as intellectual predecessors on whose shoulders new knowledge is built (see Hyland on citation strategies, 1999). Physics might regard reference to the author/researcher as taboo, whilst educational researchers might refer to themselves as the lens through which research is seen, or as the actual focus of the research, using the first-person pronoun 'I' (see Hyland 2002 on authorial presence). In the hard-pure subjects such as medical science, publications representing knowledge are likely to include statement of methods, data that is measurable and of significant quantity, and claims to be generalisable. In the soft-pure subjects such as history there may be little or no attention to the methods of the historian, the least interesting part of the data is likely to be that which can be counted and measured, and findings may be retold using the structures of narrative or storytelling (see Wingate, 2012 or Bazerman, 2000 on academic genres).

Given these cultural differences, and the gulf between one culture and the other, Mila's dilemma is unsurprising. She has traversed from a hard-pure subject to a soft-applied one. In this everything has changed: the way texts are structured, the verbs used to cite references, the way claims are made, and whether or not she should use the first-person pronoun I, all of which indicate deep aspects of disciplinary ideology. What makes this additionally difficult, is that these values and ways of expressing them are often so deeply internalised that they are rarely made transparent.

Knowing yourself

becoming a different person

In our vignette, Mila is required to confront former beliefs which are no longer helpful, to rethink not only how she is learning but what knowledge itself is, and to reshape herself into an agile and reflective professional able to learn through uncertainty. In 2010, 55 subject disciplines in the UK higher education sector referred to 'reflection', or synonyms of reflection, within their subject benchmarks of graduate competence (Quality Assurance Agency, 2010). How this is defined across pure-applied, soft-hard disciplines is varied. In Entwistle's cross-disciplinary study at the University of Edinburgh (2009), academics interpreted the term 'reflection' as the capacity to link learning and theory with real-life situations and contexts (p. 59). Other disciplines regarded a critical and analytical approach to data as the core of reflection (Entwistle, 2009). The objects of reflection varied between self, text, ideas, practice or the external world, depending on disciplinary standpoint. Yet what they all have in common, is their engagement with 'knowing' as personal change: a shift from first response to another that is deeper, more engaged, more critical, resonant and self-aware.

These changes are much more than subject knowledge; they are in fact nothing short of transformative. In his iconic text *The Idea of a University* (1852), Newman expanded on the idea of a liberal education as being not about reading great books but, rather, about "learning to think" and "enlargement of the mind" (Ker, 2011, p. 23). These views form the precursor to 21st century visions of university as the birthplace of "large concerns and large future-oriented possibilities" (Barnett, 2004, p. 61). Though different in era and language, across two centuries there is a shared perception of the ennobling potential of higher education study, and its capacity to transform. Mezirow (2018) explains transformative learning as

> a critical dimension of learning in adulthood that enables us to recognise and reassess the structure of assumptions and expectations which frame our thinking, feeling and acting.
>
> (Mezirow, 2018, p. 90)

This is the journey Mila needs to make across the several borders she crosses from one discipline to another, from pure to applied and from first degree to professionalisation. It is not the one she had contracted into, taking her core first discipline with her, along with the assumptions and predispositions that came from these first learning experiences. Whether explicitly or not, she has opted into multiple new ways of knowing: knowing her subject discipline and its hidden cultures; knowing herself in order to rethink unhelpful blocks and beliefs; knowing her future professional self and realigning herself towards that. These are many borders to cross, and many new bridges to build, and many stages between confusion and success.

Learning maps: what does it mean to know something?

Whilst there can be no fast track for these multiple new ways of knowing, a useful starting point is to appreciate what they actually are, what is hidden and what is explicit, and where assumptions need to be reconsidered. The thinking tasks in Tables 5.2 and 5.3 help to guide readers through the questions that would be useful to ask, either as a student navigating a new programme or as an educator making these choices transparent for students newly arriving to the subject.

Hidden and explicit knowledge

Higher education institutions make their view of knowledge visible through course descriptions, programme handbooks, mission statements and assessment criteria.

98   Ways of knowing

Draw up a long list of answers to this question:

- Where can I find out what knowledge is valued in this institution/programme?

Choose one of the documents or websites which are readily available to you and analyse it using Table 5.2, which guides you to ask:

- what kind of knowledge is made explicit?
- what kind of knowledge is not made explicit?

Table 5.2 Hidden and explicit knowledge

	Explicit knowledge	Hidden knowledge
Praxis: professional/practical skills Professional competences		

Transferable skills:
    Generic skills: e.g. teamwork,
    problem-solving		

Disciplinary knowledge:
    Soft or hard?
    Pure or applied?		

Personal transformation:
    Knowing yourself
    Recognising beliefs and assumptions
    Transforming beliefs
    Manifesting change through actions or practice		

Expecations and conventions:
    in writing
    in spoken communication		

Table 5.3 Teaching sessions and learning tasks: analysing the match

	Column A Learning tasks	Column B Teaching sessions
Professional and 'real-world' applications		
Reflection and self-awareness		
Disciplinary scholarship and knowledge		
Research originality: qualitative		
Research contribution: quantitative		
Knowledge of the literature		
Hidden literacies: writing skills		

Map your analysis in the relevant Box 5.2, which guide you to recognise the kind of knowledge that might be required. It is likely some of the boxes will be left blank, whilst others will be filled, giving you a clear map of the explicit emphasis of the course programme and its view of knowledge. It may also provide a map of the difference between what is made visible in the documentation, and hidden agendas under the surface.

Teaching sessions and learning tasks: analysing the match

How far do teaching sessions prepare for learning tasks, and value the same kind of knowledge?

- Find your most recent assessment activity, either one you have set as an educator or prepared as a learner. Analyse this learning task using the questions in Table 5.3 column A.
- Think about the teaching sessions which prepare for or lead to this assessment. An analysis of these teaching sessions will be in column B.
- Using Table 5.3, suggest an approximate weighting from 1–5, with 5 being 'very important/very highly valued' and 1 being 'not valued at all'.
- Do you notice any patterns, matches or mismatches?
- Do these mismatches present dilemmas and if so, can you resolve them?

Navigating polarities

Think about your current learning/teaching situation as a whole; the kind of experiences you have as a learner/educator, the kind of sessions you teach or engage in and the kind of tasks you set or perform. How clear are you what kind of knowledge lies at the centre of these experiences? Think about the polarities below and plot where you think your experience lies along each spectrum.

⟵——————————————⟶ Knowing as body of knowledge vs knowing as ongoing and continuous
⟵——————————————⟶ Knowing as measurable vs knowing as unquantifiable
⟵——————————————⟶ Knowing as disciplinary expertise vs knowing as personal transformation
⟵——————————————⟶ Knowing for divergence and innovation vs knowing for fitting in and compliance
⟵——————————————⟶ Knowing as certainty vs knowing as uncertainty
⟵——————————————⟶ How is this approach to knowing demonstrated?

In the kind of assignments set
In the way judgements are given

In the way standards are set
In the way teaching is managed

Further topics for reading and reflection

There are several sites online in which students share their stories and experiences of studying across borders. Here are a sample of these: www.goabroad.com/articles/study-abroad/study-abroad-stories;www.educations.com/study-abroad-student-stories/.

Browse through these stories and notice:

- What do the storytellers feel they have learnt as a result of their experience?
- What do the storytellers feel they know as a result of their experience?
- What is specific and distinctive about each story?
- What are the collective themes which you might wish to develop as a researcher?

References

Arcimaviciene, L. (2015) 'EU universities' mission statements: what is popularized by metaphors' *SAGE Open*, 5 (2), pp. 1–12 doi:10.1177/2158244015584378.

Atherton, A. (2003) 'The uncertainty of knowing: an analysis of the nature of knowledge in a small business context', *Human Relations*, 56 (11), pp. 1379–1398.

Barnett, R. (2004) 'The purposes of higher education and the changing race of academia', *London Review of Education*, 2 (1), pp. 61–72.

Bazerman, Charles (2000) 'Shaping written knowledge: the genre and activity of the experimental article in science'. WAC Clearinghouse Landmark Publications in Writing Studies. The WAC Clearinghouse. https://wac.colostate.edu/books/landmarks/bazerman_shaping/(originally published in1988 by University of Wisconsin Press).

Beagon, U., Dervilla, N. and Eabhnat, N. (2019) 'Problem-based learning: student perceptions of its value in developing professional skills for engineering practice', *European Journal of Engineering Education*, 44 (6), pp. 850–865.

Becher, T. and Trowler, P.R. (2001). *Academic tribes and territories: intellectual enquiry and the culture of disciplines*. Buckingham: SRHE and Open University Press.

Button, G. (2010) *Disaster culture: knowledge and uncertainty in the wake of human and environmental catastrophe*. Abingdon: Routledge.

Cavallone, M., Manna, R. and Palumbo, R. (2020) 'Filling in the gaps in higher education quality: an analysis of Italian students' value expectations and perceptions', *International Journal of Educational Management*. 34 (1), pp. 203–216.

Clifford, V., Adeunji, H., Haigh, M., Henderson, J., Spiro, J. and Hudson, J. (2011) Report on Brookes student learning experience project: fostering interculturality and global perspectives at Brookes through dialogue with staff. Oxford Centre for Staff Learning and Development: Oxford Brookes University.

Dicker, R., Garcia, M., Kelly, A., and Mulrooney, H. (2019) 'What does 'quality' in higher education mean? Perceptions of staff, students and employers', *Studies in Higher Education*, 44 (8), pp. 1425–1441.

Entwistle, N. (2009) *Teaching for understanding at university: deep approaches and distinctive ways of thinking*. Basingstoke: Palgrave Macmillan.

Hardjanto, T.D. (2016) 'Hedging through the use of modal auxiliaries in English academic discourse', *Humaniora*, 28 (1), pp. 37–50.

Hill, J., Walkington, H. and France, D. (2016) 'Graduate attributes: implications for higher education practice and policy', *Journal of Geography in Higher Education*, 40 (2), pp. 155–163.

Hyland, K. (1999) 'Academic attribution: citation and the construction of disciplinary knowledge', *Applied Linguistics*, 20 (3), 341–367.

Hyland, K. (2002) 'Authority and invisibility: authorial identity in academic writing', *Journal of Pragmatics*, 34 (8), pp. 1091–1112.

Jalongo, M.R., Boyer, W. and Ebbeck, M. (2014) 'Writing for scholarly publication as "tacit knowledge": a qualitative focus group study of doctoral students in education', *Early Childhood Education Journal*, 42 (4), pp. 241–250.

Ker, I. (2011) 'Newman's idea of a university and its relevance in the 21st century', *Australian e-Journal of Theology*, 18 (1), pp. 19–32.

Kratochwil, F. (2018) *Praxis: acting and knowing*. Cambridge: Cambridge University Press.

Laugesen, E. and Østergaard, J.A. (2015) 'Latent autoimmune diabetes of the adult: current knowledge and uncertainty', pp. 843–852 Wiley Online Library https://onlinelibrary.wiley.com/doi/epdf/10.1111/dme.12700 (Accessed: 26 June 2021).

Matthews, K.E. and Mercer-Mapstone, L.D. (2018) 'Toward curriculum convergence for graduate learning outcomes: academic intentions and student experiences', *Studies in Higher Education*, 43 (4), pp. 644–659.

Mezirow. J. (2018) 'Transformative Learning Theory'. In Illeris, K. (ed.) *Contemporary theories of learning*. Abingdon: Routledge, pp. 90–105.

Newman, J.H. (2015) *The Idea of a University*. 1852. London: Aeterna Press.

OIRA Office of Institutional Research and Assessment (2017) Examples of Mission and Vision Statements in Higher Education, Centenary University www.centenaryuniversity.edu/wp-content/uploads/2017/01/Examples-of-Mission-and-Vision-Statements-in-Higher-Education.pdf(Accessed: 26 June 2021).

Quality Assurance Agency (2010) Honours Degree Benchmark Statements. Available at: www.qaa.ac.uk/academicinfrastructure/benchmark/honours (Accessed: 21 November 2010).

Rindova, V. and Courtney, H. (2020) 'To shape or adapt: knowledge problems, epistemologies, and strategic postures under Knightian uncertainty', *Academy of Management Review*, 45 (4), *Special Topic Forum The Implications of Uncertainty: For Management and Organization Theories* https://doi.org/10.5465/amr.2018.0291 (Accessed: 26 June 2021).

Salager-Meyer, F. (2011) 'Scientific discourse and contrastive linguistics: hedging', *European Science Editing*, 37 (2), pp. 35–37.

Scott, D., Hughes, G., Evans, C., Burke, P.J., Walter, C. and Watson, D. (2013). *Learning Transitions in Higher Education*. London: Palgrave Macmillan.

Spiro, J. (2013) 'The reflective continuum: Reflecting for change and student response to reflective tasks', *Brookes eJournal of Learning and Teaching*, 2013.

Spiro, J. (2014) 'Learning Interconnectedness: internationalisation through engagement with one another', *Higher Education Quarterly*, 68 (1), pp. 65–84.

Spiro, J., Henderson, J. and Clifford, V. (2012) 'Independent learning crossing cultures: learning cultures and shifting meanings', *Compare: A Journal of Comparative and International Education*, 42 (4), pp. 607–619.

Trowler, Paul (2008) Beyond epistemological essentialism: academic tribes in the 21st century. In *The university and its disciplines*, Carolin Kreber (ed.). London: Routledge, pp. 181–195.

University of Edinburgh. (2020) 'Definition: what are graduate attributes? [online]. Graduate attributes'. Available at: www.ed.ac.uk/graduate-attributes/what (Accessed: 26 June 2021).

Williams, K., Wooliams, M. and Spiro, J. (2020) (2nd edition) *Reflective writing*, Basingstoke: Palgrave Macmillan.

Wingate, U. (2012) 'Using academic literacies and genre-based models for academic writing instruction: a 'literacy' journey', *Journal of English for Academic Purposes*, 11 (1), pp. 26–37.

6 Learning events
What happens in learning/teaching events?

Most readers will identify with lecture, seminar, class, tutorial and supervision as traditional labels that describe how learning happens in higher education. At face value it might seem that we share understanding of what these 'typical' labels mean, and what kind of behaviours are expected from learners and teachers. Yet, insider stories show that these learning events mean different things to different people, and in different places. This chapter explores not only the range of meanings attached to each of these typical higher education learning domains, but the confusion experienced by their participants when assumptions are unfounded and teacher and learner expectations conflict.

The chapter derives its knowledge from more than 100 student and teacher stories gathered through learning diaries, field notes, interviews and focus groups between 2011 and 2021, and across four separate projects. These are:

- *Reflection in the Round* (RIR) with 38 student learning diaries and 10 annual focus groups of students on one-year postgraduate progammes between 2011 and 2020. In addition, teacher field notes track learning activities and learner responses during the same period. The project is published as Spiro (2013) and crystallised into teaching materials as Williams, Wooliams and Spiro (2020).
- *Fostering Interculturality* (FIC) with 16 participants, both staff and students, who identified as international, discussing their experience of crossing cultures in semi-structured interviews and focus groups. This project is published as Clifford et al. (2011) and Spiro et al. (2012).
- *Learning Interconnectedness* (LIC) with 50 international first degree students between 2010 and 2014 sharing weekly journals about their experiences of learning across cultures and languages. In addition, teacher field notes track cross-cultural learning activities and learner responses in the same period, 2010 to 2014 (Spiro, 2014).
- *Crossing Study Borders* (CSB) with 24 staff and students who identified as having crossed borders in learning and teaching, interviewed between 2020 and 2021 and published here for the first time.

Most of the stories in this chapter were gathered before the 2020 to 2021 Covid-19 pandemic forced school and college closures and demanded that

DOI: 10.4324/9780429426261-6

both students and educators rethink their idea of learning events and learning spaces. Whilst many of the critical incidents here form a snapshot of experiences in physical spaces, they also shed light on how we use learning spaces in general: our comfort zones as learners and teachers, the social pragmatics that make events work, the way we pick up clues about who should do what in each setting, and what happens when these comfort zones fail to be helpful.

Learning about learning events from insider stories

Our view of learning events has been irrevocably changed by the global crisis of the Covid-19 pandemic that drove learning away from physical settings such as classrooms and lecture theatres, and into virtual spaces. Whilst blended and fully online learning has been an option for two decades, the pandemic has imposed new pressures to replicate the qualities of best learning in virtual spaces, and rapidly. This new imperative has divided educators between those prepared to step outside their comfort zones and see the new virtual classroom as a chance to review their approach to learning and learning spaces; compared to those who are biding time, waiting for the disturbance to return to 'normal'. Some educators responded to the impact of post-covid learning "as an opportunity for an educational revolution" (Ferdig and Pytash, 2021, p. 9) and a welcome incentive to rethink and refresh ways of teaching. The term *hybrid learning* describes a middle way in which learners and educators might move between real and virtual learning events and spaces, drawing on the best opportunities of both. Hybrid learning entails:

> Higher education institutions re-imagining themselves for the future, retaining those elements of their traditional model that work well and bringing in online learning where it makes sense to do so. (Patton, 2021, p. 11)

What are, then, these 'traditional models'; what does work well about them and what does not?

What is a 'lecture'? Who does what?

Within the many stories of learning across borders, 'lecture' was a term widely used to describe learning events, and yet rarely was it described without accompanying confusions and frustrations. Though the online medium offers some respite for students who experienced inequities in real classrooms, teacher-centred and transmissive forms of discourse are just as problematic when transferred from real to virtual settings.

> Traditional teacher-centered schooling did not work for so many students and bringing those same approaches to online learning did not succeed either. On the other hand, students who struggled to learn in traditional

settings, those who were bullied, stereotyped, or faced microaggressions due to their race, gender, beliefs, or other differences, and students who had health issues or other needs that made going to school challenging found that they could excel in online learning settings. (Ferdig and Pytash, 2021, p. 9)

Descriptions of the lecture, gathered from three projects over ten years, fall into several 'lookalike' events. If the lecture looks like 'theatre', learners expect to be passive, and the lecturer is the entertainer. If the lecture looks like 'marketplace', learners come and go whilst the lecturer sells their knowledge as something to take or leave. If the lecture is 'board meeting' it becomes a place where structured participation is expected. If the lecture is 'soap box' it becomes a place of high rhetoric, campaigning, heckling and persuasion. Another distinction is between the lecture as 'free-floating', disconnected with a specific syllabus, optional and non-assessed; versus the lecture as 'embedded' into the course, integral to study, compulsory and assessed. These might be useful snapshots of difference; but to illustrate the further complexity of lecture as a label, many of the stories describe 'lecture' with the same characteristics as 'seminar' and as synonymous with 'class'. These two labels will be reviewed in the next section of this chapter.

Broadly, the opportunity for misunderstanding between these interpretations is the extent to which learners take responsibility and become active contributors, and the extent to which educators enable that. The story below describes Kirsten's dilemma as her view of a lecture collides with her students' view, as she crosses study borders from the UK to China. She brings with her the expectation of lecture as seminar – an interactive exchange between learners and teachers; meanwhile, for her learners, their previous experience and expectations suggest that lecture is theatre, listening respectfully, responding silently if not uncritically.

> This was a partnership degree, whereby the first three years were taught in China, there was content delivered both in person and online in students' second and third years, and they then came to the UK for their fourth and final year, joining in with the standard UK-based final year of the degree. I generally take a very interactive approach to teaching, and realised, when faced with a stage, a microphone, and a group of very obedient students, that they were going to find that an interesting new challenge! I spent a little time talking to them about their usual methods of teaching and learning, what usually happened in their classes. At first, they were almost embarrassed to be asked to speak, and it took me a while to get across to them that I really wanted to hear their opinions, and that I was there to learn about Chinese education as well as to teach them psychology. Eventually, they started to talk a little more, and told me that usually their lecturer would come and read to them from the front of the class, and they were not expected to speak. I realised from

the things they were saying that speaking up was difficult, because they needed to 'save face' – no getting it wrong in public! (CSB, Kirsten)

In Kirsten's version of a 'lecture' the teacher would set the tone for how it might be managed, whereas for her students, 'lecture 'conferred authority on the lecturer, and implied performance rather than audience participation. The room was set up, the students briefed, to match these predetermined conditions. This did not mean change was not possible. As she continues her story, Kirsten explains how she changed the dynamics of the learning event from lecture-as-theatre to lecture-seminar by making the new ground rules and expectations clear. In this new learning event, both learners and teachers ask questions, both learners and teachers participate.

> I realised that I take for granted that students know how to interact in class, and that they expect to make mistakes, because that's how they learn. I teach them that – and over time, they learn to believe and trust that they can learn by trial and error in a safe classroom. For UK students, there are challenges in interaction, but I always build in safety nets, and they quickly learn to get the most out of these interactions. This made me realise that for international students studying in my classes, that safety and scaffolding towards interactivity may have been missing, especially with this perception of an 'authoritative' teacher, and that they may actually be missing out even back at my home university. It made me realise how much of what I consider 'normal' in the classroom is actually socially constructed. (CSB, Kirsten)

Alistair had the same experience in South Africa:

> In terms of what the students expected from me as a teacher it was clear that they wanted to be lectured at and told what they needed to do in order to pass the module. The students were surprised that I wanted to engage them in conversation and exercises in what they had timetables as lecture classes. This also impacted on my expectations of the students. Getting the balance of expectation right was fun to do and enable the students (and me) to discuss why they were taking my module and what it was that they hoped to learn during the module. I got the impression that this was not the kind of conversation that students normally had with academics. (CSB, Alistair)

In both Kirsten and Alistair's stories, the issue is not so much the learning itself, as the pragmatics of the learning event and changing this to empower students to behave differently. This can be difficult, when physical space separates the teacher from the students, and rows or tiers separate students from one another. Here is Pattie describing her teaching in China:

> Classrooms reminded me of primary school – desks screwed into the floor, in rows. I had to stand on the stage to teach, raised higher than the students, they stare at you if you get off the stage. (CSB, Pattie)

A characteristic of 'performance' is that it functions like entertainment, with no obligation on the part of the audience.

> You can go to any lecture – so if your class has 20 students 120 might show up if they feel like it. You can never tell how many will show up. Chances are students are coming in just to hear you, they won't know what you are talking about. (CSB, Pattie)

Alison describes the same phenomenon in Greece. She describes this as 'promenade theatre', similar to the marketplace or to the Greek orthodox church.

> In Athens my first experience was a shock. I had presentation all ready to go hardly anyone in the room just tutors chatting time was running on so I said shall I start I realised the culture was the students waited outside smoking and chatting until the lecture actually started so they filtered in ones and twos and as they arrived shouted to their mates on Greek – I found this really hard to cope with everything I said was translated if they wanted they just strolled out like a marketplace I discovered the Greek orthodox church is just the same they go on for three hours and people come and go so it's like a promenade theatre. I did adjust to it but it threatened my sense of mutual respect between me and the student a certain form of transmission tutors just said that's what they do. (CSB, Alison)

In the 'marketplace' the lecturer is 'touting their wares' with no sense of relationship being created between themselves and the student consumers, nor long-term investment in one another. In this situation, neither have high expectations of the other. Alison describes students surprised at the effort she was putting into her lecture preparation:

> I requisitioned a data projector took matters into my own hand but even collecting the projector it was covered with dust asked for a cloth and covered it with olive oil. I was lugging a computer around, the students couldn't believe I was there in advance, prepared and ready to go at the start of the lecture their expectations were quite low the lecturers were academics with books and books but the focus was their research- the students were at first a bit disconcerted. (CSB, Alison)

In the lecture-as-theatre, the audience tends to participate in silence. They might appreciate, respond, feel and receive but without (usually) joining in with the performance. Many of our teachers describe their culture shock, confronted with silent audiences. We saw earlier how Kirsten's students *"were not expected to speak"*. Kirsten's students explained to her their fear of *"getting it wrong in public"* and of needing to *"save face"* in front of others. Thus, silence might well be a result of a lecture-as-theatre pragmatics. But there are many other reasons too. Many of the stories from 'surveillance' cultures describe outspoken expression of opinion as taboo. Alison in China, Alistair in Romania, Anna in Russia and the Czech Republic describe the presence of 'supervisors' in classes that create fear of standing out, and a preference to comply, or even be invisible. For those students who have lived through cultures of surveillance and censorship, fear of open discussion is inevitable and silence simply self-preservation. Changing the pragmatics may be unachievable until the conditions are felt to be safe, and the new freedoms of thought and belief have been carefully nursed and navigated. Alison describes her experience of silence in Magdeburg, East Germany shortly after the end of the Berlin Wall:

> Students remained absolutely silent through the whole session but they would not speak I like sessions to be interactive and lively. Half the faculty vaunted themselves as east/west = my link person said these students are all East German their parents were brought up in the regime and they learnt not to speak out they learnt to be invisible in the public domain. The tutors said they had done their best but underlying fear that someone is listening to you they would have had family taken away because you didn't fit the pattern. (CSB, Alison)

However, our insider stories suggest several other reasons too for silence including being underprepared; being shy; being unfamiliar with the pragmatics of debate and discussion; fear of losing face. Another is directly a result of the *"boring"* lecturer. Winnie describes lectures in a French university: *"It was all lectures, no discussion, all static learning. The lecturer stood and delivered, they made no effort to make anything engaging"* (CSB, Winnie). Silence is an appropriate strategy when the lecturer has failed to create opportunities for any kind for dialogue.

Given the varied interpretations of the lecture, there are varied protocols too for arrivals, departures and attendance. As 'marketplace', there is the option of coming and going, as in Alison's analogy. As 'theatre' you take your place at the start of the session and wait for the performance to begin. In some settings, such as Anna's in Russia, the lecture theatre is the domain of the lecturer so polite behaviour is to wait outside the door until he/she arrives. The lecture could have the quality of a rock festival, as in settings where students wander in and out to see if it's worth staying longer: or it could have a closed-door policy whereby admission or departure is awkward or prohibited once the session has started. Physical aspects of the setting provide clues: whether the lecture theatre door remains open or closed during the session, whether the lecture space has a stage that confers distance and authority on the speaker, whether the lecture room carries the buzz of dialogue or the hush of theatre. It may be that, after the enforced revolution driving learning online caused by the Covid-19 pandemic, these kinds of misunderstandings in real space may be a thing of the past; yet the misreadings between student and teacher, and the need to clarify the pragmatics of learning events, whether in real or virtual space, will always remain important.

Seminars and classes

The only non-contentious definition of 'seminars' from our insider stories, was that this was a smaller group event than the lecture. Yet 'small' remains a relative term. For Alistair, 'small' seminars in China entailed dividing a cohort of 150 into three groups of 50; for Carmel in Saudi Arabia, 'seminars' were in groups of 12 as a maximum; and for Andrea in Oxford a 'seminar' was a discussion within a small tutorial group of up to three. Some of our insiders didn't use 'seminar' as a term at all, but rather 'class' as a catch-all for all kinds of learning events – lecture, tutorial, seminar – and many saw no distinction between seminar and class, using them interchangeably. So, for the purposes of differentiating this section from the one above, we shall look at those insider stories which do describe 'class' or 'seminar' as learning events in smaller groups than the lecture.

Beyond this broadest of features in common, insider stories about seminars suggest two sources of conflict. The first concerns the purpose of seminar: as social therapy, or as participatory learning. We met Carmel in an earlier chapter, describing her 'class' in Saudi Arabia in which the students came to class to eat and socialise. For Carmel's learners, the class/seminar was one of the few places where they could meet as women in a place that was socially safe to be informal and unveiled, and where subject learning was of secondary importance. The very possibility of being together socially was its purpose. For Carmel, she had hoped the class/seminar would be the place where learning happened with students sharing responsibility for learning and taking the process seriously.

In contrast, several of our insiders characterise the class/seminar as equally, if not more, serious a learning event than the lecture. They describe it as a place where more is expected of them, and there is more collective responsibility for the learning: for example, *"in a seminar I ask questions which I never would in a lecture"*, and *"in a seminar when the teacher asks questions we actually answer them"* (RIR). Rhetorical questions, false questions which are answered by the teacher, seem to be expected strategies in the lecture but not in the seminar/class. Several explain that they prepare much more carefully for seminars, since there they feel a collective responsibility to others: *"I wouldn't turn up at the seminar without doing the reading, but I often go to a lecture without preparing, I feel I can be invisible there"* (RIR). *"I would feel bad skipping seminars because we work with other students then, we are much more seen*" (RIR). Peer pressure carries the power, both in the best-case learning event, and in the less optimal one that Carmel finds herself in. It will need a strong steer to turn this around, especially single-handedly, and entails Carmel making most of the compromises.

The second conflict in perceptions is how far learning is co-created with other learners, and how far it's controlled by the teacher. Those who expected to learn from the teacher and found the learning was with other students, were frustrated, disappointed, even angry. An RIR participant tells us:

> I don't understand why it is interesting to listen to what the other students are thinking when I came to study to hear the people who are expert. (RIR)

Several students in the RIR project revealed they were unsure of the rules of the seminar as compared to the lecture.

> We do all this that we talk in groups to our neighbour and say what we think but I don't know what I am meant to say. In the lecture I know what I am meant to do, but I am never sure why I am talking to the other students. Am I meant to write notes or not? (RIR)

However, the disappointment is also experienced in reverse; where a student is hoping for a student-centred learning opportunity in seminars, and fails to experience this:

> In the class we were from at least 8 different countries but we never once in class had a chance to find out about this, we were always looking at cases theoretically from what it said in the papers we read. I thought it was such a missed opportunity when we had all that experience just sitting there in the class. (RIR)

Learning from one another/learning from the teacher, however, is a difficult balance to find. For one RIR participant there was too much focus on the discussion of set texts and not enough on student experience. For another student the reverse was the case. For her, the seminar had a tendency to be *too* student-run and lose its centre as a learning event. For this student the seminar tended to become "*a kind of therapy session*" (RIR):

> Specifically the problem was the seminar was used as a place where we prepared for our assessed work, so it became competitive and individualistic. It became a place where everyone really expressed their panic and concerns about their own project rather than learning something new together, so the lecturer was all the time dealing with people's worries. (RIR)

The student stories suggest that, even where learning is more informal, there is still a strong need for structure, clarity and purpose, and this is likely to be even more the case as these transactions move to virtual settings. The insiders who expressed most disappointment were those who didn't quite know what they were meant to do or why; and who, at the end of the seminar/class, felt nothing had been learnt or achieved. By analogy, the educators who felt most frustration were those, like Carmel, who could not achieve any of their learning goals, and whose approach was consistently thwarted by conflicting expectations. Some of our educators, such as Kirsten and Alistair, have given us examples of changing their learners' expectations and shifting the pragmatics of their class – from silent theatre to exchange and dialogue. Yet every situation needs to be reassessed in terms of: what can be changed for the better, and what simply cannot be changed? How far can even small changes make a difference?

Tutorials and supervisions

In some settings, tutorial, seminar and class are used interchangeably; but for the purposes of this section, tutorial and supervision are here used to describe one to one or small group interactions, between student and lecturer. Tutorials and supervisions map themselves along several polarities: from formal to informal, from optional to integral, from pastoral to content-specific, from teacher-controlled to co-operatively managed.

Optional, pastoral and informal tutorials, in theory, appeared to be valued, but in practice the insider stories suggest lack of clarity as to their purpose, and lack of take-up. Emanuel (CSB) describes the discovery, moving from France to Canada, that drop-in meetings with lecturers were available to clarify lecture information or check assignments. Students had to 'opt in', even find out by accident, that these were offered. The students in Currant's study (2021) of BAME students in a middle-England institution, describe their awkwardness in taking up the offer of tutorial help. There was a fear of losing face, admitting weakness, and the systems were unclear. Several students in the data say that they never availed themselves of a tutorial throughout their first-degree study. *"There seemed no reason why I should. I was never sure the purpose of a tutor who didn't actually teach me anything"* (RIR). At the reverse end of the spectrum are teacher accounts of mismatched expectations *"when the student read my office hours as free therapy. I realised I was out of my depth and referred the student to the student counsellor. I had to work out very clearly what my boundaries were"* (RIR). Unstructured tutorial spaces and encounters thus seemed to be the least effective from both student and tutor perspectives.

In contrast, Andrea describes the role of tutorials at Oxford, as opposed to her university in Germany. At Oxford University the tutorial was the central place where learning happened, focused content-based dialogue with a subject-specialist, and an integral compulsory part of learning. The tutorial was structured around set tasks, or set written assignments, and the tutorial was a place for thorough debate of content areas. Tutorials of this kind were a surprise for those students who had never experienced it before:

> The first time I treated the tutorial like a lecture, I could take it or leave the preparation and reading. I was so embarrassed when I realised the tutor just wasn't prepared to fill in the gaps I should have filled in myself, that nothing happened unless I had something to contribute. I never forgot that first bad tutorial and always worked for them afterwards. (RIR)

Supervisions, as a label, were generally interpreted as one-to-one meetings focused on a specific project: a dissertation, thesis or assignment. Insider stories of 'supervision' suggested a much clearer 'contract' between student and supervisor. "*I know I have to prepare for a supervision, I have to have clear ideas about my project and send in some writing in advance*" (RIR). For some, this focused supervision experience was transformative. One informant described supervision

> as the best learning experience I had. In my first degree I never spent time with a tutor but for my second degree the supervisions for my project were really helpful and I felt I was being treated as an individual in my learning for the first time. (RIR)

Anna (CSB) describes her transition to supervision for a higher degree as

> waking up. In lectures I would never have spoken or asked questions; but one to one, working with a supervisor who was focused on my project and my development, I actually realised what it was I wanted to research and to say. (CSB, Anna)

These accounts suggest interactions where student and teacher expectations are in harmony. Both seemed clear as to the contract between them: the balance between student contribution and teacher attention. Where this contract is broken on either side, there was cause for frustration and disappointment on both sides. One university teacher participant explained,

> it was really hard to say '*If you haven't read the article and have nothing to say about it, I suggest you go away and come back when you have read it*'. I felt awful doing that, but I learnt to in all kinds of diplomatic ways. (RIR)

Conversely, students complained where they expected and failed to receive prompt support and feedback.

> I was so excited at the idea of having a tutor, but I was never really clear how much feedback I could expect. When I did send some work in advance of an assignment he told me to send it to the module leader. (RIR)

Learning events 113

Learning events, then, repeatedly return to the question of clarity; clarity as to the kind of contract between teacher and learner, the balance of power and responsibility, and the way this will be reflected in the balance of teacher talk and student talk.

Learning about learning events through the literature lens

Here is Akio's story from the Reflection in the Round project, describing critical moments in a class where he was constantly 'wrong-footed' by misunderstood expectations.

> In the class I was ready to take notes. I was confused when the lecturer said to answer some questions. I thought the question was not a real one. When the lecturer then said my name to answer the question I was completely shocked. I didn't expect to answer, and I couldn't think quickly. The lecturer went on to someone else but I felt embarrassed and upset.
>
> Later she said we should work with others to answer another question, there was more than one answer, and we should choose in the group the best one. The other students in the group kept changing what they thought. I was confused and was quiet. I thought there was one right way but I was upset because I wasn't sure what that was and I didn't think the other students knew either. I think if there was one right way the teacher should tell us.
>
> At home I am a good and serious student. We don't ask questions because that is disrespectful to the lecturer. Also it means you haven't understood properly. But in this class I kept making mistakes, and I didn't understand what the lecturer wanted. (RIR)

Taking turns

I thought the question was not a real one.

We see that Akio had carried into the class-as-seminar, the protocol and expectations of the lecture. This is a new kind of discourse, of which he has had little experience and no preparation. The literature suggests he is not alone in finding the transition both surprising and difficult. Mukorera and Yotanga's study of undergraduates in Alberta (2017) is one of very few that tracks interactive learning over time. Their study found that first year students tended to prefer working in isolation, either one to one with a tutor or on their own in response to lectures, whilst second and third years shifted to valuing more social learning with others. These are new forms of behaviour to be learnt, and new expectations as to who does what in the learning situation.

To help us appreciate more exactly what these different expectations are, it is useful to look at forms of classroom analysis. Walsh (2011) divides classroom discourse into four modes. Although his main focus is the language learning classroom, the four modes are relevant when applied across other disciplines too. They reveal the way purpose and pedagogic goal impact on who is expected to do what. One of the most revealing ways to differentiate learning events concerns who takes turns to talk, and how long those turns are. Akio is accustomed to the class or lecture being conducted in a 'managerial' mode. Here the teacher transmits information and has a long and extended 'turn' to talk. In this contract, as the teacher adopts their extended turns, students are not required to participate and are offered minimum chance to contribute. Table 6.1 illustrates that this is one amongst several kinds of discourse the learner is likely to find in a classroom setting.

The pragmatics of the seminar are very different from the managerial approach the learner is expecting. In Akio's example, the teacher started with a number of direct questions, initiating an idea, waiting for a response and offering brief feedback. When Akio does not respond she moves briskly on and invites a response from a student ready to provide a prompt answer. However, the class then progresses to a problem-solving stage, with students given longer 'turns' to talk, and questions being more open-ended. What looks to Akio like lack of clarity, is in fact a process of negotiating knowledge and arriving at co-created understanding.

Table 6.1 Classroom modes of discourse (Walsh, 2011, p. 113)

Mode	Pedagogic goals	Interactional features
Managerial	To transmit information	A single extended teacher turn An absence of learner contributions
Materials/text or content focus	To elicit responses in relation to texts/materials To check and display answers To clarify when necessary To evaluate contributions	The use of scaffolding Extensive use of the patterning: Initiate/Respond/Feedback
Skills and systems focus	To provide learners with practice in skills and sub-skills To display correct answers	Extended teacher turns Display questions Teacher echoes Clarification requests
Classroom context	To enable learners to express themselves clearly To promote fluency and confidence talking about their subject	Extended learner turns Short teacher turns Minimal repair Content feedback Scaffolding Clarification requests

This is a kind of interaction that Akio has not experienced before and at this early stage it does not seem to him to lead to learning, which is still perceived as something transmitted from the lecturer to the learner intact. There is a big leap from this view of learning and interaction to the one he is being asked now to adopt, and to make this leap he will need to understand the process, as well as trust its purpose.

Kinds of talk

The other students in the group kept changing what they thought.

In an extensive comparison between learning in three countries, England, France and Denmark, Osborn et al. (2003) identified three different kinds of discourse which typified learning cultures. Whilst we will not, in this chapter, ascribe them to specific places, it is interesting to place these three modes side by side and consider the conflict in moving from one to the other (see Table 6.2).

Akio's expectation of learning is that he should '*fit in*'. This means that becoming visible is awkward, and asking questions suggests weakness, or entails interrupting the teacher in her entitlement to long 'turns'. In contrast, the learning event he now enters fosters collaboration and eventually personal growth; the learner takes longer turns, and the teacher gradually steps out. The questions are different in these settings: from questions that ask for clarification, or that expect finite answers, to questions that open debate and lead to negotiation. Osborn et al. (2003) ascribed the differences in 2003 to national culture, the influence of peers and local culture, and the influences within the individual lives of learners. At the time of writing those findings, globalisation and mass schooling were creating new expectations and cross-cultural notions of best practice. This is all the more so as this book goes to print in 2022, with global online interactions as real and present as local ones. In Akio's class, response to the new way of interacting no longer divides along

Table 6.2 Three kinds of talk (derived from Osborn et al., 2003, p. 215 and Walsh, 2011, p. 113)

	Mode 1 Co-learning	*Mode 2* Individual learning	*Mode 3* Fitting in
Location in Osborn study (2003)	Denmark	England	France
Features of the learning discourse	Collaborative/consensus	Differentiation	Solidarity/lack of difference
Kinds of talk	To solve problems collaboratively To negotiate To reach agreements	To compete To express and compare personal opinions	To clarify knowledge To display shared knowledge To reach common standards

116 *Learning events*

national or cultural boundaries, but rather divides between those who have become familiar with a new kind of discourse and whose expectations have adapted to these, and those who have not.

Self-esteem and knowing what to do

> *I felt embarrassed and upset.*

In Akio's estimation, the lecturer has not delivered what he would define as helpful learning. Wilkerson and Gisjelaer's (1996) study in Maastricht found that students who feared they were failing also felt the tutor was not doing what he/she ought to do. The more they feared failure, the less highly they evaluated their tutor. Clearly there is a circularity about this finding; is the problem that the student has low self-esteem, or that the teacher is not enabling learning, and how is it possible to break this unvirtuous cycle?

Studies suggest that student sense of wellbeing is highly connected with a sense of rapport with their university teachers. De Souza et al. (2019) studied the acclimatisation of 680 Brazilian and Portuguese university students to a new university culture and found those who perceived their university teachers to be supportive also had a greater sense of wellbeing and a greater sense of their university's preparedness for them. Students in Hong Kong (Morrison and Evans, 2018), asked to evaluate the effectiveness of their university teachers, arrived at similar criteria. Students most valued teachers that helped them develop critical thinking and who gave them clear explanations with concrete and practical examples. Akio, then, is not alone in finding his self-esteem affected by unclear explanations. He needs instructions that take him through the learning steps and the satisfaction of succeeding, not only in the eyes of his teacher but in his own estimation as well.

Comfort and discomfort zones

> *I am a good student.*

Akio's comment "*I am a good student*" suggests self-esteem on the one hand, but on the other a possibility that his view of himself is fixed, and resistant to change. The higher education teacher who happily does the same thing for many years, as it seems to work well, could be seen as similarly inflexible. The Covid-19 pandemic's impact on teaching provided a critical learning curve for higher education teachers. We have seen that 'traditional' learning events do not seamlessly move from physical to virtual settings.

> In terms of logistics, remote learning is incredibly difficult – people don't realize how much more time it takes teachers. You don't have that instant feedback, you don't have the ability to scan the room, but I think the mindsets were [already] there: 'I know how to set the stage to help students'. (Will, 2020, online)

Just as Akio has learnt a way of interacting and is uncomfortable with a new expectation, lecturers who were accustomed to a 'managerial' approach that worked well in real space have needed to rethink this in the light of a covid-safe world. This digs deep into ways that learning is perceived and managed, into the very 'weltanschauung' of learners and teachers. Dron (2021) describes his conversation with a science lecturer who

> patiently explained that he has classes with hundreds of students and fixed topics that they need to learn, and he really didn't see it as desirable or even possible to depart from his well-tried lecture format.
>
> What he actually wanted was for someone to make (or tell him how to make) the digital technology as easy and as comfortably familiar as the lecture theatre, and that would somehow make the students as engaged as he perceived them to normally be in his lectures, without notably changing how he taught. The problem was the darn technology, not the teaching. (Dron, 2021)

A report based on teacher responses in the US to the pandemic (Will, 2020) suggests that teachers can no longer remain within comfort zones, which were unhelpful in real spaces, and even less so in virtual spaces. Amongst the recommendations are the need to make support targeted and instructions explicit, so learning activities are crystal clear; building in clear opportunities for speaking, which may have happened in a more unplanned way in real spaces; and helping to "build resilience and independence", so learners can manage their schedules better and know what needs to be done and when. Claiming to place the learner at the heart of the learning event, and actually doing so, however, are sometimes different things. Uiboleht et al. (2019) studied 33 undergraduate student responses to different kinds of learning environment. They found that, even where teachers claimed to have a student-centred approach to learning, the actual learning environments they created were widely variable; and only those which genuinely engaged the students in learning activities, and focused on learning rather than delivery of content, were experienced as positive. What is interesting in this study, is that university teachers varied in their actual adoption of a learning-centred approach, even where they claimed to be espousing it. It is perhaps taking account of resistant learners, or those new to the learning encounters, that might make the difference: in other words, bearing in mind learners such as Akio for whom the new setting is a learning leap, and who needs practice and time in these new kinds of interactions.

Reviewing studies across subject disciplines, we see that higher education educators are rethinking learning events to include forms of engagement that students do favour: students taking responsibility, talk as discursive and open-ended, modes of learning as co-constructive and developmental. Table 6.3 offers a sample of these different learning events designed to support students.

Table 6.3 Learning events and subject disciplines

Subject discipline	Learning event	Learning focus	Research study
Music	Seminar	High-stakes teacher performance and portfolio assessments were a major focus of seminar content. We recommend incorporating activities into the seminar that support continued pedagogical growth and socialisation into the profession. (Baumgartner and Council, p. 11)	Baumgartner and Council (2019)
Pharmacy	Journal club	Classroom Seminar and Journal Club (CRSJC) model and explains potential benefits of implementing the use of various review and research articles published in reputed journals and periodicals through this model in order to study the syllabus topics in depth and upgrade the knowledge, quality and standards of postgraduate pharmacy students. (Dahiya and Dahiya p. 69)	Dahiya and Dahiya (2015)
Metallurgy	Reciprocal peer assessment in tutorials	Opportunities for synergistic peer learning, healthy competition among students, self-directed learning, (Matinde p. 1)	Matinde (2019)
Sports development	Student-led tutorials	The tutorless tutorial A platform for student learning designed to increase active learning prior to participation in more traditional and tutor-led modes of university teaching. (Hayton p. 12)	Hayton (2019)

These learning events reframe the discourse so students have a chance to take the lead, to develop their skills as team players and leaders, and to step into the shoes of their teachers as initiators and assessors of ideas and knowledge. Yet Matinde's study (2017) shows that response is not always favourable. In the peer assessment tutorials, there were many of the same blocks as Akio experiences:

> low level of trust among peers, anxiety over year marks, time constraints, and discomfort due to perceived incompetency when compared to their peers. (Matinde, 2017, p. 1)

Are students such as Akio ready for these very different kinds of learning events? Hermann's (2014) study suggested that students who stayed with a surface view of learning were less likely to appreciate being responsible participants. In her study:

> students relying on surface approaches to learning seemingly are the ones least likely to respond to tutorials in the way they were intended. (Hermann, 2014, p. 591)

Moving from a transmissive lecture to student-led tutorials, journal clubs, and reading circles require many changed expectations: how discourse takes place, where responsibility lies between teacher and learner, and what learning actually means. As a slowly learnt transition, it needs time for trust to build, its purposes to become apparent and its processes clear.

Learning maps: what happens in learning/teaching events?

Using Table 6.4 and these reflection questions, explore how you define learning events.

Defining learning events

- What are your expectations of these learning events?
- What is your experience of these learning events?
- Is there any difference between these two? What do you need to do/know/change to accommodate this difference?
- In which of these settings, as a learner, would you:
- feel most comfortable to ask questions?
- have opportunities to talk to other students about your work?
- as a student have an opportunity to present your work?
- feel you have most control and involvement as a student?
- What would be the physical clues in the classroom that suggest which learning event is taking place?

Defining the learning contract

Now use Table 6.5 to explore your learning contracts.

120 Learning events

Table 6.4 Defining learning events

	Lecture	Seminar	Class/Session	Tutorial	Supervision
Formal and controlled by the teacher					
Interactive (students talk/ask questions)					
Small groups (less than 12)					
Large groups (more than 12)					
One to one					
Subject based only					
Pastoral issues					
Open to the public/drop-in					
Marketplace, rock festival, theatre					

Table 6.5 Defining the learning contract

	Lecture	Seminar/class	Tutorial	Supervision
To read and prepare in advance				
To take notes				
To participate in discussion				
To attend every session				
To submit written work in advance				
To set the agenda				
To ask questions				
To answer questions				

- What is the contract between student and tutor in each of these settings, according to your expectations?
- What is the contract between student and tutor according to your experience?
- What is the difference between these two and what changes would help to bridge this difference?

Defining student talk

Finally, use Table 6.6 and these questions to explore aspects of student talk.

Table 6.6 Defining student talk

	Lecture	Small classes Tutorials/seminars
To display		
To respond to content		
To solve a problem		
To be critical of ideas or content		
To check meaning		
To negotiate with others		
To develop your personal ideas		
To think aloud		
To socialise with peers		

- What is the purpose of student talk in these settings, in your experience?
- What are your expectations of student talk in these settings?
- What changes and compromises would you need to make the bridge the difference between these two?

Further topics for reflection and reading

How useful, do you think, are case studies of particular groups of students in a particular time and place? Below are four case studies of seminars in different parts of the world.

- What is unique and specific about each case study?
- What universals and shared themes and questions are suggested?
- How might you conduct a similar study into one kind of learning event in your study setting?

Al'Adawi, S.S.A. (2017) 'Exploring the effectiveness of implementing seminars as a teaching and an assessment method in a children's literature course', *English Language Teaching*, 10 (11), pp. 1–14.

Clarke, K. and Lane, A.M. (2005) 'Seminar and tutorial sessions: a case study evaluating relationships with academic performance and student satisfaction', *Journal of Further & Higher Education*, 29 (1), pp. 15–23.

Harris, H. and Myers, D. (2013) 'Student perceptions of integrative field seminar: a comparison of three models', *Administrative Issues Journal: Education, Practice, and Research*, 3 (2) [online]. Available at: https://eric.ed.gov/?q=EJ1057088&id=EJ1057088 (Accessed: 26 June 2021).

Liu, B., Xing, W. and Wu, Y. (2019) 'Students' interaction and perceptions in a large-enrolled blended seminar series course', *Turkish Online Journal of Educational Technology*, 18 (3), pp. 88–96.

References

Al'Adawi, S.S.A. (2017) 'Exploring the effectiveness of implementing seminars as a teaching and an assessment method in a children's literature course', *English Language Teaching*, 10 (11), pp. 1–14.

Baumgartner, C.M. and Council, K.H. (2019) 'Music student teachers' perceptions of their seminar experience: an exploratory study', *Journal of Music Teacher Education*, 29 (1), pp. 11–25.

Clarke, K. and Lane, A.M. (2005) 'Seminar and tutorial sessions: a case study evaluating relationships with academic performance and student satisfaction', *Journal of Further & Higher Education*, 29 (1), pp. 15–23.

Clifford, V., Adeunji, H., Haigh, M., Henderson, J., Spiro, J. and Hudson, J. (2011) *Report on Brookes Student Learning Experience Project: Fostering Interculturality and Global Perspectives at Brookes through Dialogue with Staff*. Oxford Centre for Staff Learning and Development: Oxford Brookes University.

Currant, Neil James (2021) *"My Stomach Churns": Belonging and Strategies for Belonging for BME Students in a White University*. Unpublished EdD thesis: Oxford Brookes University.

Dahiya, S. and Dahiya, R. (2015) 'Class room seminar and journal club (CRSJC) as an effective teaching learning tool: perception to post graduation pharmacy students', *Journal of Effective Teaching*, 15 (1), pp. 69–83.

De Souza, S.B., Veiga Simão, A.M., da Costa Ferreira, P. (2019) 'Campus climate: the role of teacher support and cultural issues', *Journal of Further & Higher Education*, 43 (9), pp. 1196–1211.

Dron, J. (2021) 'Are experienced online teachers best-placed to help in-person teachers cope with suddenly having to teach online? Maybe not' [Blog] Jon Dron's home page. Available at: https://jondron.ca/are-experienced-online-teachers-best-placed-to-help-in-person-teachers-cope-with-suddenly-having-to-teach-online-maybe-not/ (Accessed: 5 April 2021).

Ferdig, R.E. and Pytash, K.E. (2021). 'What teacher educators should have learned from 2020'. Association for the Advancement of Computing in Education (AACE): The Learning and Technology Library. Available at: www.learntechlib.org/primary/p/219088/ (Accessed: 6 April 2021).

Harris, H. and Myers, D. (2013) 'Student perceptions of integrative field seminar: a comparison of three models', *Administrative Issues Journal: Education, Practice, and Research*, 3 (2) [online]. Available at: https://eric.ed.gov/?q=EJ1057088&id=EJ1057088 (Accessed: 26 June 2021).

Hayton, J.W. (2019) 'Helping them to help themselves? An evaluation of student-led tutorials in a higher education setting', *Journal of Further and Higher Education*, 43 (1), pp. 12–29.

Hermann, K. (2014) 'Learning from tutorials: a qualitative study of approaches to learning and perceptions of tutorial interaction', *Higher Education*, 68 (4), pp. 591–606.

Liu, B., Xing, W. and Wu, Y. (2019) 'Students' interaction and perceptions in a large-enrolled blended seminar series course', *Turkish Online Journal of Educational Technology*, 18 (3), pp. 88–96.

Matinde, E. (2019) 'Students' perceptions on reciprocal peer tutorial assessment in an undergraduate course in process metallurgy', *Education Sciences*, 9 (1). https://doi.org/10.3390/educsci9010027 (Accessed: 26 June 2021).

Morrison, B. and Evans, S. (2018) 'University students' conceptions of the good teacher: a Hong Kong perspective', *Journal of Further & Higher Education*, 42 (3), pp. 352–365.

Mukorera, Sophia and Nyatanga, Phocenah (2017) Students' perceptions of teaching and learning practices: a principal component approach. *Alberta Journal of Educational Research*, 63 (2) pp. 120–138.

Osborn, M., Broadfoot, P., McNess, E., Planet, C., Ravn, B. and Triggs, P. (2003). *A world of difference? Comparing learners across Europe*. Maidenhead, Berkshire: Open University Press.

Patton, Renee (2021) How universities can fit into a hybrid learning future. *Future of Education Technology*, MediaPlanet, p. 11.

Spiro, J. (2013) 'The reflective continuum: Reflecting for change and student response to reflective tasks', *Brookes eJournal of Learning and Teaching*, 2013.

Spiro, J. (2014) 'Learning interconnectedness: internationalisation through engagement with one another', *Higher Education Quarterly*, 68 (1), pp. 65–84.

Spiro, J., Henderson, J. and Clifford, V. (2012) 'Independent learning crossing cultures: learning cultures and shifting meanings', *Compare: A Journal of Comparative and International Education*, 42 (4), pp. 607–619.

Uiboleht, K., Karm, M. and Postareff, L. (2019) 'Relations between students' perceptions of the teaching-learning environment and teachers' approaches to teaching: a qualitative study', *Journal of Further & Higher Education*, 43 (10), pp. 1456–1475.

Walsh, S. (2011) *Exploring classroom discourse: language in action*. Abingdon, Oxfordshire: Routledge.

Wilkerson, L. and Gisjelaers, W. (eds.) (1996). *Bringing problem-based learning to higher education: theory and practice*. New Directions for Teaching and Learning, No. 68, San Francisco: Jossey-Bass.

Will, M. (2020) 'Six lessons learnt from 2020', *Education Week*. Available at: www.edweek.org/technology/6-lessons-learned-about-better-teaching-during-the-pandemic/2020/11 (Accessed: 5 April 2021).

Williams, K., Wooliams, M. and Spiro, J. (2020) (2nd edition) *Reflective writing*. Basingstoke: Palgrave Macmillan.

7 Learning spaces

How do I experience campus and virtual spaces?

This chapter looks at the way learning places/spaces make a difference to teaching and learning. It seems straightforward to suggest libraries are for studying, classrooms for teaching and student union bars for socialising. Yet increasingly, in 'home-like' study settings, or those with a holistic vision of spaces, social and study settings overlap and assumed demarcation of spaces has to be revisited. The stories shared in this chapter suggest that nothing can be taken for granted in our interpretation of the physical world, as we move from one space to another.

In earlier chapters we also mentioned the year that physical classrooms closed due to the Covid-19 global pandemic 2020–2021, a crisis which took to a new level our relationship with online learning. Our stories of transitions in space thus need to include, not only moving across cultures, regions and languages, but also moving from built classrooms to virtual ones. How do expectations from one setting conflict with another, and what can we learn from the surprises, matches and mismatches? Our stories come from three studies first described in Chapter One: *Crossing Study Borders* (CSB), the *Learning Interconnectedness* study (LIC) and the *Reflection in the Round* (RIR) project. In addition, educator responses to the Covid-19 year have been gathered through the means of an online international symposium held at Oxford Brookes university, *Teaching and Learning in Virtual Space* 2020–2021. These represent in-the-moment dynamic responses from educational 'frontline workers' to the changed relationship with online learning during the year campuses closed and the world stayed at home.

Learning and teaching in campus spaces

Student and teacher stories from our three main studies confirm that buildings do make a difference to wellbeing and sense of belonging. This will not be an unusual perception; feng shui, holistic and home-like design, are founded on the knowledge that spaces affect feelings. More will be said about these ideas later in the chapter. The narratives show the impact of changing places from one built learning environment to another, and the impact of these changes on wellbeing, safety, learning and identity. For ease of referencing, we shall refer to the term

DOI: 10.4324/9780429426261-7

'campus' to describe the physical place of study, whether a single building or a complex of buildings scattered over a number of hectares or even different parts of the city.

Learner stories of campus spaces

The happiest students were those whose new campus included safe and culture-appropriate places for socialising, easily marked as such and easy to find. Those mentioned include sports centres, music practice rooms, exhibition spaces, prayer rooms and rooms dedicated to quiet. These were described as "*grounding*", "*helpful*", "*my go-to place*", and importantly as places where friendships were found and forged, and where wellbeing was nurtured (LIC).

> Where I met my best friends in my first year was not in class, but playing netball. We would chat in the changing rooms and then sit by the drinks machine chatting and drinking coke. That's where I most bonded with people and not in the lectures or classes where I didn't really at all. (LIC)

Places that honoured religious cultures helped students bring personal identity into the campus space. "*I liked that there was a Moslem prayer room and it gave me a sense of home and being myself*" (LIC). For one participant who explained her tendency to panic at noisy, hectic spaces, the prayer space became a lifeline. "*If I needed to escape from all the big noise I would go to the prayer room. It helped me to feel calmer and it became an important place for me to prepare*" (LIC). Places of personal peace were those that had the deepest connections with home. One of the participants described finding a Japanese tea ceremony room in her new institution. "*It felt like a very safe place to be and I was very happy to find it and it made me feel less homesick*" (LIC).

Conversely, where these spaces did not exist, students felt more acutely the separation from other students, homesickness and the struggle to form supportive networks. Many of our stories reveal that the physical spaces themselves were causes of separation and isolation. It is not so much the worry of getting lost on a big new campus, but the worry of finding social spaces that were comfortable, safe and in harmony with personal and religious beliefs. Anna (CSB) describes the experience of moving from a small local college to a large international university on a multi-hectare campus with buildings spread a mile in either direction.

> I had never appreciated the importance of small scale. In my first college, I bumped into class friends in the corridor, in the café, in the library, I knew everyone who made the campus work and they knew me by name, the caretaker, the librarians, the office administrators. I felt very visible, and when I had to take two weeks off for a family bereavement when I came back loads of people had noticed I hadn't been there. Six months

> later I was on this big campus. The classes were huge, the administrators were miles from the teaching, the teaching was miles from the library, I was running between them all and I never saw anyone twice. I really thought in the first week, 'how am I going to manage?' (CSB, Anna)

From 16 international students in one year group of data, none had been into a local home. A possible reason for this, according to their stories, is that the learning spaces simply hadn't encouraged friendships between them and home-based students (RIR).

> After the class we had to leave the classroom. Then maybe some would go to smoke or have coffee. There was a small smoking hut on the campus and I think they made friends there but I didn't smoke. There was a student union place but it was locked during the day when the bar was closed, everyone disappeared so I never got to know anyone but my two study abroad friends I always sat with. (RIR)

> Some of the students said: "*if we stayed in the class afterwards and talked maybe I would get to know them, but there was this way of everyone rushing out at the end*" (RIR).

We have seen in earlier chapters, that one reason for "*rushing off*" after class included being a commuter student, living at a distance from study, and other work or family commitments. But other reasons emanated from the space itself. Students describe classrooms opening onto narrow corridors with no natural light, unconducive to lingering for long; or classes where another group was waiting outside the door to use the room, and there was pressure to leave promptly. This lack of physical space for forging relationships after class was a direct cause of distance and loneliness. Students who described homesickness and loneliness in their early months in the new setting, often connected this with lack of a physical setting where they felt comfortable to socialise.

> I would like to have talked to the others but how to do it? It was a big campus and I would never see them afterwards. Sometimes in the library but we mustn't talk there. I began to feel shy. (RIR)

For students already finding it hard to acclimatise, these all represented "*problems of where to go. Where did everyone go after class?*" (LIC). Chapter 2 told the story of one student who did discover that both her peers and tutors spent time in the student bar; but for her as a non-drinking practising Muslim, this was simply not an acceptable option.

Several of our stories describe the impact of separated spaces: as international students, for example, being separated from students local to the area or culture. Whilst this separation was often well-meaning, with mission statements suggesting that these forms of separation allowed for targeted support to certain groups, it was not necessarily how it was experienced. Aidan, whom we met in earlier chapters, describes his experience as an international student in Japan:

> I was put in a bubble. It was double-edged; they were trying to accommodate you, but it feels like you are being protected, segregated. We were in a building separating us, there were staff just for us, so everything we did was separate to the 'real' Japanese experience. It was because we were there to study Japanese, so the locals obviously didn't need it. (CSB, Aidan)

Aidan describes these enforced 'bubbles' as counter-productive to the main purpose of his travel: to fit in with the local culture. He implies that it was equally daunting for the local students to come into this bubble as it was for international students to leave it. To move in either direction the students needed an extra spurt of self-confidence. Whilst Aidan appreciated the rationale for this decision, still it did not help his sense of distance from his new place of study, as seen in Chapter 2 where we discussed his experience of living in a separate bubble from his Japanese peers.

For Aidan, the social spaces became essential for breaking down this distance. He did have the courage to join an international club, which included local students, and through this made Japanese friends. Through these friendships he was able to venture into a local home.

> We stayed with a friend in Nagano to go to a festival which happened every 4 years. We staying in his house, all his family were staying too. About 10 of them. It was a traditional Japanese home with tatami mats and sliding doors up a mountain, we slept on futons.
>
> The biggest cultural mistake I made was gift-giving. Gifts are huge – they fed us, put us up for several nights and we showed up empty-handed. Our friend was too humble to mention we should have brought a gift. We were oblivious at the time. (CSB, Aidan)

In spite of his cultural error, Aidan is unusual in being able to bridge the gap between himself and local students and enter into a local home. A more common experience is Carmel's, whom we met in earlier chapters teaching in Saudi Arabia. Before teaching she was a study abroad student, and for her, contact with the local community could be edgy and threatening:

> I was there as a study abroad student for 4 months – every single thing was different; toilets, where you buy food, how you address people, how you dress, the sandstorms – So I gave less attention to the educational differences.
>
> The professors became our support, they would talk in Arabic for us, we were dealing with so many barriers. Our friend was being harassed

and the professor took the phone and said: 'I am her father'. (CSB, Carmel)

Physical spaces facilitate or hinder studying together too. In earlier chapters, we compared student groups that continued their learning together outside the classroom as opposed to students who scattered at the end of the class and rarely met in between classes. Andrea (CSB) describes her experience of crossing between these two kinds of student groups and noticed the benefits for students whose academic conversations continued organically between sessions because they lived together: problems were resolved, reading was shared, and anxieties about assignments were reduced. Buildings offer clear clues as to whether this kind of collaborative learning is encouraged or not. Bookable meeting rooms, booths and 'pods' where students can discuss work with peers, soft seating and coffee machines all suggest an ethos in which social and study spaces meld together. The students in the *Learning Interconnectedness* project reported the most successful shared study happened when there were spaces encouraging this: *"we would meet in the student café where there were tables with sockets to plug in and you could pull a screen round you to have private discussions"* (LIC). Another said, *"I did all my writing in the student cafeteria. I worked there much more than in the library"* (LIC). Cafeterias in many of the stories were the favoured workplaces. Students liked the relaxed atmosphere, the lack of pressure, the buzz of other people around them when they felt *"safe"* at a table of their own, with a place to charge their laptop, and the noise stayed as a background buzz. One student expressed her disappointment moving from one institution to another and ascribed her academic difficulties to the changed use of spaces.

> Where I did my first degree the café was absolutely where I did my best work, and loads of my friends did too. When I did my study year abroad the café was noisy with an echo that gave me a headache; the tables were small and wobbly and absolutely not conducive to sit for long, and anyway you were miles from the nearest place to charge your laptop. You felt odd too because people were literally there to eat and drink, and noone else was just hanging out there working. (LIC)

Libraries were significant spaces, even if not always the preferred place of study. An LIC participant described the library *"like a mausoleum. It was cold, and no-one spoke. I felt literally chilled when I went to the library and I didn't go much"* (LIC). In contrast, for another LIC student it felt like a safe place, a haven for escaping too much noise and movement, and somewhere to settle and feel safe, similar to the Japanese tea ceremony room that she also liked. Thus, the library as a place of quiet study partly depends on preference for silence or the quiet hum of conversation. Libraries that offered both, with an organic flow between silent study and social interaction, were much appreciated:

When the library introduced a small sitting room inside where you could have coffee from machine, use photocopier and talk a bit I liked that and used it more. (LIC)

The educators amongst the storytellers were most aware of the impact of space on their teaching and the students' learning. The size of a room made a difference to interactions. Bridget describes the allocation of a "*little room*" in her school in China to meet students, in lieu of being allowed to meet them as a large group. This seemed like an explicit way of limiting conversation:

I was in school for a couple of weeks I said I would be happy to speak but they didn't want me to speak to any of the faculty alone so I was allocated a little room and they came to me with questions I wasn't allowed to ask them questions. (CSB, Bridget)

Alternatively, spaces could be experienced as too large for comfortable teaching too.

The classes were in this cavernous room meant for about a 100 people. About 25 students took the class and I would say the room was a huge obstacle at first to getting it right. The students were used to it but I am convinced it made them more passive, more distant from me and one another, and much less happy to engage in discussion. (LIC)

Thus, the most careful teaching and learning plans are subject to the limitations of space and can easily be subverted by them. Even though perceptions may turn the same space into a heaven or a hell, pure logistics can make a place viable for learning or not. In one case:

I was running a class in a college in India in the hottest season. When the fans were turned on, all the handouts which had been carefully sorted flew all over the room. My clearest memory was running round the room with the students picking them up from the floor and dumping everything in a pile on the table. (CSB, Anna)

The teachers mention the following features, which made a space conducive to teaching and learning. The room:

- fits the student numbers (neither too big nor too small)
- does not set up a barrier, platform or distance between teacher and students
- allows for interaction between students (for example, chairs that can be moved into groups or organised for face-to-face dialogue)
- allows everyone to be visible to one another, both students and teacher
- allows a shared screen or board to be visible to everyone

- does not have an echo that escalates sound
- has natural light

Learning in campus spaces: theorising insider stories

Here we compare vignettes of Carmella and Tanya, two friends moving from a small college to a large university campus (LIC). Carmella and Tanya's stories give us two contrasting perceptions of campus spaces, and an opportunity to view spatial theories through the prism of their experience.

> I loved the big campus. I liked the big open spaces between buildings, so I got fresh air and exercise just being there, and it always lifted my spirits. I spent the day around the library and café, there was a bookshop and bank so I had everything to hand, I played squash in the sports hall, it was my bubble. The only thing was I had to calculate more time to get to classes as the distances were further. Compared to being in the small college where I was it was great, more cosmopolitan, more like living in a mini city. (Tanya)
>
> I really missed my other college. There, it felt safe, everything flowed organically, so you would go from class to a café and to the library and they were all near to one another. You knew people, you met them around the place so it was easy to make friends, you were visible and it felt like my second home. In the big campus everything took much longer, you never saw anyone twice, it was like being in a huge airport terminal, and at night I didn't know who was around and I didn't feel safe. (Carmella)

Three ways of looking at space

my bubble vs I didn't feel safe

Tanya and Carmella saw the same space yet interpreted it in opposite ways. It is interesting to analyse these differences using three notions of city spaces, formalised by Lefebvre (1991). Lefebvre's *spatial triad* has influenced thinking about built spaces up to the present day (see Brown, 2020 and Alzeer, 2018). These notions interweave what is concrete and visible, with what is felt, experienced and believed. Table 7.1 explains *perceived space, conceived space* and *lived space*, and can helpfully be applied to the case of Tanya and Carmella.

In terms of *perceived* space, for Tanya the open spaces between the buildings, and their scattering across a landscape replicated for her the experience of an optimal urban space, where she could freely move and access the facilities she needed. After the small scale of her previous college, it represented 'growing up' and independence. In contrast, for Carmella the perceived space represented a loss of home-like safety and familiarity. The open spaces, rather

Table 7.1 Three ways of looking at space (derived from Lefebvre in Brown, 2020)

Lefebvre concept	Explanation
Perceived space	What space represents for a person symbolically and personally; what it triggers in terms of memories, associations and emotions.
Conceived space	The physical properties of the built environment, and how we perceive that physical space: for example, is a staircase too high to climb? Is a quadrangle a place to mingle or to escape?
Lived space	How the space is actually used, lived in, and appropriated for our own purposes.

than beckoning opportunity and freedom, beckoned in the unknown and unsafe. Underpinning this, we might find that the two friends are on a different point in the journey towards acclimatisation, with Carmella at the point of dis-integration from what she knows and believes, and Tanya at a point of euphoria and re-integration with the new (Pederson, 1995 and Adisa, 2019).

Studies suggest that homesickness impacts students differently, depending on how early the learner is in this cycle. Götz et al. (2019) asked students on study exchange to record their feelings every few days. Their findings show that none of the predicted factors had the expected impact on homesickness: openness to experience, voluntariness, previous stays abroad, support from host university, geographical distance, co- and host national identification, language proficiency. Rather, homesickness "peak(ed) immediately after relocation", and then gradually faded away. For our purposes, this suggests that change of place, the physicality and unfamiliarity of this, had more of an impact than we might have predicted. We might predict that Carmella's symbolic association of the new campus with lack of safety and loneliness would gradually be revised as it becomes more familiar.

In terms of *conceived space*, the physical properties of the small campus were envisaged differently by Tanya and Carmella. The proximity of spaces with different functions, such as library, office and classroom, were conceived of as convenient and pleasant by Carmella. For Tanya, they were conceived of as parochial and claustrophobic. For Carmella, they enable her to be visible; whilst for Tanya, they hindered becoming invisible and reinventing herself as an adult. The direct built space represented different values for each of them. Jessop et al.'s study (2012) sought correlations between student perceptions of physical spaces and of learning events. Their study suggests that students who had traditional views of teacher-centred learning, also had more limited views of how spaces might be used, "constraining their imagination of fresh possibilities" (Jessop et al., 2012, p. 189). They suggest that spaces themselves represent instead boundaries: so, the more traditional lecture theatre and classroom spaces may "re-inscribe hierarchical, teacher-centred approaches" (Jessop et al., 2012, p. 189). Carmella, in expecting these traditional spaces, may also be projecting her expectation of traditional learning approaches, whilst her new campus is in fact rethinking spaces for learner independence.

In terms of *lived space,* Tanya is building connections with the new spaces by using them fully: jogging daily round the sports fields, sitting on the lawn between classes, shopping in the campus grocery and bookshop, preparing classwork in the library or in the café. Carmella lives in the space differently because its symbolic value for her is different, at least at the start of her stay. With a more traditional view of learning and teaching, she confines herself to the traditional learning-teaching spaces such as the library and classroom, rather than availing herself of the other spaces for socialising, studying collaboratively or developing wellbeing more generally. In other words, Carmella does not connect with these spaces as long as she does not actually live in them and use them.

Campus as home-like spaces

> *my second home vs a huge airport terminal*

What Carmella expects from her first, happier college experience are 'home-like' qualities, and instead she finds the equivalent of an airport lounge: echoing and cavernous, with everyone on the move. Her sense of discomfort compares to many other students leaving home for the first time to study. Janning and Volk (2017) surveyed 256 students at a US residential college and noticed that their view of 'home-like spaces' changed as they moved from pre-college to college and to imagined future homes. The study categorised their perceptions of home into four: physical, social, personal and temporal. What was perceived as 'home-like' in each of these categories changed through the different stages in their life.

Alzeer's (2018) study of Emirati women learners highlights the cultural specificity of these home-like qualities. She describes the way in which Emirati women 'appropriated' campus spaces, by finding places that were safe to 'sit on the floor', a social practice which consolidated friendships and marked 'togetherness'. For Alzeer, the study shows the value of campus spaces that combine the contemporary with the traditional and culture specific. Home-like spaces represent safety, welcome and identity. Nasir and Al-Amin (2006) for example, suggest that "the practice of Islam in the college setting is at once intensely personal and painfully public" (Nasir and Al-Amin, 2006, 22), and a prayer room is critical to their feeling of being "identity-safe".

Space, then, is a zone of potential comfort or discomfort, and it has high stakes at times of danger. Mazmanyan and Lupo (2020) describe how students refused to leave Lied Library during the horrific gun assault three miles away at Las Vegas Nevada in 2017. Nine students who sheltered in the library were asked: *What measurable features of a shared space make it feel safe, and what can be done to increase that sense of safety?* (Mazmanyan and Lupo, 2020, p. 110). They reported "feeling safe in areas they were most familiar with, in areas where campus police were known to patrol, and in areas with fewer entrances and more ways to lock themselves into the space" (Mazmanyan and Lupo, 2020, p. 112). The safe places were those that offered both refuge and escape, as well as being visible to others who might help and bear witness. We can see that Carmella's sense of discomfort might be explicable with reference to these specific features: she has not yet found a place of refuge which has the features of familiarity, nor does the presence of others yet give her a sense of safety. We have some evidence that students gravitate to the most familiar and 'lived in' spaces where they have limited time on campus. Bauer (2020) tracked the movement of commuter students and found their tendency to return to the same safe spaces, with the library as a preference.

So, Tanya and Carmella are both projecting onto the spaces around them their own values regarding identity, safety and wellbeing.

Holistic spaces and campus learning

> *big open spaces and everything flowed organically*

In our two stories, Tanya specifically refers to the "*big open spaces*" of the campus, and "*lives*" in them as part of her daily activities. She enjoys the holistic quality of the campus, where buildings flow naturally in and out of open spaces. Scholl and Gulwadi (2015) envisage the holistic campus as "networked landscapes that foster learning" with a flow between buildings, roads and natural landscape. Their proposal is that this natural landscape is a "learning resource for its students" and has the potential actively to replenish "cognitive functioning" (Scholl and Gulwadi, 2015, p. 53). We saw in the section above that where these places were not to be found, and 'flow' between spaces was not present, students felt their wellbeing as well as their learning to be compromised. In the virtuous circle, the presence of safe spaces with a 'flow' between them gave students a sense of contentment and wellbeing, leading in turn to successful learning. It is interesting to seek out campus spaces where this virtuous flow is demonstrated, both in the buildings themselves, and in student response to them. Wood, Warwick and Cox (2012) gathered staff and student responses to three innovative new buildings at the University of Leicester and arrived at the DEEP framework, which categorises the qualities of the holistic campus. We explain the DEEP framework with reference to Tanya's experience at her holistically planned campus in Table 7.2.

Krajewski and Khoury (2021) tell the story of an Australian university, which experimented with a "soft room" without any hard furniture or technical equipment. Their changes are 'dynamic' and 'participatory' in the ways suggested by the DEEP model: the room is changed to encourage students to unlearn their expectations about teaching spaces and relationships, and to take greater learning risks as a result.

134 Learning spaces

Table 7.2 The DEEP concept of spaces

Quality Wood, Warwick and Cox (2012)	Description	Tanya and holistic space
Dynamic	The space adapts to changing seasons, needs, pedagogies.	One large hall space is at different times in the year: a dance studio; an exhibition hall; a theatre; a pop-up bookshop; a cabaret; a graduation dinner venue.
Engaging	Spaces encourage activity and involvement and opportunity to take responsibility.	There is gallery space which encourages Tanya to set up a photography exhibition related to her area of study.
Ecological	Sustainable and environmentally friendly open spaces.	Tanya helps in the planting of trees in a new arboretum designed to renew the environment for indigenous wildlife.
Participatory	The potential for participants to develop and change the space.	One open space at the front of the college theatre is adapted for a Tai Chi class once a week.

Carmella and Tanya's stories bring together new ways of envisaging the campus. Making the journey from one physical space to another is not only a matter of change in architecture. We have seen the multiple changes which are in fact taking place; in how safety is perceived and experienced, where well-being and identity are best expressed, what pedagogies are suggested, and what kinds of interactions are encouraged. Campus maps are very much the surface of a dense deep structure of feeling and being. It might help Carmella, in our vignettes in this section, simply to know that her sense of displacement is not surprising, given the great deal of learning and adaptation needed as we shift from one physical setting to another.

Learning and teaching in virtual spaces: stories from 2020 to 2021

In this section we share responses to the exceptional circumstances of 2020 to 2021, the study year when learning for the whole world moved from classroom to online spaces. The voices we shall hear come from open forum online discussions as part of the *Reflection in the Round* project, with participants not identified individually but by cohort (2020); higher education educators responding to the invitation from Oxford Brookes University School of Education to share experiences in *Theorising the Virtual* through the pandemic;

and pre-symposium online focus groups meeting weekly between January and May 2021. The symposium invitation elicited responses from teachers in a rich array of subject disciplines including nursing, food science, art, children's literature, theology and modern languages, and from Hawaii, Canada and the UK. Since the presentations are shortly to be, or are already, in the public domain, the data is included in the reference list at the end of this chapter. Through these, we have a dynamic snapshot of how learners and teachers responded to the transition from concrete learning spaces to virtual spaces with unplanned backdrops such as kitchens, bedrooms, cats and dogs, background noise of rumbling trains or traffic. We have yet to fully understand the implications of this, as the world has taken a leap forward in its online learning experience. These 2021 accounts are thus just a starting point in what is likely to be an 'educational revolution' in our relationship with virtual learning spaces.

Learning and teaching stories of virtual spaces

On the one hand, the new online environment has been an equaliser: its newness means everyone is equally learning new technological skills, both teachers and students, both first culture and second culture. It also minimises the difference between students who have travelled to their classrooms, across streets, cities, country borders and oceans. Many students returned home and continued studies from sitting rooms, kitchens, bedrooms, spaces shared with homeschooling children, partners, family pets. Some students who had felt overwhelmed by the space, noise and hecticness of campus life, felt in some ways safer and more connected in the online setting.

> I liked everyone was there with their names. I learnt some names for the first time. I felt safer because I went home and studied from my parents' house, so that feeling of confused wasn't so much. (RIR)

On the other hand, the online learning world has been a great divider, splitting participants between those able to access the technologies economically, socially, intellectually, and those not able to. Although backgrounds in 'zoom rooms' can be manipulated, participants may be embarrassed about the personal space around them, fail to have that personal space, are subject to the interruptions and disruptions of home life. The experience starkly separates those who have good learning conditions, and those who do not.

> Challenges included competing for a device with the students, low bandwidth internet connection and the six-hour time lapse. Every evening, I looked forward to reading the replies from my tutors and they did not disappoint me. I felt I wasn't 'out of sight out of mind' and I realise now how it kept me motivated to stay on the course and to meet assignment deadlines. (CSB, Bridget)

Several of the students returned home and conducted learning from a bedroom.

> I'm in my bedroom, working on my bed, it's the only space, I haven't put on make-up, I'm not dressed like I was going out or I would going to college. No way am I going to turn on the camera. (RIR)

Childs et al. (2021) describes a survey of 250 university teachers at Durham University (UK), reflecting on their transition from campus to virtual teaching during the global pandemic. The survey suggests a spectrum of responses that fall between two extremes. On the one hand were those who felt the new online learning worlds heralded an educational revolution, with the chance of new technologies leading to fresh ways of achieving goals. On the other hand, were those who begged *"never again"*. Childs' survey bears out the importance of ideology in the educator's response to online learning. Where there was strong opposition to online learning, it was often accompanied by the view that online interactions are less valid than in-person ones, and community cannot be built in this way. In contrast, those who found the new online space to have potential and value, also believed that rapport could be established this way, learning could be achieved and the new technologies could create new ways of building community.

Gosia Sky (2021) describes her own transition as an educator, adapting a module in sociolinguistics to the new virtual medium. She describes the impact of these rapid and urgent changes on teacher workload, digital know-how, session planning and preparation. How ready the educator might be to adopt these changes depends on the several factors suggested by Mark Childs: believing learning can be done effectively and communities can be built successfully online. It is important to believe this, in order to imagine learning transferring successfully from physical into virtual space.

Nick Swarbrick with Mat Tobin (2021) use Google Earth to take the viewer/learner into the physical locations in children's literature. Rachel Payne (2021) describes a project in which artist teachers are walked virtually around the site of an iron age settlement. Wendy Johnston (2021) at John Moores University describes translating work placements for her food science students into virtual placements.

> The changes from physical to virtual placements has tailored in real life opportunities and highlighted real world applications of knowledge and skills, has improved digital literacy, has harnessed student motivation and ensured students have applied what they are learning to real world contexts. (Johnston, 2021)

However, it is not only the educator making the leap into a new space. Marion Waite (2021) describes the "inner work" students must do in making the required pedagogical transitions. She describes the impact of pre-prepared online videos on a cohort of student nurses, and the importance of "psychological balance". This balance is what comes about when the listener is able to pause and reflect, rather than feeling dominated by the resources – for example, an overlong video over which they feel little control.

> Our findings imply that it is not possible to generalise the experiences of involuntarily online learning but there is a need to understand how cultural resources, such as videos might assist students to develop their understanding of the target concepts and how to learn online. In doing so, such resources might be useful for students to overcome contradictions caused by their transfer to online learning and development as learners. (Waite, 2021)

The accounts here suggest that the shift into learning online has potential to be innovatory where this potential is embraced and internally accepted by both teacher and learner. However, it does not come without some costs, and the change from physical to virtual classrooms entailed the following changes in expectation and behaviour:

1. The expectation that *students would be visible*: teachers came to recognise that students had reasons for not wishing to be visible during a session, and they needed to respect this, even when it ran counter to their own preferences.
2. The capacity to monitor overall progress of small group discussions: breakout room technology meant teachers could only join one breakout group at a time, so a visual overview of small group activity was not possible.
3. The expectation that students would respond to *verbal elicitations*: the technology meant speaker role needed to be allocated more formally, and thus student participation and questions, especially in larger groups, were best moved into an online chat tool.
4. The expectation of how much *content* should be prepared and presented in advance of the session: attention span and absorption of information seemed to have more limits in online than in face-to-face meetings. As a result, more material was prepared in advance, including mini lecture clips, tasks and readings.

In parallel, students also reported changes in expectations and behaviour:

1. Between session contact with teacher: "*that the teacher would keep in touch with us between sessions with online chat or some one-to-one meetings, to make sure we were OK*" (RIR).
2. Between session contact with class: "*that the class would find ways of keeping in touch like in WhatsApp groups*" (RIR).
3. Advance preparation of content: "*that things like the lectures and readings we did in our own time so the sessions would be a chance to meet and talk*" (RIR).

138 Learning spaces

These are starting points in a rapidly changing relationship between physical and virtual learning worlds. However, what they do suggest is that we might ask, not only what can technologies do for learning and teaching, but also how must we change what we expect, how we behave and what we believe to be possible as we adopt these new 21st century learning spaces. Can we bring into the online classroom the best of the built world: a place with the potential to be home-like and holistic, dynamic and participatory, lived in symbolically, emotionally and personally?

Learning maps: how do I experience campus and virtual spaces?

In this section we apply the ways of analysing space to your own setting, either learning or teaching. We are also inviting you to consider the difference between the actual spaces you use, and the ideal spaces you are seeking.

Campus places: learning within walls

Use Table 7.3 to explore the following questions:

- Where is your *preferred* place for each of these activities?
- Where are the places you *actually* use where you now teach/study?
- What is the difference between these two?

Table 7.3 Campus places

	Library	Classroom	Cafeteria	Student Union	Somewhere else?
Discuss work with your peers					
Read for your subject					
Prepare papers/ assignments					
Talk to friends					
Talk to your tutor					
Preferred place to eat and drink					
Time in between lectures/classes					
Feel most relaxed/calm					
Feel most creative/ energetic					
Feel safest					

Table 7.4 Optimal learning conditions

A place to:	Open air/ spaces	Buzz of people	Silence	Public space café, bar	Private space table	Food and drink	Table/chair	Soft furniture
Relax								
Meet friends								
Study with friends								
Prepare a class								
Write an assignment								
Discuss personal issues								
Discuss study/ work issues								

140 Learning spaces

Take your analysis deeper by answering these questions, using Table 7.4.

- What conditions do you like for each of these activities?
- It will be interesting to compare your own optimal conditions with others that you know or think you know. Ask a friend, peer or colleague to respond to these questions, and compare your responses.
- Where do you find each of these conditions in your current teaching/learning situation?

Virtual learning: learning without walls

Virtual learning has its own optimal conditions, which also vary for learners. Explore by considering the following questions and recording your responses in Table 7.5.

- While learning online, which of the study conditions were you able to find?
- Which were you not able to find and how did you deal with this?

Making the transition from campus to virtual spaces: what changes do you make?

Think about Table 7.6 from your own perspective as a student or as a teacher.

- In making these observations about your own use of space and your feelings about space, is there anything you need to change in order to create the best conditions for your learning or teaching?
- Which of these changes are viable?
- Which of these changes are not viable? Can the space be made more acceptable, or exchanged for a preferable alternative?

Further topics for reflection and reading

Another space for learning and teaching is neither on campus, nor virtual, but outside either of these in field trips, work placements, study abroad or the community.

Below are case studies of learning in these different settings and spaces.

- What is different about learning in the workplace or community, as compared to inside an explicit educational setting?
- How can better connections be made between what is learnt inside higher education and what is learnt outside in other settings?

Table 7.5 Optimal conditions in virtual learning

My 'real' place for virtual learning	Natural light	Buzz of people	Silence	Public space café, library	Home space family, flatmate	Food and drink	Table/chair	Sofa/bed/ cushion
Ideal								
Actual								

Table 7.6 Making the transition from campus to virtual spaces

As a student	Campus space	Virtual space	As a teacher
View a video lecture in advance			Make a recorded mini-lecture available in advance
Read the literature and do tasks in advance			Make readings and tasks available in advance
Work in small groups			Divide class into small groups for discussion and problem-solving
Present and lead discussion			Set up opportunities for students to present and be the teacher
Ask questions about tasks and assignments			Provide opportunities for questions and discussions
Exchange ideas and thinking after class			Encourage after-class discussion opportunities
Dress and prepare to be seen by others			Expect students to be visible/to attend

Gerloff, A. and Reinhard, K. (2019) 'University offering work-integrated learning dual study programs', *International Journal of Work-Integrated Learning*, 20 (2), pp. 161–169.

Hardwick, L. (2013) 'The place of community-based learning in Higher Education: a case study of Interchange', *Journal of Further and Higher Education*, 37 (3), pp. 349–366.

Smith-Tolken, A. and Bitzer, E. (2017) 'Reciprocal and scholarly service learning: emergent theoretical understandings of the university–community interface in South Africa', *Innovations in Education and Teaching International*, 54 (1), pp. 20–32.

References

Adisa, T., Ajibade, M.B., Gbadamosi, G. and Mordi, C. (2019) 'Understanding the trajectory of the academic progress of international students in the UK', *Education and Training*, 61 (9), pp. 1100–1122.

Alzeer, G. (2018) 'A perspective on women's spatial experiences in higher education: between modernity and tradition', *British Journal of Sociology of Education*, 39 (8), pp. 1175–1194.

Bauer, M. (2020) 'Commuter students and the academic library: a mixed-method study of space', *Journal of Library Administration*, 60 (2), pp. 146–154.

Brown, W. (2020) 'A new way to understand the city: Henri Lefebvre's spatial triad' [online]. *This City*. Available at: https://this-city.medium.com/a-new-way-to-understand-the-city-henri-lefebvres-spatial-triad-d8f800a9ec1d (Accessed: 6 May 2020).

Childs, M., O'Brien, R. and Nolan-Grant, C. (2021) *'Practical theorising and the new teaching experience: understanding the different responses to online teaching'*, Theorising the virtual online research conference. Oxford, UK, 26 May.

Gerloff, A. and Reinhard, K. (2019) 'University offering work-integrated learning dual study programs', *International Journal of Work-Integrated Learning*, 20 (2) pp. 161–169.

Götz, F.M., Stieger, S., and Reips, U.D. (2019) 'The emergence and volatility of homesickness in exchange students abroad: a smartphone-based longitudinal study', *Environment & Behavior*, 51 (6), pp. 689–716.

Hardwick, L. (2013) 'The place of community-based learning in higher education: a case study of interchange', *Journal of Further and Higher Education*, 37 (3), pp. 349–366.

Janning, M. and Volk, M. (2017) 'Where the heart is: home space transitions for residential college students', *Children's Geographies*, 15 (4), pp. 478–490.

Jessop, T., Gubby, L. and Smith, A. (2012) 'Space frontiers for new pedagogies: a tale of constraints and possibilities', *Studies in Higher Education*, 37 (2) pp. 189–202.

Johnston, W. (2021) *'From physical to virtual: the emergence of an authentic work-related learning experience'*. Theorising the virtual online research conference. Oxford, UK, 26 May.

Krajewski, S. and Khoury, M. (2021) 'Daring spaces: creating multi-sensory learning environments', *Learning and Teaching*, 14 (1), pp. 89–113.

Lefebvre, H. (1991) *The Production of Space*. Oxford: Blackwell.

Mazmanyan, K.L. (2020) 'Student perceptions of the library during times of terror: exploratory research surveying students affected by the October 1 shooting and their impressions of safety in the academic library community', *College and Research Libraries*, 81 (1) pp. 109–121.

Nasir, N.S. and Al-Amin, J. (2006) 'Creating identity-safe spaces on college campuses for Muslim students', *Change*, 38 (2), pp. 22–27.

Payne, R. (2021) *'Settlement'*, Theorising the virtual online research conference. Oxford, UK, 26 May.

Pedersen, P. (1995) *The five stages of culture shock: critical incidents around the world*. Westport, CT: Greenwood. Randel.

Scholl, K.G. and Gulwadi, G.B. (2015) 'Recognizing campus landscapes as learning spaces',*Journal of Learning Spaces*, 4 (1), pp. 53–60.

Sky, G. (2021) *'Teaching an undergraduate sociolinguistics module during the Covid pandemic'*, Theorising the virtual online research conference. Oxford, UK, 26 May.

Smith-Tolken, A. and Bitzer, E. (2017) 'Reciprocal and scholarly service learning: emergent theoretical understandings of the university–community interface in South Africa', *Innovations in Education and Teaching International*, 54 (1), pp. 20–32.

Swarbrick, S. (2021) *'Going beyond the immediate page'*, Theorising the virtual online research conference. Oxford, UK, 26 May.

Waite, M. (2021) *'Learning through a crisis: the experiences of involuntary online learning for undergraduate nursing students'*, Theorising the virtual online research conference. Oxford, UK, 26 May.

Wood, P., Warwick, P. and Cox, D. (2012) 'Developing learning spaces in higher education: an evaluation of experimental spaces at the University of Leicester', *Learning and Teaching: The International Journal of Higher Education in the Social Sciences*, 5 (2) pp. 49–72.

8 Kinds of assessment
What do learning and assessment activities mean?

Assessment is the main event where students become accountable to their learning. This is the most critical meeting place between what has been taught and what has been learnt, and the place where mismatches between these two will be most clearly exposed. Given the importance of this end-goal in the learning process, transparency of expectations is vital; yet it is here where misunderstanding, disappointment and even despair are most played out. This chapter will look at three kinds of ambiguity: whether assessed competences are explicit or hidden; whether the purpose of an assessed task is to comply with received knowledge or to demonstrate the creative, original or personal; and whether tasks are designed for learning, or to measure learning. There are many opportunities here for misunderstanding, and in addition assessment tasks take many forms and the labels used to define them are varied. The stories in this chapter explore the gap between what higher education teachers expect from learning activities and how learners interpret or misinterpret those expectations when the assessment culture is new and unfamiliar.

Learning about assessment from insider stories

As throughout this book, the stories in this chapter derive from learning diaries, field notes, interviews and focus groups between 2011 and 2021, and across four separate projects. These are:

- *Reflection in the Round* (RIR) with 38 student learning diaries and 10 annual focus groups of students on one-year postgraduate progammes between 2011 and 2020. In addition, teacher field notes track learning activities and learner responses during the same period. The project is published as Spiro (2013) and crystallised into teaching materials as Williams, Wooliams and Spiro (2020).
- *Fostering Interculturality* (FIC) with 16 participants, both staff and students, who identified as international, discussing their experience of crossing cultures in semi-structured interviews and focus groups. This project is published as Clifford et al., (2011) and Spiro et al., (2012).

DOI: 10.4324/9780429426261-8

Kinds of assessment 145

- *Learning Interconnectedness* (LIC) with 50 international first degree students between 2010 and 2014 sharing weekly journals about their experiences of learning across cultures and languages. In addition, teacher field notes track cross-cultural learning activities and learner responses in the same period 2010–2014 (Spiro, 2014).
- *Crossing Study Borders* (CSB) with 24 staff and students who identified as having crossed borders in learning and teaching, interviewed between 2020 and 2021 and published here for the first time.

Assessment opposites 1: explicit and hidden literacies

The accounts reveal that students experience so many varieties of learning activity and assessment, it is hard for them to recognise coherence or consistency in what they are expected to do. Annabel describes her US first degree assessment tasks as "*lots of shorter assignments: 5 reading responses, a quiz, a class presentation, a group project – there were many more moving pieces, more things graded*" (CSB, Annabel). Assessment tasks broken into many parts and dispersed through the programme seemed to offer different kinds of learners the chance to succeed:

> In the US there are many different ways of gauging your learning as you go along – it gave people a chance to do well. That system did work better for some people, it was possible to process things one at a time. (CSB, Annabel)

The outcome of these tasks was unambiguous, and success could be achieved by focus on content knowledge explicitly covered in the taught sessions.

In contrast, moving to a higher degree in Europe, there were fewer but longer tasks, and the predominant ones were discursive papers of 3000 words:

> much longer than anything I had done before, and the bulk of the feedback was all for that one assignment. It allowed me to focus in more depth. I prefer fewer, to go more in depth studying – also it fosters honesty between students and professors. Instead of pretending to be an expert in everything I am going to focus on one topic, it helps to shape my learning a lot more than if I had to write on everything. (CSB, Annabel)

She compares the two kinds of assessment, the first requiring breadth, the other depth:

> In (my first degree) some assignments I write a reading response, turn in your notes, I was always able to express my point of view but it didn't have the depth and it all added up to less than half the final grade. Here with fewer assignments it changed the way I thought about my learning,

building towards breadth and topics we found interesting. One or two projects/assignments that carry a lot of weight – helps me to focus on channelling my learning. (CSB, Annabel)

The challenge of the longer written pieces, however, seemed to be that 'hidden skills' were required for success, which went over and beyond the subject content itself. Annabel's lecturers/educators attended to the disciplinary content, but the writing itself was not explicitly taught. Jake, too, at an elite UK university, experienced the same sense of a missing or hidden agenda:

Cambridge had assumed we could all write readable prose. Nothing linguistic had been specifically taught or named. I had no idea what a 'dangling modifier' or a 'topic sentence' might be. Cambridge (unlike Oxford and the US) had decided that language was not a legitimate part of an English degree, the study of which might have introduced us to some of the specificities of language analysis and how to construct our writing. (CSB, Jake)

For Bridget, this was an issue she noted making the transition from first degree to higher degree. Somewhere in this journey, there was an assumption that she had acquired these hidden skills.

Though the tasks were clarified, the how to write them, the academic style was not even mentioned and I realised only later that there seemed to be an assumption that the cohort of mature students knew or understood or were able to write academically – language style, mechanics, critical and being concise. (CSB, Bridget)

The sense of disconnection between content, and writing about content, continued as she moved into her next institution. The split agenda was taught by different teachers and in different parts of the university.

This appears to be the case in my current place of work where subject content is taught by the professionals, but the critical writing of academic essays is left it to the Learning Development Unit. Moreover, it is for the students to approach and arrange learning sessions with the LDU themselves. These students are fortunate in a way as I had to self-teach through discovery learning especially the referencing style. I had a photocopied guide which I religiously followed to get my references accurate. (CSB, Bridget)

The writing conventions of the subject discipline were described in Chapter 4 as 'tacit knowledge'. Annabel, Jake and Bridget describe their encounter with this tacit knowledge, as they sense something is expected in their written assignments, which has not been fully revealed. Though ways of explaining knowledge in writing is deeply embedded into disciplinary norms, still their subject teachers did not regard it as part of what they needed to teach.

However, prescriptive and confining writing rules are equally problematic. Winnie, for example, found herself moving from Canada where there was an element of freedom and creativity in writing tasks, to France where the reverse was the case. She found herself confronted by precise rhetorical rules, and criticised for not abiding by them:

> in the French way: taking essay conventions in French and transforming them. There were strict rhetorical moves and only that was good writing – you must do it our way. I prefer the information to be more of a guide when I write, less direct, less prescribed, less scripted. (CSB, Winnie)

These stylistic changes are not only surface ones about adding citations or changing pronouns. They also impact on the kind of person one presents through writing. We met Gerda in earlier chapters, for whom the 'hedged' and 'polite' way of writing were a personal jolt for her as she moved from a German to a UK programme of study.

Subject disciplines can create writing islands, with intolerance of the conventions on other islands. For example, Jake shows two different approaches to footnotes on two sides of the Atlantic:

> The Americans were training to be professionals and their notion of professionalism meant that anything unprofessional was to be avoided. Footnotes acquired a new status; at Cambridge they were regarded as excrescences of dubious value. In the US they were signs of serious intent. Citations and bibliographies were essential if one was to be taken seriously. (CSB, Jake)

This difference in approach is also symptomatic of disciplinary culture. Humanities subjects such as history and philosophy, for example, use footnotes to list references and expand the main text; whilst social sciences such as education embed both citations and authorial comment within the main text. Although these different conventions suggest deeper differences in attitude to knowledge and to authorial voice, surface manifestation in citation practice is enough to cause confusion. Students crossing from one discipline to another describe not only these conflicting conventions, but also the assumption of their teachers that there is only one correct version.

> I had the footnotes in my essay marked all through with an x: these comments should go into your argument/do not use footnotes etc. I was completely confused and asked to see the tutor to say: in my other programme I have to use footnotes all through, whenever I cite someone. This tutor was completely unsympathetic He just said: well we don't do that. How come two subjects do things so differently? (RIR)

As we have suggested all through this book, expectations often reveal themselves only when they are breached. Where we are taught one way of being appropriate in speaking and writing, alternative ways can be surprising, even shocking. Expectations are often taught as rules or taboos, such as how direct one should be, whether or not one should refer to oneself, or how close to an original text one is permitted to be. Katya, for example, describes her embarrassment at realising her idea of appropriacy is completely different to the one held by her fellow students:

> In terms of a mismatch regarding study skills, when I moved from Poland to America, one of the most unexpected discoveries concerned the concept of paraphrasing. In one Composition class, the teacher asked us to read a passage from a book and summarise what it said. It was a task I had been familiar with so I did it quickly and was quite proud of the result, so despite my usual misgivings about speaking out (because I was embarrassed about my accent), I volunteered to read it aloud. The teacher was pleased with it but one student attacked me for replicating the unnatural language of the original instead of putting it in my own, more natural, words. Then they proceeded to read their own version, which sounded more natural but unsophisticated to me. I did feel like a fraud afterwards, although couldn't quite appreciate why at the time.
>
> In my home country, when working with other people's ideas, it was encouraged to convey them as closely as possible to the original, to honour the author and stay true to their message. In the US (and the UK), however, it meant risking accusations of plagiarism, which was pretty shocking to me to realise. It took a while to understand that using your own words, style and sentence structure did not mean a disregard for well-established knowledge, which I had much respect for, but a preference for original thinking and a more personal style of writing. My home education taught me to separate creative writing from academic writing; this new cultural context expected me to be creative within academic writing. (CSB, Katya)

The differences Katya describes may arise from subject discipline, but also from local preference and practice. The critical point here, however, is that these national/local/disciplinary preferences are often so deeply internalised by those who own them, they have not been made explicit. Both teacher and student may firmly believe that there is only one way that content can be expressed in language; and find to their surprise that there are other variations, and perhaps both are right within certain contexts. It is these hidden cultures which need to be teased out so that educators reveal those competences critical to success, but which are not directly made known or taught.

Assessment opposites 2: compliance and creativity

Another confusion as students move from one assessment culture to another is whether a piece of work should demonstrate content knowledge known, received and taught, staying closely to instructions and criteria; or whether it leaves room for individual interpretation of the task, and expects the personal, original or creative. One participant describes the surprise of moving from compliant assessment to creative:

> the student actually creates things instead of copying, it was more open-ended – the exams we had in the States are pretty much directive – when I saw an open-ended exam I was amazed and thought – wowo how do you answer this? (In the new place) a student is not meant to write yes or no to an answer but marshall all the information and knowledge and views and things that they have and then describe them in an essay. (FIC)

Danielle describes a move in the opposite direction, from a culture that required deep learning, into another culture that assessed duplication of knowledge:

> Spain is very transmissive – here's the info, reproduce it in an essay. (Where I first studied) it's much more interactive, required deeper understanding, you can't just reproduce what other people thought, you had to understand it. Spanish style is much more literature based, a compilation of other people's thoughts. Here we are interested in what students bring to it, whilst in Spain it's how much you know about existing knowledge. (CSB, Danielle)

She describes the impact of this assessment expectation on her group of trainee language teachers, as she set tasks which required creative thinking:

> I asked them to write an original grammar game or activity which they could use with beginners. Laura wrote a grammar activity just like the one in her textbook. She explained she was practising another grammar point so it wasn't the same exercise. I tried in all kinds of ways to show what I meant by a different kind of activity, something new, invented, original, something her learners would find fun: but she never got the point and I just got these same exercise types back. (CSB, Danielle)

The invitation to think differently is not easily accepted if this has never before been the expectation. There are issues for Laura, who has never been entrusted with the chance to experiment and try out; and who in turn doesn't quite trust that this is what is being asked of her. If she departs significantly from received expectations and knowledge, how does she know if her work will be acceptable? By what standards and expectations will she then be judged?

At times, and sometimes with even greater degree of confusion, the assessment task might suggest compliance but expect creativity, or the reverse. Katya negotiates this confusion, as she crosses between Poland, the US and the UK:

> These (and similar situations) revealed an interesting difference not only between Poland and the US, but also the US and the UK In the US, learning is much more structured, but the results of this learning (e.g. essays) are expected to be much more creative and flexible. In the American college and university I attended, I could really explore my ideas not constricted by form and even topic – it was allowed to stick quite loosely to the essay question, for example, or even produce your own take/reflection on the topic (it was quite similar in Poland as well). Conversely, in the UK the learning process is much less rigid, in the sense that attendance/participation is not compulsory and expectations placed on students are not very high, but the results/essays must adhere to strict criteria in order to receive a good grade. (CSB, Katya)

Her confusion is not only about crossing from compliant to creative assignment tasks, but that even within the institution there is a mismatch between what is suggested on the surface, and what outcomes are actually rewarded.

Even in creative disciplines such as art, music, architecture and creative writing, students expressed frustration that some aspects of the assessed tasks were inauthentic. Art students in the *Learning Interconnectedness* project (LIC) were frustrated by the pressure to articulate ideas in words. One participant commented on this problem as he presented his art installation:

> I made an ice sculpture that would slowly melt into a bucket while it was being exhibited. For me, the installation was obviously about climate change but my tutor kept saying Talk us through this. It seemed to be this art college thing, to talk it through. At school I could just make things, but at art college here I had to use words all the time. If I'd wanted to use words I wouldn't have chosen an art degree. Words aren't the way I say things. I wanted the object to do the talking. (LIC)

Almost all students described the expectation that their creative work be accompanied by a 'rationale' or analysis, explaining how their work had been conceived and informed by current practice. This included the many forms of creative task listed below:

- art installation
- art objects/exhibition
- materials writing
- creative writing: poems, story, memoir
- architectural and engineering design
- musical performance or composition

A creative writing tutor explained her position on this:

> Yes it is about doing whatever you want to do, but you have to know why you're doing it. It's hard to sort out, but really the best creative writers in

the group yes they did work intuitively but they also knew what they were doing and why and could explain it. (RIR)

The invitation to be original and creative is inspiring as a learning activity but takes on a different form as an assessment activity. For the teacher in RIR, the creative writer needed to reveal mindfulness about the craft of writing, and how this had been subverted, adapted, personalised, transformed by the writer; yet this requires a form of articulation which is not necessarily the student's chosen way of 'talking', as we have seen for the LIC participant. There are other problems too, suggested by students who made a transition from literature-based assessment tasks to creative tasks.

- *If I really do my own thing creatively, how can I be assessed?*
- *When I see our work side by side, I simply don't understand why some of us got good marks and others didn't – and that's even when it's me that got the good mark!*

The answer to these questions lies in the clarity of the assessor. The teacher in RIR explained that the best students "*did work intuitively but they also knew what they were doing and why and could explain it*". That certainly explains ways in which a rationale or reflective analysis might be assessed: but not the creative work itself. Is the success of a creative work the way it is received by its viewers, or the way it was conceived by its creator? Is it a matter of taste or a matter of reasoned measurement? Is technical skill sufficient without vision, or conversely is vision realisable without technical skill? What is the optimal meeting point between these two and who is equipped to see this; the artist, the informed practitioner-expert, or the lay observer? These questions have been debated over centuries, and, as with all our questions in this section, there are no easy answers, except to suggest that the questions need to be asked continually and the answers never assumed.

Assessment opposites 3: learning vs measurement of learning

Another area of potential confusion described in our learner and teacher stories concerns the purpose of learning activities: whether they are designed to be part of learning process and development, or whether they are designed to measure what has been learnt and place a student's skills or knowledge against a set standard.

Andrea describes the process at her elite UK university, of weekly essays that mimic the kind of essays to be written in an end-of-term exam. This system makes a clear distinction between activities designed for learning and development, and those designed to yield a final grade. The formative, or learning activities, led to tutorial discussions and tutor feedback but no formal grade; whilst the exam leads to a formal grade but no discussion or feedback.

> The exam system has to be properly scaffolded. The students in Munich and Oxford get more formative feedback even though their assessment is not cumulative – essays don't fall into final degree classification They write three essays in three hours in the exam, they basically get 6 lots of formative feedback for this paper and 8 lots for the other papers on the same kind of essay as in the exam; then in addition there are collections which are practice exams which are handwritten exams which are the kind they will have to do. (CSB, Andrea)

This supported progress towards the exam is unusual, however. Gerda describes her own experience of exams in Germany:

> at the end of the semester there was a very big official exam, you are set a proper paper and that you had to pass. There was no formative – not when I was studying, that may be different depending on the degree.
>
> I didn't mind there was no formative assessment and you didn't know until the end when you took the exam. I was a bit carefree, much more carefree, it was something I wanted to do, not 100% but the other option wasn't available, you study, you take your exam and hope you pass. The first six weeks you do nothing, go to the lectures, then you start to panic and work for the exam. I thought I am just so glad I am not going to school anymore, I have much more freedom, I didn't think twice about it. (CSB, Gerda)

Gerda had no experience of formative feedback or tutor scaffolding towards the exam; nor did she expect this. In other words, assessment was not the place where any learning took place, only measurement of learning. She was surprised to move to another system in her UK institution, where tutors gave copious feedback to learning tasks and expected her to pay more attention to this than to the actual assignment grade. In addition, these learning tasks were not leading *towards* a formal assessment, but actually *were* the formal assessment. This meant rethinking tasks as not only final displays, but rather part of a cycle of development.

> Lots of the people in the class got their work back and just looked at the grade and just said, OK I passed. At first, I thought that and then I learnt it was important to look at what the tutor said because that way you learnt and got a better grade next time and all of it added up to your result. (CSB, Gerda)

Many of the stories report this conflict between notions of assessment, from both the student and tutor perspective.

> I would spend so long explaining what could be done to improve, justifying the mark I had given and explaining how to improve: it was very

disheartening to realise most of the students only looked at the grade. I saw the assignment as something that would help them to learn but they saw it as just something they wanted to pass. (RIR)

Carmel's class of women students in Saudi Arabia also regarded assessment tasks as a time to vie for grades rather than to learn. Carmel designed an assessment activity in which students presented to one another on a topic covered during the term.

> One part of their course they had to do a presentation – they would bribe you, bring you a gift on the day of their presentation, wear a nice abaya, beads, the room was full of perfume, gifts, dress up really smartly with lots of makeup and jewellery, would want marks on the day and they wanted full marks. Saudis love to get full marks – anything less in useless. (CSB, Carmel)

The difficulty for Carmel in crossing this study border, is that because the activity is assessed, it has changed its authenticity; it is no longer an activity which inspires sincere best effort and learning, but rather desire for best grade by whatever means.

Labelling a learning activity as an assessment, can fundamentally change learners' approach to the task. Anna (CSB) for example, describes:

> setting up a series of thinking points in an online forum. I intended these to be a chance for the group to pick up on points of interest from the session and begin choosing a topic they wanted to develop in their assignment. But because I used the phrase 'planning for the assignment' there was a kind of group panic that I was going to assess their online contributions. The following year I dropped that phrase and said: a chance to develop your ideas informally. It completely changed their attitude to the discussion and made it much safer. (CSB, Anna)

Thus, terminology is critical and does not always translate across settings. Jake (CSB) describes moving from the UK to the US: in his first degree, *"essays that had been the mainstay of my school and university life were non-existent. Nobody used the word and nobody knew what it meant"*, whereas in reverse, *"I had little notion of what an 'assignment' might be. I thought it was some kind of meeting"* (CSB, Jake). Jake describes the essay in contrast to the assignment, as he gradually discovered the differences:

> It was different, because there was a wider range of assignments than there were 'essays'. An assignment might be a number of different projects, such as: a quiz, a translation, a research presentation. The essay was an invitation to exhibit your general literary awareness/knowledge, encouraged an ostentatious display of historical/literary knowledge

154 Kinds of assessment

whereas the assignment was more directed, more elementary, about demonstrating what you knew or what you could find out, more focused and more detailed. (CSB, Jake)

It is not always clear from label alone, whether a learning activity is a final graded piece of work, or work that is intended to be formative and progressive. For example, *term paper, test, assignment, submission,* suggest final graded pieces; whilst *formative assignment, set tasks, class exercises, online forum* suggest activities as part of a learning process. Yet this distinction is far from being clear cut. In a study culture where learning process is tracked and assessed, the latter list may all constitute the 'moving parts' of assessed activities. We have seen that some tasks are designed for learning, such as the practical projects Danielle set for her trainee teachers. Other tasks are designed to elicit final grades, such as the exams described by Gerda and Andrea.

The questions that might most help to understand the purpose of learning activities are these: Will the activity lead to feedback that might help *my development as a learner*? Or does it lead to a final grade that measures my learning, and which represents *the results of my learning*? To confuse one for the other can lead to missed opportunities. To misread formative activities might mean missing the chance to learn from feedback, focusing instead on the final grade; while to misread a final grade task might mean not giving it the effort needed to showcase best abilities and to represent where one has arrived as a learner.

Learning activities through the literature lens

The vignette below is a composite of situations showing what happens when the aim and purpose of assessment tasks fail to convey themselves to the student. The confusion that results can make a difference between successful study and dropping out altogether.

> Faisal came from a transmission style of learning at a traditional college in Saudi Arabia. He was an assiduous student, reading everything the teacher suggested and memorising his lecture notes. His grades were always excellent. When he came to study in a Canadian university his first task was to write a reflective diary about his reading now and in the past. He wrote a list of books he had read at school and copied the short summaries from the back of the books. He was told this piece of work had failed because he had not used his own words and had not explained his personal responses to the books. The second task was a literature review on a chosen topic. This time he brought his own personal responses and feelings into the piece. But again, he did badly, being told that in a literature review it was not appropriate to refer to himself, and he should instead focus on the opinions and

Kinds of assessment 155

information he found in his reading. For the third task, he had to write a research proposal. This time he explained carefully what he found in his reading, focusing only on what he had read. Again, he received a bad mark: he was told in a research proposal he should present his own research question, and not depend on the ideas of others. Faisal wrote in his diary:

> The feedback from one task doesn't seem to work for a second task. Every task seems to have its own different set of rules, and I am meant to guess what these are. I only find out the rules when I have broken them.

Assessment and levels of thinking

the feedback from one task doesn't seem to work for a second task

We can empathise with Faisal's confusion as he navigates his way through all these different kinds of assessment. Faisal's vignette refers to a reflective diary, literature review and research proposal, whilst the participants in this chapter have mentioned translations (Jake), paraphrases and summaries (Katya), presentations (Carmel), short quizzes, reading responses and tests (Annabel), and practical activities (Danielle). How do newcomers to these assessment types navigate all these uncharted new kinds of activity, especially if their handbooks and study guides give limited advice? Surgenor (2013), in a study of multiple assessment tasks across subject disciplines, found that module handbooks didn't really distinguish clearly between types of tasks, and study guides tended to fall back on a traditional and limited number of assessment types, such as the essay. It is, then, unsurprising that students in one study (Struyven et al., 2005) questioned the fairness of these assessment varieties, and favoured straightforward tasks such as multiple choice where expectations were clear.

However, 'knowledge-based' memory tasks such as multiple choice are not a solution. Assessment needs to be aligned to the higher levels of thinking appropriate in higher education, such as those at the tip of the pyramid in Bloom's taxonomy (1956). Iowa State University developed a refinement of this taxonomy, which since its first conception has formed a useful way of classifying thinking, from more mechanical levels such as memorising, to more complex and independent levels such as creating and evaluating (CELT, 2021). As shown in Table 8.1, assignment tasks map themselves over these ways of thinking, either explicitly, directing students to the level of thinking expected; or implicitly.

Faisal's new tasks are finding varied ways to activate his skills of differentiating (for example between past and present reading habits in his reading diary), analysing and organising (for example the literature on a topic in his

Table 8.1. The Cognitive Process Dimension – categories, cognitive processes (and alternative names) (CELT, 2021)

Cognitive level	Examples of thinking/learning
Remember	<ul><li>recognising (identifying)</li><li>recalling (retrieving)</li></ul>
Understand	<ul><li>interpreting (clarifying, paraphrasing, representing, translating)</li><li>exemplifying (illustrating, instantiating)</li><li>classifying (categorising, subsuming)</li><li>summarising (abstracting, generalising)</li><li>inferring (concluding, extrapolating, interpolating, predicting)</li><li>comparing (contrasting, mapping, matching)</li><li>explaining (constructing models)</li></ul>
Apply	<ul><li>executing (carrying out)</li><li>implementing (using)</li></ul>
Analyse	<ul><li>differentiating (discriminating, distinguishing, focusing, selecting)</li><li>organising (finding, coherence, integrating, outlining, parsing, structuring)</li><li>attributing (deconstructing)</li></ul>
Evaluate	<ul><li>checking (coordinating, detecting, monitoring, testing)</li><li>critiquing (judging)</li></ul>
Create	<ul><li>generating (hypothesising)</li><li>planning (designing)</li><li>producing (construct)</li></ul>

literature review), critiquing, planning and generating new ideas (for example in his research proposal). These might be not only new kinds of tasks, but also new kinds of expectations. Studies (such as Reimann and Sadler, 2017; Bose and Rengel, 2009; Norton et al., 2019) show us that educators are continually striving to design varied and innovative forms of assessment that enable these higher levels of thinking. We know that best assessment activities are also learning activities that stretch and challenge the learner. Sambell et al. (2013); for example, bring together educator insights as they strive for excellence in aligning assessment with learning. Thus, a regress to a closed and safe quota of assessment tasks is neither likely nor desirable. Painful as this may be, Faisal may need to meet his assessors halfway, making himself open to change, as they clarify and scaffold these new expectations.

Assessment and academic text types

every task seems to have its own set of rules

One helpful way of making sense of these many assessment types is to identify clusters of tasks that share similar characteristics. The Strategies in Scottish Higher Education (ASSHE) project surveyed assessment practices across 22 Scottish higher education institutions (Hounsell et al., 1996) and arrived at a long list of assessment types. This long list has been fine-tuned by Gillett and Hammond (2009) in a study at one university across multiple disciplines. They arrived at six ways of classifying assessment types, according to the kind of activity, the medium of expression, and who is the assessor. Table 8.2 reframes these six classifications as questions we can ask about assessment activities, comparing the multiple-choice test and a research proposal as two very different kinds of learning activity.

Table 8.2 Six questions about task types: derived from assessment strategies in Scottish higher education (Hounsell et al., 1996) and from Gillett and Hammond (2009)

	Six questions about assessment activities	*Multiple-choice test*	*Research proposal*
Task type	What kind of activity is the learner engaged in?	Multiple choice, IT based	Piloting of data collection tools (interviews, survey) Literature search Creating a rationale or hypothesis
Medium	In what way is achievement expressed, over and above the written word?	One-word/phrase written answers to test items	Written paper Timeline of actions Table mapping ideas Chart showing relevant statistics
Who assesses	Who is involved in assessing achievement in addition to the assessor?	Centrally assessed	Peer assessment (piloting tools) Self-assessment Tutor assessment
Cognitive demands	What kind of intellectual processes are elicited by the assessment task?	(Bloom's taxonomy) Remembering Understanding	(Bloom's taxonomy) Applying, analysing, evaluating, creating
Time span	Is the assessment a single snapshot or developed over a period of time?	A single snapshot	The first step in a sequence of activities developed over time and leading to an extended dissertation
Work-related	How does the learning activity relate to real-world tasks and activities?	Minimal	Simulates real-world project design

158 *Kinds of assessment*

These questions help to reveal why more complex assessment tasks are necessary, despite their variation. They are nearer to real-world problems and tasks (and often actually are real-world tasks) and enable higher levels of thinking appropriate for the workplace and for higher education achievement. However, whilst this might be true, it does not precisely help Faisal to know what his final piece of work might look like. For this, he may need a different approach that offers concrete information at the level of language and organisation.

The British Academic Writing in English (BAWE) analysed 3000 assessments in three UK universities which had received 'good' grades above a 2:1 classification or merit standard (Nesi 2012; Nesi and Gardener, 2006). This project focused on the purpose of each kind of assessment and arrived at five categories, which differentiate between levels and kinds of tasks. Table 8.3 identifies these five purposes and maps them against a variety of assessment types as well as against the levels of thinking which they are likely to enable.

Nesi's (2012) five categories might explain why the expectations in each of Faisal's tasks are so different. The reflective task focused on the way reading has impacted on his own development as a student (WOO); whilst the research proposal focused on the way reading might influence the design of a research project (BRP). The connecting thread in the first is the student himself, whilst the connecting thread in the second is the research. This will change how information is organised, how the literature is referred to, and how the author reveals himself in language.

Assessment and academic discourse

> *I only find out the rules when I have broken them*

The confusion may be further compounded by rubric, which leaves room for ambiguity. Studies into higher education suggest rubric can make a significant difference to student success, and yet assessment descriptors are often unclear and ambiguous (for example Reddy and Andrade, 2010 and Sherre et al., 2020). Rubric may not, for example, clearly enough flag up the kind of thinking that is expected, the specific genre or text type being invited, or the linguistic conventions which that might imply. For example, Faisal's tasks were labelled as reflective diary and literature review, yet their actual descriptors were not distinctly different:

> Prepare a reflective diary entry in which you compare your reading at school, and reading in your current studies. What influenced and interested you at school? What influences and interests you now?

Whilst Faisal's assessors might consider the significant words in this descriptor to be *reflective diary*; for Faisal who has never met such a label, the significant words are *reading at school, reading in your current studies.* In other

Table 8.3 Five assessment purposes mapped against genres (derived from Nesi (2012), Gillett and Hammond (2009) and Bloom (1956))

Purpose (Nesi, 2012)	Genres (Gillet and Hammond, 2009; Wingate, 2012)	Cognitive levels (Bloom, 1956)
Demonstrate Knowledge and Understanding (DKU)	Literature review Book review Summaries Article critique Literary criticism	Foregrounding the literature and current knowledge Recognising patterns, gaps and significance in the literature
Develop Powers of Independent Reasoning (DPIR)	Essay Debate	Comparing Contrasting Evaluating Speculating Balancing pros and cons Developing theory and hypotheses Arriving at reasoned conclusions
Build Research Skills (BRS)	Research proposal Research rationale Research design Methodology Analysis of research findings Abstracts Dissertations and theses Research paper	Understanding current research in the field Applying understanding to the formulation of new questions Evaluating research tools and literature Analysing research findings Creating new methods and/or theory
Prepare for professional practice (DPP)	Reports Project designs and proposals Case studies Simulated work settings such as mock trials, patient diagnosis, project designs (law, nursing, engineering)	Applying knowledge and ideas to practical situations Describing and analysing situations Solving practical problems Creating new designs and solutions to problems and situations
Writing about oneself (WOO)	Reflective diaries Observation notes Auto-ethnography Personal narratives Action research projects	Interpreting one's actions, ideas and experiences Exemplifying achievements Inferring hidden meanings and connections Comparing past and present actions

words, Faisal reads this as demonstrating knowledge and understanding (DKU) whilst his assessors intended it to be writing about oneself (WOO).

The reverse error took place when we turn to Faisal's literature review. Here his assessors intended him to demonstrate knowledge and understanding of a particular field (DKU) prior to drawing up a research design. In the sample rubric below, however, there are some phrases which can be misread as a trigger to WOO (writing about oneself), especially if the most recent assignment required this. These phrases are in italics:

> Review the literature which informs *your research question*, showing the link between current relevant knowledge in the field and *your research intentions*.

At surface value, no description has explained that the intended text is to be qualitatively different from the first one. In addition, two references to *your/your*, and the word *intentions* appear to suggest writing about oneself. Faisal's confusion is that they look very much the same to those untrained in the interpretation of these different kinds of rubric.

Misunderstanding, then, can lie on the surface in the language and can hinge on a single word or phrase. Clear rubric is helpful; but also, concrete examples of what the expected text type actually looks like. There are many helpful analyses of language in academic text types: such as report writing language (Jackson et al., 2006); journal articles (Murray, 2013), submission letters (Swales, 1996) and dissertation acknowledgements (Hyland, 2004). However, even more valuable than a case-by-case analysis, is the capacity to ask the right questions about what kind of language is deemed successful, where examples can be found, and how wide is the scope for re-inventing. In Table 8.4 are four questions which are amongst those systematically asked and answered by discourse analysts in their interrogation of different text types. The column on the left lists the questions, and the column on the right indicates the kind of responses typically found in successful student assessments such as those in the BAWE data (Nesi, 2012), or in academic publications such as those analysed by Hyland (1999, 2002 and 2013).

If we apply these questions to different assessment tasks, their distinctive differences are highlighted. In a series of Tables (8.5 through 8.8), the transcript of a talk about work in progress versus a research abstract summarising the completed project are set side-by-side as Box A and Box B. Both tasks relate to the same content: how students with different first languages engage with one another in class. However, the first task is an informal talk to an audience of peers about first ideas for a project, whilst the second is a written piece designed to simulate formal submission to a research journal. At a macro level, this means they will be organised differently. The talk is organised to explain a concern or question, and to think through potential solutions. The research abstract is organised to match the formal house style of research journals; establishing the area of research and showing how the author intends to make a new research contribution. Table 8.5 shows these differences as they relate to the parts and purpose of the tasks.

It is clear from the examples in Table 8.5, that the two kinds of text also take different approaches to revealing the author. In the more informal talk,

Table 8.4 Four discourse tools for analysing texts

Questions Spiro (2021)	Examples Nesi (2012), Hyland (2013), Cheung et al. (2018)
1. How are the *different parts (moves)* indicated and what is their purpose?	Typical 'moves' might be: • Establishing the terrain: *Doctoral writers* … • Connecting with the community: *Studies show that/Literature suggests that* … • Establishing a gap: *However, few studies* … • Occupying the niche: *This study aims to* … • Explaining the process: *Data was gathered* … • Showing significance: *The study reveals* … • Evaluating: *However, although, whilst* …
2. Is there *a reflective I* and how does the author reveal or occlude her presence?	Authors may hide their presence through: • Passive forms: *the research was conducted* … • -ing forms: *Having collected the data* … • 'It' clauses: *It is important to note* …
3. How and where are *opinion/judgement/values* revealed?	• Opinion might be hedged in verb choices: *Claims that, suggests that* … • Verb forms suggest speculation rather than judgement: *it may be/might be/could be* … • Adjectives suggest evaluation: *It is important/interesting/clear/unclear* …
4. How are other authors/literature *cited and referenced*?	Literature may be cited: • At the start of the sentence: *Rogers (2020) notes* … • In parenthesis at the end: *… (Rogers 2020)*. Verbs reveal author attitude to the literature: *comments, suggests, claims, states, confirms* …

the author refers to herself in several ways. In contrast, the research abstract hides the author, although her actions and opinions are actually present implicitly throughout, both seen in Table 8.6.

The tasks, of course, will go on to apply a wide range of strategies for hiding and revealing the author, but we can also see that the author's opinion and values lie under the surface even where these are not explicitly self-referenced, as shown in Table 8.7.

Table 8.5 Discourse question 1. How are the different parts (moves) indicated and what is their purpose?

Box A: transcript	Box B: research abstract (Spiro, 2014)
Describe a situation I teach classes in which 12 or more different languages are spoken. **Identify a problem** I noticed that learners created their own separate silos with the people who seemed most familiar. **Respond to the problem** So I began asking myself, how can I help this exchange to happen?	**Establish the terrain** This study explores the view that student engagement with one another is critical in the internationalisation mission. **Establish current state of knowledge** The literature is rich in its discussion of policy, institutional meanings, and student voice. **Establish a niche** However, it offers us less insight into how internationalisation might be translated into classroom practice. **Occupy the niche** The study shares examples of four small-scale projects, which trial ways of designing interaction into classroom tasks.

Table 8.6 Discourse question 2. Is there a reflective I and how does the author reveal or occlude her presence?

Box A: transcript	Box B: research abstract (Spiro, 2014)
VISIBLE AUTHOR Start sentence with 'I' *I teach/I noticed* Ask oneself question *How can I help this exchange to happen?* Vary position of I in sentence As shown in the two examples above	HIDDEN AUTHOR Passive forms *It **is intended*** 'Empty' subject pronouns: *it offers us less insight into* Opinions without personal agency *student engagement with one another **is critical** in the internationalisation mission.* Noun phrases, not pronouns: ***This study** explores the view that ...*

Our final discourse question, in Table 8.8, asks how literature is cited in a piece of writing. The two examples in Box A and B both refer to the same background reading. However, in Box A the reference come first and is the focus of attention: in Box B, the idea comes first, expressed in the author's own words. A literature review that stays too consistently with the strategy in Box A, will leave little room for the author's own ideas and thread of connection. For Faisal to know this might make the difference between a literature review that fails for being descriptive and dependent on the words of others, to another that succeeds because he has allowed room for his own thinking to emerge.

Table 8.7 Discourse question 3. How and where are opinion/judgement/values revealed?

Box A: transcript	Box B: research abstract (Spiro, 2014)
Evaluative language: negative created their own *separate silos* with the people who seemed most familiar (adjective/noun) **Evaluative language: positive** how can I *help this exchange to happen*? (verb/adjective)	**Evaluative language: importance** student engagement with one another *is critical* in the internationalisation mission. (adjective) **Evaluative language: absence** However, it offers us *less insight* into how internationalisation might be translated into classroom practice. (comparative adjective/noun)

Table 8.8 Discourse question 4. How are other authors/literature cited and referenced?

Box A: transcript *The literature is cited first and the idea follows.* (Spiro, 2021)	Box B: research abstract *The idea is explained first in the writer's own words, and the citation follows.*
Wenger (2010) first named these co-constructed sites as communities of practice, identifying three key characteristics: a joint enterprise, mutual engagement, and shared repertoire.	Sharing work in progress with peers works well when there is a shared endeavour, mutually agreed ground rules, and equal power and incentives. Wenger identifies groups with these qualities as *communities of practice* (Wenger, 2010)

So, we see that there are patterns worth noticing, that may give students a closer match with target kinds of writing. These ways of writing are far from self-evident, and as our vignette notes, the rules are often revealed only in the breaking of them. This section has suggested ways of making tasks transparent by asking questions about levels of thinking, assessment purposes, characteristics of different assessment types, and questions about language. Most importantly, these are ways of recognising hidden goals, and unpacking expectations in thinking, acting and writing that lie under the surface of assessed activities.

Learning maps: what do learning and assessment activities mean?

Mapping assessment alongside four discourse questions

If you are a student, select one assessment task you are working for currently.

- What kind of written work are you expected to do? Can you identify a text type or genre, such as report, research paper, reflective diary, article critique, book review?

164   Kinds of assessment

- Find a successful example of this text type: either in course information, in the library, through learning support, from your peers, or ask your teacher to suggest where you can find one.
- In Table 8.9 are four discourse questions. Analyse the sample assignment using these four questions. Your answers will give you a clear indication of the kind of writing you are expected to do in order to be successful.

If you are a higher education teacher, select one assignment you are currently preparing.

- What text type are you expecting your learners to write: for example, research paper, book review, literature review, critique, reflective notes, evaluation, report.
- Where are successful examples of this text type to be found? For example, a repository of successful past student assignments, published examples of the text type you could direct your students to in the library or online, study resources?
- In Table 8.9 are four discourse questions. Analyse one of these sample texts using these four discourse questions. How can you draw on your answers to provide your students with clear guidance as to the qualities of a successful assignment?

Table 8.9 Using the four discourse questions

Questions	A successful example of your assessment type
1. Is there *a reflective I* and how does the author reveal or hide (occlude) her presence?	
2. How (and how often) are other authors/literature *cited and referenced*?	
3. How are the *different parts (moves)* indicated and what is their purpose?	
4. How and where are opinion/judgement/values revealed?	

Mapping assessment alongside polarities

As a student, review your assessment task again and plot the underlying expectations along these four polarities. If you are not sure of the answer, how could you find this out? Who would you ask, or which resources would you refer to?

As a higher education teacher, think about the assessment task you are planning. How do you conceive of it along these four polarities? Is there anything you do, or might need to do, to make sure these assessment goals are transmitted to your students clearly?

Compliance ⟵————————————⟶ Creativity
Explicit qualities ⟵————————————⟶ Hidden qualities
Assessment for learning ⟵————⟶ Assessment for measurement of learning
Single snapshot (periodic) ⟵————⟶ Developed over time (process)

Further topics for reflection and reading

Group assessment

- What is your view of group assessment? How can group assessment be constructed so it is fair for each individual? What do you think are the problems and advantages of this kind of assessment?
- After formulating your own ideas, compare them to these papers which explore the value of and problems of group assessment.

Daba, T.M., Ejersa, S.J. and Aliyi, S. (2017) 'Student perception on group work and group assignments in classroom teaching: the case of Bule Hora University second year Biology students, South Ethiopia – an action research', *Educational Research and Reviews,* 12 (17), pp. 860–866.

Ellis, R.A. (2016) 'Students' approaches to groupwork in a blended course, associations with perceptions of the online environment and academic achievement – when is learning engaged?', *Education and Information Technologies,* 21 (5), pp. 1095–1112.

Moore, P. and Hampton, G. (2015) '"It's a bit of a generalisation, but …": participant perspectives on intercultural group assessment in higher education', *Assessment and Evaluation in Higher Education,* 40 (3), pp. 390–406.

Exams

The fashion in assessing by exams varies. Some institutions favour it because it ensures there are no problems of plagiarism or late submission, and because it provides a kind of equality of experience.

On the other hand, some institutions have axed exams as playing to memory and surface learning, rather than continuous development, deep learning and focus on process. Exams are also tests of qualities that are not connected with subject competence, such as stamina, capacity to cope with pressure, and reading/writing speed.

- What is your position, and what is the position of the study context where you are now?
- After formulating your own ideas, review the papers below, which show different student responses to exams.

Pilcher, N., Smith, K. and Riley, J. (2013) 'International students' first encounters with exams in the UK: superficially similar but deeply different', *International Journal of Teaching and Learning in Higher Education*, 25 (1) pp. 1–13.

Tait, C. (2010) 'Chinese students' perceptions of the effects of Western University examination formats on their learning', *Higher Education Quarterly*, 64 (3), pp. 261–275.

References

Bloom, B.S. (ed.) (1956) *Taxonomy of educational objectives: the classification of educational goals.* New York: David McKay.

CELT (2021) 'Effective teaching practices: revised Bloom's taxonomy', Center for Excellence in Learning and Teaching, Iowa State University [online]. Available at: www.celt.iastate.edu/teaching/effective-teaching-practices/revised-blooms-taxonomy/ (Accessed: 12 May 2021).

Bose, J. and Rengel, Z. (2009) 'A model formative assessment strategy to promote student-centered self-regulated learning in higher education', *US-China Education Review*, 6 (12), pp. 29–35.

Cheung, K.Y.F., Flander, J., Stupple, E., Nairn, J. and Play, M. (2018) 'Academics' understandings of the authorial academic writer: a qualitative analysis of authorial identity', *Studies in Higher Education*, 43 (8), pp. 1468–1483.

Clifford, V., Adeunji, H., Haigh, M., Henderson, J., Spiro, J. and Hudson, J. (2011) *Report on Brookes student learning experience project: fostering interculturality and global perspectives at Brookes through dialogue with staff.* Oxford Centre for Staff Learning and Development: Oxford Brookes University.

Daba, T.M., Ejersa, S.J. and Aliyi, S. (2017) 'Student perception on group work and group assignments in classroom teaching: the case of Bule Hora University second year Biology students, South Ethiopia – an action research', *Educational Research and Reviews*, 12 (17), pp. 860–866.

Ellis, R.A. (2016) 'Students' approaches to groupwork in a blended course, associations with perceptions of the online environment and academic achievement – when is learning engaged?', *Education and Information Technologies*, 21 (5), pp. 1095–1112.

Gillett, A. and Hammond, A. (2009) 'Mapping the maze of assessment', *Active Learning in Higher Education*, 10 (2), pp. 120–137.

Hounsell, D., Mcculloch, M. and Scott, M., (eds.) (1996) *The ASSHE Inventory: changing assessment practices in Scottish higher education.* Sheffield: University of Edinburgh and Napier University in association with the Universities and Colleges Staff Development Agency.

Hyland, K. (1999) 'Academic attribution: citation and the construction of disciplinary knowledge', *Applied Linguistics*, 20 (3), pp. 341–367.

Hyland, K. (2002) 'Authority and invisibility: authorial identity in academic writing'. *Journal of Pragmatics*, 34 (8), pp. 1091–1112.

Hyland, K. (2004) 'Graduates' gratitude: the generic structure of dissertation acknowledgements', *English for Specific Purposes*, 23 (3), pp. 303–234.

Hyland, K. (2013) *Disciplinary discourses.* Michigan: Michigan Classics.

Jackson, L., Meyer, W and Parkinson, J. (2006) 'A study of the writing tasks and reading assigned to under-graduate science students at a South African university', *English for Specific Purposes*, 25 (3), pp. 260–281.

Moore, P. and Hampton, G. (2015) '"It's a bit of a generalisation, but ...": participant perspectives on intercultural group assessment in higher education', *Assessment and Evaluation in Higher Education*, 40 (3), pp. 390–406.

Murray, R. (2013) *Writing for academic journals.* Maidenhead: Open University Press McGraw-Hill Education.

Nesi, H. (2012) *Genres across disciplines.* Cambridge: Cambridge University Press.

Nesi, H. and Gardener, S. (2006) 'Variation in disciplinary culture: university tutors' views on assessed writing tasks', in Kiely, R., Rea-Dickens, P., Woodfield, H. and Clibbon, G. (eds.) *Language, culture and identity in applied linguistics*, London: BAAL/Equinox., pp. 99–118.

Norton, L., Floyd, S. and Norton, B. (2019) 'Lecturers' views of assessment design, marking and feedback in higher education: a case for professionalisation?', *Assessment and Evaluation in Higher Education*, 44 (8), pp. 1209–1221.

Pilcher, N., Smith, K. and Riley, J. (2013) 'International students' first encounters with exams in the UK: superficially similar but deeply different', *International Journal of Teaching and Learning in Higher Education*, 25 (1) pp. 1–13.

Reddy, M.Y. and Andrade, H. (2010), 'A review of rubric use in higher education', *Assessment & Evaluation in Higher Education*, 35 (4), pp. 435–448.

Reimann, N. and Sadler, I. (2017) 'Personal understanding of assessment and the link to assessment practice: the perspectives of higher education staff', *Assessment & Evaluation in Higher Education*, 42 (5), pp. 724–736.

Sambell, K., McDowell, L. and Montgomery, C. (2013) *Assessment for learning in higher education.* Abingdon: Routledge.

Sherre, R., Beer, C. and Lawson, C. (2020) 'The importance of clarity in written assessment instructions', *Journal of Further and Higher Education*, 44 (2), pp. 143–155.

Spiro, J. (2013) 'The reflective continuum: reflecting for change and student response to reflective tasks', *Brookes eJournal of Learning and Teaching*, 2013.

Spiro, J. (2014) 'Learning interconnectedness', *Higher Education Quarterly*, 68 (1), pp. 65–86.

Spiro, J. (2021) 'Why do I write this way? Tracking the stylistic leap from professional to academic writing' in Zyngier, S. and Watson, G. (eds.) *Pedagogical stylistics in the 21st century.* Basingstoke: Palgrave Macmillan, Chapter 14, in press.

Spiro, J., Henderson, J. and Clifford, V. (2012) 'Independent learning crossing cultures: learning cultures and shifting meanings', *Compare: A Journal of Comparative and International Education*, 42 (4), pp. 607–619.

Struyven, K., Dochy, F. and Janssens, S. (2005) 'Students' perceptions about evaluation and assessment in higher education: a review', *Assessment & Evaluation in Higher Education*, 30 (4), pp. 325–341.

Surgenor, P.W.G. (2013) 'Measuring up: comparing first year students' and tutors' expectations of assessment', *Assessment & Evaluation in Higher Education*, 38 (3) pp. 288–302.

Swales, J.M. (1996) 'Occluded genres in the academy: the case of the submission letter', in Ventola, E. and Mauranen, A. (eds.) *Academic writing: intercultural and textual issues*, Amsterdam: John Benjamins Publishers, pp. 45–58.

Tait, C. (2010) 'Chinese students' perceptions of the effects of Western University examination formats on their learning', *Higher Education Quarterly*, 64 (3), pp. 261–275.

Wenger E. (2010) 'Communities of practice and social learning systems: the career of a concept', in *Social learning systems and communities of practice*, Blackmore, C. (ed.) London: Springer, pp. 125–143.

Williams, K., Wooliams, M. and Spiro, J. (2020) (2nd edition) *Reflective writing*. Basingstoke: Palgrave Macmillan.

Wingate, U. (2012) 'Using academic literacies and genre-based models for academic writing instruction: a "literacy" journey', *Journal of English for Academic Purposes*, 11 (1), pp. 26–37.

9 Kinds of feedback
What does feedback mean?

The assessment activity is just one part of a continuous process. It establishes a 'station' on the route towards accreditation and validation – of knowledge, skills, development. There is, in some way, no more critical moment in the study process than the one where marks are received. Even the most sanguine and experienced of students will feel invested in this moment. It validates not only work that has been done and completed but points the way to next steps: what needs to be done in order to improve, or what new doors have now been opened. All the emotions are engaged with this: sense of fair play, self-esteem, aspiration, disappointment, elation, hope and despair. Yet this most emotional of moments is also the time when measurements are in place, quantitative evidence is being gathered to establish standards, and a student's whole cycle of learning is synthesised into a set of numbers.

As throughout this book, the stories in this chapter derive from learning diaries, field notes, interviews and focus groups between 2011 and 2021, and across four separate projects. These are:

- *Reflection in the Round* (RIR) with 38 student learning diaries and 10 annual focus groups of students on one-year postgraduate progammes between 2011 and 2020. In addition, teacher field notes track learning activities and learner responses during the same period. The project is published as Spiro (2013) and crystallised into teaching materials as Williams, Wooliams and Spiro (2020).
- *Fostering Interculturality* (FIC) with 16 participants, both staff and students, who identified as international, discussing their experience of crossing cultures in semi-structured interviews and focus groups. This project is published as Clifford et al. (2011) and Spiro et al. (2012).
- *Learning Interconnectedness* (LIC) with 50 international first degree students between 2010 and 2014 sharing weekly journals about their experiences of learning across cultures and languages. In addition, teacher field notes track cross-cultural learning activities and learner responses in the same period 2010–2014 (Spiro, 2014).
- *Crossing Study Borders* (CSB) with 24 staff and students who identified as having crossed borders in learning and teaching, interviewed between 2020 and 2021 and published here for the first time.

DOI: 10.4324/9780429426261-9

Learning about feedback from insider stories

Chapter 8 suggested that assessment activities could be split into two types: those that lead to developmental feedback as part of a cycle of learning, in contrast to those that lead to a final grade. Chapter 8 also suggested the confusion that may occur when tutor and student have different expectations about which kind of assessment activity is happening: for example, when teachers design activities for development, whilst their students pay attention only to the final grade. This section divides itself between these two processes: firstly, the many ways students receive and tutors give developmental feedback; and secondly, the many ways final grades are used and interpreted. As with all the chapters, these varieties of feedback and grading are seen through the prism of first encounters, as students translate their assessment experiences from one culture or context into another.

Kinds of feedback

We have noted above and in Chapter 8, that one kind of assessment is designed to measure learning whilst another is designed to scaffold development. Whilst the first, summative kind of assessment usually yields a mark or grade, there are multiple ways that formative feedback might be given and received: through class activities, in a one-to-one tutorial or discussion, as generic points for a whole class or feedback focused on the individual, as peer review or self-assessment. Any one of these is confusing if encountered for the first time, and if they conflict with what is expected.

Andrea describes a variety of different approaches to formative feedback as she moves from Munich to Oxford, and between a traditional university and a modern university. In Munich *"we had grades all the way through, you get issued a blue paper book and for every course you do you get a piece of paper which the tutor signed and that is basically your proof of study"*. The taught steps led to grades as indicators of level and attendance, rather than developmental feedback. In some cases, comments were written on exam papers, and these were read in a structured *"viewing session with all the papers and the students can look at the comments on the paper"* (CSB, Andrea).

In contrast, at the UK university Andrea moved to, the final grade was scaffolded with *essays* or *collections* at several stages on the journey, each supported with feedback.

> All the essays are discussed in the tutorials and with feedback. The collections also have feedback attached to them. The tutor meets with them and discusses the collections. (CSB, Andrea)

Here she indicates two ways feedback was shared: the first is discussion in small groups, so feedback becomes part of a dialogue, and not just between student and assessor, but between students and tutor as peers. The other is the more traditional kind with written feedback "*attached*" to the task, as a private exchange between tutor and student.

This kind of formative feedback can be received either as a learning opportunity, or as judgement, depending on what has shaped student perceptions. Gerda, in Chapter 8, describes how much she valued formative written feedback in her new institution, compared to final grade assessments:

> When I was studying with those big exams you just got an exam and that was that – you passed it and went on to the next.
>
> What I liked with the assignments I learnt from each assignment and each comment. S has marked my essay to death, I like it. my referencing was not that great. I really like it that I could look and think, that what it was, if I had done that, and then done that, I would have got a better grade. She even went through the dots in referencing. Someone else said they don't even look at the feedback because they don't like to be criticised. I thought it very helpful I like that through feedback. The next time I go back and I think the next time I have to balance it better, this approach I find, if you really want to learn that is the much better approach. (CSB, Gerda)

Gerda shows, in this account, that she is open to learning from feedback and in fact values it as a tool for her own development. This compares to some of her peers who construe feedback as 'criticism' and prefer to avoid it. We saw in Chapter 8 that some teachers express frustration when students look only at the final grade and are reluctant to see feedback as a chance to learn. This may not, however, be accountable only to the sensitivity of the learner. Winnie describes feedback in her French university as "*punitive, it's about what you have done wrong. There is no rubric, matrix, criteria*" (CSB, Winnie). What Winnie implies here is that feedback should be principled and relate to skills and knowledge which have been explicitly defined.

Feedback, as we have seen above, is not necessarily helpful unless its systems are clear and its judgements fair and transparent. Where developmental feedback is not explicitly part of the expectation, it can be missed altogether. Emanuel discovered, simply through word of mouth, that he was entitled to feedback from teaching assistants in his Canadian university.

> Once I realized this feedback process was available it was very pleasant because it enabled me to write better essays. However it did feel a bit unfair that no one had said this was possible. In general I feel that these sorts of processes should be made very clear by the University and everyone should be informed of them. This creates a more level playing-field. (CSB, Emanuel)

These learner stories do suggest that, where feedback is a known pathway towards learning, and systematically connects with transparent learning goals,

172 *Kinds of feedback*

learners are pleased to make this transition. However, to do so they need to carry with them a learning mindset, so they are open to doing things differently as a result. We also see in this section a spectrum of feedback from detailed written comments to a signature in a notebook; and from punitive private comments directed at the student to discussion in groups where feedback becomes part of dialogue.

Feedback and language

We also saw in the section above, the contrast between comments written as negative and punitive, as in Winnie's case, in contrast to comments that were detailed but constructive, as in Gerda's case. Gerda trusted her feedback as reliable and criteria-related and was therefore able to learn from it; whilst Winnie clearly did not. This section draws from participant stories in our four projects – *Learning Interconnectedness* (LIC), *Reflection in the Round* (RIR), *Fostering Interculturality* (FIC) and *Crossing Study Borders* (CSB) – to discern where the language of feedback confused or even offended, and where it induced trust and enabled learning.

The stories describe critical incidents related to specific words in feedback. Here is Anna's story of a class in Switzerland:

> I wrote in the feedback something like: This is a very good piece of work and you have understood the ideas very well. It's a shame though you didn't finish your paper and it seems to end in the middle of a sentence. I said a lot more about why the paper was good even though unfinished. However, the only thing the student saw was the word *shame*. She was absolutely devastated. She kept repeating it as I had really insulted her. I explained it meant more like *unfortunately* but she just wouldn't hear of it. I now fully appreciate I made a mistake and feel very bad about it. (CSB, Anna)

Here the learning was sharply on the part of Anna as teacher, and she describes becoming much more mindful after that about the cultural connotation of words she chose in feedback. She learnt that feedback language needs to be face-saving, and words which have false friends in other languages, or which have different weight and history in another culture, are best avoided.

However, feedback language that is too hedged and polite can also be confusing. This is Grace's story:

> The feedback seemed to me very good. It said how I had answered the question and I had made some good reading. Also I had a mark just it was pass. It said: you might consider seeking help with your language with the Academic Support Unit (ASU). (RIR, Grace)

Grace did not recognise that *you might consider* was a polite way of saying: *you must*. She thus ignored this advice. Rather than points being listed with negative structures, such as *you have not, you do not*, they were listed as recommendations using modal forms: *you may, you might, you should*. No verbs suggesting compulsion were used: such as *you must, you have to* or imperatives such as *please consult the ASU*. Words carrying negative judgement were also carefully omitted, such as: *not good, lack of, failure to, unsatisfactory*. As a result, the feedback continued to be interpreted as positive and Grace did not read them as points that she needed to attend to, until her grades changed from borderline to direct fails. Only the grade was sufficiently unequivocal to flag up that she had been misreading her feedback.

Other terms critically important for success also proved to be problematic. Across multiple subject disciplines (including nursing, education, design and technology, engineering, law, history, economics), students were asked to be more *reflective* and *critical* yet were unclear about what these terms actually meant. Their expectations were tested both by the rubric (as we saw in Chapter 8), and then by feedback, as confusion continued from first encounter into written submissions. Several feedback points directly conflicted with myths and expectations about being *reflective*.

The reflective 'I'

> *You have tended to refer to 'I' all through without varying your style*

This was confusing feedback for several students whose expectation was: "*to be reflective I have to use I all through*" (RIR). On the contrary, writing reflectively does not mean 'I' should monotonously be placed at the front of every sentence. To do so is not only repetitive stylistically, but also suggests the author is focused only on themselves. Simply changing what comes first in the sentence also changes the reader's focus of attention. Hyland (2002) suggests ways that the author changes their position in the sentence and hides or 'occludes' themselves linguistically. Phrases such as "*it is important/interesting/significant that*" suggest the author's evaluation is the subject of interest. Phrases such as "*having said that/noting that/seeing that*" introduce the author's own actions without drawing attention to the author. These strategies are not dishonesty or lack of rigour; rather they give a text stylistic variety and allow the writer to draw attention not only to themselves but to their ideas, actions, sources of knowledge or judgements.

Building an argument

> *You have made claims based on your thinking without really developing or explaining your ideas*

A common assumption is that reflective tasks do not need to have the same kind of rigour as research or literature-based tasks, and they do not have any internal rules or conventions. Yet, as in any rigorous piece, an opinion that has not been explored is no more successful in a reflective piece than in a literature-based piece. Qualities such as capacity to evaluate, acknowledge causes and sources of opinion, and recognise different perspectives, are as critical in a reflective piece as any other. Similarly, claims which are not justified and evidenced are equally suspect in a reflective piece as any other. In this, discourse markers are helpful in opening up ideas into critical and reflective directions: *although, because, while, having said that, on the other hand*. The language of speculation also suggests the author is open to the possibility of alternatives: *it may/might/could/be*. (See Hyland, 1999 on citation strategies in academic writing.)

Connecting reading with writing

> *You have not referred to any of the supporting literature to show you are aware of your connection with the wider literature*
>
>   the piece was reflective so I thought you just had to say what you felt. (LIC, Greta)

Another common assumption is that reflection about self and reference to supporting literature are two conflicting positions, and that one should never refer to others in reflective pieces, and by reverse analogy, never refer to oneself in literature-based pieces. As suggested above, opinions in a reflective piece need to be interrogated as in any rigorous piece of writing, so literature that expands, supports, develops or evidences, shows that the writer sees themselves as part of a wider community, to which he/she can both learn and contribute. Discussing literature reflectively (rather than critically) suggests that the literature links in some way with personal experience. For example:

> My experience of peer review is shared by X.
> X describes a similar situation to mine.
> I found x helpful.
> X's model of team learning has been useful because …

Taking this latter example, it is also interesting to recognise that many of the students experienced the terms *reflective* and *critical* as interchangeable, with feedback doing little to unravel for them the differences. Students struggled when their feedback told them they were displaying reading, rather than drawing on it for a reason as part of an argument or discussion. They struggled too, with the distinction between describing their reading, and responding to it critically. One of the most presiding myths about *being critical* is that this means *being negative*; and this is particularly problematic where a learner has internalised the sacrosanct quality of the published written word. One participant (LIC) writes "*I have been told I must be critical. But who am I to look for things an author should have done better? The author knows much more than I do*". Assessment tasks which are literature-based do include agendas which are not always explicit. With some of the learning tasks, such as an annotated bibliography or results of a literature search, showing familiarity with a literature is sufficient. With other learning tasks, such as an article critique, book review or research paper, there is an expectation that the literature be evaluated, selected to build an argument, and connected to create coherence. To mistake one kind of literature-based task for the other is a source of confusion and disappointment. Here is a typical example, shared in the RIR study:

> I had done all the reading on the list. I had done everything the teacher asked. I read everything and in my paper I explained it. But still I got a bad mark. (RIR)

For this student, the task of writing about a topic with reference to the literature entailed *listing, summarising* and *describing* what he had read. These are useful skills, but only for certain text types such as a sample bibliography or synopsis of a book. Higher levels of thinking, however, are implied in the concept of criticality such as: *evaluating, analysing, debating, identifying, creating* (Bloom, 1956). These deeper ways of thinking may have been explained, listed in criteria, even modelled, but this may not be enough: *being critical* contains within it multiple sub-skills which need ideally to be modelled, developed, and internalised slowly over time. Where there has not been this process, students may default back to unhelpful myths about key words such as *reflective* and *critical*, which blind them to different and new definitions.

Feedback and criteria: anatomising assessment activities

If the student with the disappointing grade for his literature review searched the course documentation, he might have found the following explanation of the task, correlated to Bloom's higher levels of thinking (1956):
In the literature review the student should be able to:

- Evaluate the contribution of a reading: strengths, gaps, connections, new ideas, precedents
- Identify the relevance of readings, and parts of readings, to a topic, theme or argument
- Analyse the content and qualities of readings
- Debate issues found in readings drawing on reasoned and balanced analysis
- Create links and connections with a research question, topic or theme
- Recognise patterns and connections with a wider literature
- Create new theory and hypotheses informed by the literature

These assignment criteria might, perhaps, have been spelled out in several places, including course handbooks, assignment descriptions, or teaching material. In practice, however, the more detailed and precise the criteria, the more it may need 'translation' by the assessor. One academic (who echoes the experience of several) describes:

> students asking questions where the answer is in the handbook. Our handbooks get longer and longer, more and more detail, more and more explanation, but the more there is in the handbook the harder it is for students to work out what's important. For students who have never met these detailed handbooks and lists, they would just much rather come and talk to us. (CSB, Karen)

Criteria may be difficult to interpret, not only because the language and concepts are unfamiliar but because multiple suggestions make it harder to extract the more important from the less important. The best feedback can flag up what is important for an individual and clarify the missing steps in a longer piece of work. This is particularly helpful in longer assessed pieces, such as dissertations and research projects.

Many participants in the *Learning Interconnectedness* (LIC) and *Reflection in the Round* (RIR) projects cited the dissertation as the biggest challenge in their studies, not only because of its length, but also because of the many parts that built up towards the whole. The dissertation seemed to be a great equaliser, in that it was seen as a major hurdle to most students whether studying in their home culture and first language or whether they were in a new country, culture and language. Several cited feedback as the most helpful way of learning what needed to be done at each stage, whilst acknowledging that the feedback also caused frustration and disappointment. Below is a compilation of typical feedback comments from different stages of the dissertation process, along with student responses to these derived from LIC and RIR.

Refining the question

> *You need to refine your research question so it is practical and realisable*
> this made the question much smaller than I had wanted it to be, but then I realised I could never have answered my original question, it was far too wishy-washy and general. So though I hated making my question smaller, in the end the revised question was one I could actually answer. (RIR)

Selecting the literature

> *Your literature doesn't really relate in a focused enough way on your research question*
> I put down everything I could find about the topic but then I realised from this feedback that at least half were not going to be really useful so I started again, I chose things I need to find in the articles so they were more specific, for

example not just general about working with young people but specifically in urban areas with a high number of families on benefits. (RIR)

Targeted data

You have suggested ways of collecting data which don't precisely target the research question
My first idea was to use questionnaires because they were easy and I had fewer ethical issues, but I got so much more information by including semi-structured interviews with families, observing youth activities, and walking round the urban environments seeing what was there for them (or what wasn't). it was worth the extra work. I was really annoyed with that feedback at first as I spent a lot of time planning the questionnaire but it was right and it helped in the end. (RIR)

The meaning of grades

We know from the student stories above, that grades are often given more attention than tutor comments. This is despite the fact that the best feedback is designed to provide so much more information, such as match with criteria, steps in a task, or learner progress. It is also despite the fact that numbers alone have the potential to be relative and unfair. Academics in the *Fostering Interculturality* project (FIC) explain their frustration with this approach.

I would say the students are very motivated by marks, less motivated by what they think they'll get out of the educational experience, so they're strategic. (FIC)
There's a problem of students not coming for feedback from assessment. They tend to think of assessment as just something that they do, that they pass or they fail, they don't seem to have an idea. It's not in their culture at the minute about feeling the need to do better, feeling the need to progress, or how do they go about progressing what they can't. You're gonna leave people behind before you even get started. (FIC)

Since grades encourage the idea that a piece of work can be precisely measured, it is then not surprising some students view their efforts as divisible into measurable pieces.

A student came to see me with a 47%, 3% below the passmark. She asked 'how many extra references do I need to add to get the extra 3%?' (CSB, Anna)

The difficulty of giving a single grade for complex skills is exposed here, as teachers struggle to be fair and correlate their grades to criteria. Yet the difference between a fail and pass is not so easily atomised. As we saw in

Chapter 8 and the sections above, a pass is likely to require more complexity in thinking, for example a shift from listing and summarising to evaluating and critiquing; so, the extra 3% is not so easily explained. Nor will the extra references make any difference if the quality of thinking has not been changed. Conversely, Katya (CSB) points out that a learner who is disengaged all through the study year, can achieve a successful grade right at the end simply by ticking the competences in the criteria list in a strategic way.

> Writing well is not enough to receive a first here; in fact, writing well is almost not expected. Instead, one must definitely answer the question, know how to argue a point, and do the kind of research that is expected. At the same time, a student may be disengaged throughout the year and have few other skills but if they produce a good essay that follows the brief, they can really reap the rewards with the final grade at the end. (CSB, Katya)

What it means to reach a pass mark is a critical moment, for both teachers and learners. Yet even this is on shifting ground, varying from place to place and over time. Dared describes his move from Ireland to Australia, but also the changing approach to pass marks.

> I see some trends. It's really difficult to fail. The influence of consumerism on higher education has really changed things so when you do a course now, the pass mark for a course compared to either the progression mark or the actual real mark has shifted, so what you get is, unless you score particularly well and you get a good 2:1 or first, you may pass but it's a kind of polite way to say you have failed. There has been a big shift around standards right across the sector and that's one big change. When education was free as it was when I did my undergraduate in Australia and Ireland, the academics failed a lot more people. They could get away with it. That's a big change. (CSB, Dared)

His point, that lower grades may be interpreted as *"a polite way of saying you have failed"* also raises important questions about the relative value of numbers. Tim (CSB) describes moving from the UK to the University of Oklahoma applying his *"miserable UK approach to grading"* within the US system.

> no-one explained about grading, priorities – it was painful, they wanted me to give better grades – I was used to the miserable UK approach to grading– you need to give As all over in the US, the students expected that and were disappointed, didn't understand why not – that was difficult. (CSB, Tim)

For a British or French educator, 70% or 14/20 is in the top category. Marking grids in UK universities describe work in this category as *excellent* and distinction standard. In these European contexts the higher numbers are rarely if ever awarded, especially in the social sciences and humanities. Jake had the same experience studying and teaching English:

> Even if Shakespeare had written an essay about Hamlet he wouldn't have got higher than 80%. (CSB, Jake)

Receiving a grade widely outside your expectation has high stakes, if this is your first indicator of how you are succeeding in your new study culture. For Winnie, the first grade she received in her new French university was nothing short of shocking.

> In Canada I graduated top in my programme with A/A+. Typical top grades there were:
>
> A-85–90%
> A90–95%
> A+95–100%
>
> In France grades are like the UK – I got 14/20 (70%) and I was in tears – it was like a fail. But they told me, no that's like the top of the class. I thought anything below 90% was bad, poor performance. (CSB, Winnie)

Annabel, shares this experience, describing the difference in grading as "*one of the biggest adjustments I had to make*" (CSB, Annabel), moving from the US to the UK:

> In the US we use the top part of the scale 50–100. My grades always fell between 80–100. When I got my first grade back, my first presentation was 70%. I should have been proud, but I had a visceral reaction to 70% not what I should have felt about a distinction. I worked it out – one friend from Germany was also disappointed until she had it explained. For me 70% is middle of the way, a C – it doesn't say you are doing fantastic work. It shows me how ingrained is the grading system. Even though I knew it was different here I still had just a visceral reaction – in all my undergraduate years I never got anything under 70%. (CSB, Annabel)

What helped Annabel make this adjustment was feedback. From the feedback she could recognise what had been appreciated, and gradually she was able to attach value to this rather than to the percentage she had been awarded.

> When I read the feedback (for my 70% assignment in the UK) I knew the professor enjoyed the paper. I am getting more used to it but it was so jarring.

180   Kinds of feedback

> The feedback was so helpful – I look more now to the feedback as I am less attached to the number – I am more aware of feedback here but in the US I only looked at feedback if I didn't do well – I am more interested now in knowing what else I could do, what critiques, what suggestions for more research etc. It may be a postgraduate vs undergraduate thing, or I am a bit older. (CSB, Annabel)

Her comments reflect her changing attitudes to feedback in the course of studying. She started as an undergraduate with no interest in feedback and a fixation on the number, and developed as a postgraduate to the reverse approach, valuing feedback and learning to pay less attention to her grade.

One academic describes the mutual misunderstanding that can happen when a learner does fixate on numbers in the way Annabel describes in her early learning stages.

> Tariq comes into the room waving his assignment: '60% is no good to me. There is no point in the MA unless I get a distinction'. (CSB, Anna)

In Anna's story, Tariq may be disappointed partly because numbers are more important to him than feedback, and partly that in his home culture he might be accustomed to high grades up into the top percentiles. One academic recognises Tariq's position as a pattern:

> They've got to get a 2:1 or they're a Nobody. They're highly motivated to get a 2:1. And there's a certain segment who are highly motivated to get Firsts. And that's every year, definitely. (FIC)

However, in addition Tariq may be typical of the fee-paying culture mentioned above by Dared. A dangerous culture of 'buying' good marks may drive students to expect them and pressure educators to give them. In some cases, scholarships and funding depend on students receiving high grades, which might be unrealistic in a different grading culture. One staff participant in *Fostering Interculturality* (FIC) describes how this has creates a culture of complaint:

> There are more and more students who contact module leaders and they challenge the marks that they get. They get a mark and they just send an email saying 'Oh I'm very disappointed. I think I should get at least five points more.' This would be just unbelievable in another institution and I think it leans to the fact that we do treat students like customers so they think they can have these expectations that they will get high marks – then they are not happy because maybe on some other module they put similar effort and got a much better grade. (FIC)

Gerda has an interesting solution from her perspective as a student challenged by all these varied conventions and approaches to number.

Kinds of feedback 181

What would be interesting to explain where does the average lie that people achieve, so someone knows say 70% get an average or below, certain percent above merit, below merit, that would put it all in perspective. (CSB, Gerda)

Measuring her results against average marks in her new study context is a helpful suggestion, rather than comparing them to her former grading culture.

This section, then, has suggested that there is no straightforward way of translating feedback and grades so they work seamlessly across cultural borders. Both feedback and grades can be received in many different ways, depending on a learner's first study culture and the stage they have reached in their own development. We have seen other factors too are at play in creating bridges between assessor and learner. Feedback is dependent on words conveying clear meanings, and time and space being given for these meanings to transform into deep learning. Meanwhile numbers give the impression of objectivity, yet as we have seen, the use of them for grading is highly relative and differs from place to place. As with all the questions in this book, there are no definitive solutions but rather being open to answers that are surprising, challenging, or might lead to inner change.

Learning about feedback through the literature lens

The vignette below is based on several stories shared by both students and academic staff in the *Crossing Study Borders* project. It reveals the mismatch between student and teacher perceptions of helpful feedback, and the potentially high cost of this misunderstanding.

> Lihua received 45% for her social studies project on a festival or custom that was part of her own heritage. The pass mark was 50%. Her supervisor, aiming to be both positive and constructive, wrote:
>
> > Thank you for your interesting project about the Chinese new year. At the moment you have told me how much you enjoy the festival. I would also like to know why you enjoy it: for example how you celebrate, things you do, say, wear or eat. You can resubmit this to receive a pass grade.
>
> When it came to the resubmission date, Lihua failed to resubmit and was given a fail grade for the module. She appealed against this decision and made a complaint against her tutor for not making clear what she should do and for not giving her helpful feedback. At her appeal interview she said:
>
> > I think the grade is not fair. She never used the word fail. I thought when she said your interesting project that I had done well. She said you can

> resubmit, not you must. I did everything I was told the first time and did not understand why I should do the project again.

Meanwhile the tutor maintained her judgement and position, saying,

> I gave Lihua clear pointers for how to improve her piece of work and also explained she should resubmit.

Feedback and fairness

I think the grade is not fair vs I gave the student clear pointers

The outcome of feedback and assessment felt unfair both to Lihua as a student, and equally to her tutor who thought she had provided helpful and constructive feedback. This mismatch between tutor and student perceptions of feedback is well researched in large-scale studies such as Carless (2006) in Hong Kong, Burger (2017) in Germany and Ryan and Henderson (2018) in Australia. How can these studies and the wider literature help to unravel what has gone wrong here?

The studies tell us that Lihua and her supervisor are not alone in misunderstanding one another. In Hong Kong, for example 1740 students had a very different view of feedback, compared to the 860 staff who were surveyed (Carless, 2006). The teachers believed their feedback to be effective and helpful, whilst their students did not. A smaller study of 18 first-year students, 20 third-year students and academics (Murphy, 2010) found a similar mismatch between tutor and student views, not only about feedback, but also about realistic expectations given time constraints. This mismatch is particularly problematic where students are studying in a culture new to them. Ryan and Henderson (2018) researched the assessment experiences of 4514 students in two Australian universities. A clear pattern emerged for students studying in Australia as a second culture. Irrespective of their first language, they felt more discouraged and upset by feedback comments than their home-based peers. In addition, students receiving lower grades than expected felt *"sad, shameful and angry"* (Ryan and Henderson, 2018, p. 880) in contrast to students with higher grades. These words reflect the strong emotions attached to the assessment experience, but also the vulnerability of those studying in a new culture away from their place of first study. We have suggested from the start of this chapter that feedback is more than a stage in learning. It is also a moment of high emotion that can lead to loss of face or elation, to fear of failure and loss of self-esteem. Carless (2006) reports on students who could not bring themselves to collect assignments with low marks for fear of the negative feedback. In his study he also found a strong correlation between students with low grades and those who found marking to be unfair.

A student's sense of fairness is much more complex than a form of words or a flattering grade. Deeley et al. (2019) concluded that *"students' dissatisfaction with assessment and feedback is not a 'tame' problem for which a straightforward solution exists. Instead, it is a 'wicked' problem that requires a complex approach with multiple interventions"* (Deeley et al., 2019, p. 385). These many research studies into assessment mismatches thus tend to arrive at a multi-layered response to the problem. One example is the study by O'Donovan et al. (2019). They invited students to share examples of feedback they thought were fair and helpful, followed up with 32 interviews. The researchers identified four broad factors which seemed to affect a sense of fairness: feedback artefact, position within an assessment cycle, relationships and assessment literacy.

These are helpful categories for analysing Lihua's case. The 'artefacts' of feedback include, for example, written comments, a grid or matrix correlated to criteria, recorded comments, or a separate feedback sheet. To trust and understand this artefact and practice, using it as a tool for learning, clearly affects a student's sense of fairness. For Lihua, the 'artefact' of written comments at the end of her paper did not seem to correlate with clear criteria as to what was needed to pass or fail this task.

Secondly, feedback, which sits within a cycle of assessment and learning, including formative stages, learning activities and follow-up, leads to a better sense of fairness. However, these steps were unfamiliar to Lihua. Thus, she paid attention only to the grade as a free-standing piece of assessment not connected with what came next, and thus did not link her learning from one task to another.

A third important factor was the kind of community that had been created between peers and teachers. Where students were accustomed to learning with one another, peer assessing and sharing examples of good work, their sense of fairness was increased. Teachers who were able to build this kind of community were also fostering a culture of fairness. Chalmers et al. (2018) offer us an example of this kind of culture. A cohort of 84 students were offered the option of receiving either written or face-to-face feedback on their assignments. Face-to-face marking was chosen by 49, and written feedback by 35. Those who chose face-to-face marking found the dialogue highly beneficial, and both staff and students valued the opportunity to *"explain and justify why marks were given"* (Chalmers et al., 2018, p. 35). In Lihua's case, this kind of dialogue had not been formally created by her teacher. Students had formed their own small circles of learning, to which she had not been invited. In addition, tutorials and assessment discussions were set up informally, so again, she was not aware of these and did not avail herself of them.

The fourth area identified by O'Donovan et al. (2019) in their study, was students' familiarity with assessment language, criteria and practices. As we saw in the sections above, assessment information is not sufficient simply listed in a handbook. Learning the language of rubric, its text and subtext, unravelling the hidden expectations related to writing and reading sub-skills, all connect with a learner's ability to read assessment clearly. Yucel et al. (2014) describe an explicit assessment literacy programme developed for first-year biology students. Their study shows that this explicit practice of assessment tools did indeed enhance student success and appreciation of assessment expectations. In Lihua's case, assessment language had not been made an explicit focus of learning by her teacher, and conversely her teacher had not been fully aware that rubric or feedback language might be ambiguous. So, on several counts, these four categories are helpful for unravelling the mismatch between Lihua and her teacher. However, there may be further reasons we still need to uncover, with the help of the literature.

Contributing to this sense of unfairness, Carless (2006) also found that students felt powerless when they received judgements which did not reflect their effort, or when demands were made which seemed unreasonable. One example of this is told by Currant (2021) in his study of student narratives:

> After failing an essay, she was asked to produce an entirely new essay on a different topic. This meant she had effectively spent twice the time on this assessment than her peers because the academic felt it 'unfair' to give Michelle multiple chances at an assignment her peers did only once. Academics can see this as seeming to preserve 'academic standards' rather than the transmission of an unexamined and problematic culture (Michelle in Currant, 2021, p. 61)

Michelle would here have every reason to feel powerless. The judgements seem to be irrevocable and to give more attention to regulations than to the reality and specificity of her case. Francis et al. (2019) studied student sense of unfairness at King's College London and found that here too, *"many comments indicated a lack of student agency"* (Francis et al., 2019, p. 468) and a student sense of powerlessness within their communities. A culture of dissatisfaction and mistrust is thus not uncommon in many of the studies we have referred to. Francis et al. (2019), Carless (2006) and Burger (2017) arrive at the recommendation that more dialogue is needed between assessor and students and between peers: "assessment dialogues", tutorials, short assessment classes and other forms of collaborative follow-up to feedback. This kind of dialogue at several stages in the learning and assessment process might have made Lihua's feedback clearer.

Burger's study (2017) of 1549 students across 48 departments in a German university also found student participation in assessment helped them to internalise criteria and feel their grades were fairer. Studies suggest that students can be highly responsible when given the chance to be their own assessors and measure work against clear criteria. Scott (2017) tells us of a group assessment practice with BSc Zoology and BSc Marine and Freshwater Biology in a UK university. The students were able to apply assessment criteria accurately and constructively to assess work produced in their groups, and their capacity to do so improved over time so their judgements were increasingly accurate as a result of this dialogue. Thus, we know from these several research studies that where recommendations such as development of assessment literacies are put in place, they do have an effect and students are indeed more satisfied with the processes and feel them to be fairer.

We have seen in this section that there are many reasons assessment might be seen as unfair, and several ways a tutor might reverse this judgement. Lihua may well have felt particularly vulnerable functioning in her second culture and language; the feedback and result were more viscerally tied to her sense of survival in the new culture. Several processes may have helped her and her tutor to arrive at an understanding. These include "assessment dialogues" between peers, and between peer and tutor, such as seminars, peer review exchanges and assessment follow-up tutorials. In addition, the skills and literacies of assessment are content areas in themselves, and like all content areas need to be scaffolded, modelled, explained, defined and given time for slow and deep learning to take place. Finally, since assessment is the moment when high emotions are engaged, it needs to be seen as part of a developmental cycle with the chance to learn and change rather than as a place where final irrevocable judgements are made. These are ways of giving students a sense of agency and rebalancing a relationship in which they may find themselves to have little power or agency.

Feedback and assessment discourse

she never used the word fail

If we now turn to the language of dialogue between assessor and student, we see that there is more at stake than choice of words. Choosing words that take account of the emotions, and that seek to preserve self-esteem, leads to another kind of confusion. In Lihua's example, her feedback has not been sufficiently direct and has been hedged in the language of politeness and suggestion. Reflections about formative feedback gathered by Walter (in Scott et al., 2013) show us this difficulty is shared by other students too. In Walter's study, a group of both home-based and international students agreed that their preference was for clearly stated feedback that told them exactly what they had done right or wrong. One participant, Joanna, wrote in her journal:

> when they correct they are not very exigent. The reply I got from my essay was extremely positive and I just felt that there wasn't any comment that helped me to challenge myself and go further what I had already written. Isn't their job to force me to be better? To cast doubt on my statements? (Joanna, in Scott et al., 2013)

Studies looking more closely at the language of feedback suggest this tendency to be positive is widespread. Orsmond and Merry (2011) analysed documented examples of feedback between 19 biological sciences students and 6 of their tutors. They also found that feedback tended to focus on giving praise, and this constituted almost half the content of the feedback comments. A study in Hong Kong showed the various strategies teachers used to avoid showing disagreement in the classroom (Lopez-Ozieblo, 2018). Whilst these were non-verbal indications, still the study showed that strategies for *not saying no* were widespread and internalised. It seems to be the case that educators take particular care to avoid the negative, and for good reason. Dewaele (2016) conducted an interesting study of 30 emotion-laden words in the English language, via an online questionnaire from 1159 native English (L1) users and 1165 English foreign language (LX) users. His study found that the non-native speakers "overestimated the offensiveness of most words" (Dewaele, 2016, p. 112). Dewaele's recommendation is that first language learners be warned of the power of these words when using them in the classroom, and by extrapolation, their teachers too. To return to our vignette, Lihua's supervisor is responding with care to avoid language that might offend, and she is not alone in doing so.

Instead, the advice Lihua's supervisor gives her relates to broad suggestions about content and structure. In this she is acting in a principled way that is supported by fellow-practitioners such as Orsmond and Merry (2011). Across several studies we see that students find generic feedback to be more helpful; in other words, feedback which suggests points that can be carried over to other assignments. Song et al. (2017) reviewed 42 pieces of written work in draft and final versions and found that students were much more concerned with overall qualities such as: clarity, logical development of ideas, overall structure. Of far less concern for them were the detailed mechanics of their writing. This is unsurprising. If we look at the kind of mechanical, surface-level feedback students are given, this can be contradictory and confusing. To take one example, we looked in Chapter 8 at reflective writing and its definition in different subject disciplines. Hyland (2002) points out the contradictory advice given to novice science writers as to whether or not they should make themselves visible. On the one hand young scientists are advised to hide themselves:

> The total paper is considered to be the work of the writer. You don't have to say 'I think' or 'My opinion is' in the paper. (…) Traditional formal writing does not use I or we in the body of the paper (Spencer and Arbon, 1996, p. 26)

On the other, by other specialists, they are told to reveal themselves:

> I herewith ask all young scientists to renounce the false modesty of previous generations of scientists. Do not be afraid to name the agent of the action in a sentence, even when it is 'I' or 'we'. (Day, 1994, p. 166)

This is a confusing position for the novice student who is trying to discern what is expected of him in new kinds of assessment tasks. Drawing attention to the self with the pronoun 'I' does not make a text less objective or rigorous, nor more informal and inappropriate. Hyland (2002) studied authorial presence across a range of both novice and experienced writers. He found that novice writers and students tend to refer to themselves far less frequently than confident authors; and in addition, these references to the self are made for specific reasons: most frequently to explain a procedure, and less frequently (or in his data never) to express self-benefit or belief. In Lihua's case, the feedback her supervisor gives her suggests that she needed to relate the project to her own experience. However, there seem to have been precise ways of explaining this experience which Lihua had not appreciated.

The assessor is thus poised between two extremes: taking care to avoid the negative, which we have seen (Dewaele, 2016) carries more emotional weight for second language learners; and taking care to be direct and give clear pointers, which are generalisable to other forms of writing. Lihua's supervisor has tried to do this responsibly, but her message has failed to reach the student. A likely reason for this may be, not only the language itself, but also the failure to support the language with the kind of strategies we have suggested (see page 162–164). An interesting way to review the vignette above, is to ask: what could the supervisor have done differently? Some ideas, based on those in this chapter, include developing assessment literacies by inviting students to assess one another using the task criteria; following up feedback with group discussion, identifying steps for those with fail grades; and one-to-one conversation explaining the grade and next steps. What could Lihua have done differently? She might have referred more closely to the criteria before writing the task; compared her fail-grade work to her peers who had received a higher grade; reflected more closely on the feedback and sought the help of her supervisor where there was doubt.

Successful communication in assessment feedback does indeed mean meeting midway. Since the assessor has the power in this equation, she needs to provide opportunities for explanation, engagement, support and revision. Meanwhile, students too need to claim what agency they can, by being proactive and asking questions about the process. Importantly, they need to be aware of their own responsibility in making their assessment tasks opportunities for learning.

Learning maps: what does feedback mean?

In this section, the models, strategies, and ways of thinking about feedback discussed in the chapter will be drawn upon, in order for you to analyse your own assessment experiences.

Kinds of feedback

Review the kind of feedback you give or receive now, either as a learner or as a teacher, and track your responses in Table 9.1. What would your ideal kind of assessment be and how could you make changes in order to reach this?

Kinds of feedback

Table 9.1 Kinds of feedback

	Varieties and options	Your current assessment	Your ideal assessment
Who gives feedback? *power and agency* (Francis et al., 2019)	• External assessor • Teacher/tutor • Peer • Self		
What kind of feedback is given?	• Specific to the assignment • Generic comments relevant to all assignments		
How is feedback given? The "feedback artefact" (O'Donovan et al., 2019)	• Written summarising comments • Written in-text notes and comments • In a course booklet • In a grid/matrix • Recorded spoken comments		
How is feedback followed up? "assessment dialogues" (Carless, 2006)	• In a class discussion • In a tutorial/small group • Email or other contact		

Feedback preferences

Table 9.2 is an opportunity to conduct small-scale research into your own assessment context.

- Ask five teachers and five learners the kind of feedback they value most, using the list in Table 9.2.
- What patterns do you notice?
- What are the differences between what learners value and what teachers value?

Kinds of grades

In Table 9.3, compare the way grades are given in your current setting and two other settings. These could be other places you have taught or studied, or other places your colleagues or peers have experienced as a learner or teacher.

- What is the typical top grade band? Does the grading go up to 100% or does it stop much lower in the scale?
- What is the typical bottom pass grade? What grade would constitute a failure? Is a failure at the bottom of the scale, such as 0%, or much higher such as 50%?

Table 9.2 Feedback preferences

As a learner?		As a teacher?
	The grade	
	Feedback that explains what was right/what was wrong	
	Feedback that is positive	
	Feedback that relates clearly to criteria	
	Feedback that clearly lists points to be changed	
	Feedback that is specific to the assignment in hand	
	Feedback that identifies generic issues relevant to all assignments (e.g. citation)	
	Macro-feedback about structure, overall logic and coherence	
	Detailed feedback about surface and mechanical features such as spelling and vocabulary choice	

Table 9.3 Kinds of grades

	Typical top-grade band	*Typical bottom-pass grade*
Your current setting		
Another setting		
Another setting		

- What are the differences? Do you consider these grades to be fair? Why, or why not?

Further topics for reflection and reading

Peer assessment
- What is your experience of peer assessment?
- What do you think are the benefits of peers assessing one another? What kinds of structures and mechanisms do you think need to be in place for this to happen in a responsible and constructive way?
- What do you think are the problems with peer assessing: as a student experiencing this? As a teacher setting this up?

- Do you think it would help or hinder for this kind of assessment to be anonymous?
- Is there anything you would now change in the way you assess, either as a student or as a teacher?
- Read the articles below to expand, confirm or critique your ideas. All of these are available online.

Kaufman, J.H. and Schunn, C.D. (2011) 'Students' perceptions about peer assessment for writing: their origin and impact on revision work', *Instructional Science: An International Journal of the Learning Sciences*, 39 (3), pp. 387–406.

Mulder, R., Baik, C., Naylor, R. and Pearce, J. (2014) 'How does student peer review influence perceptions, engagement and academic outcomes? A case study', *Assessment and Evaluation in Higher Education*, 39 (6), pp. 657–677.

Panadero, E. and Alqassab, M. (2019) 'An empirical review of anonymity effects in peer assessment, peer feedback, peer review, peer evaluation and peer grading', *Assessment and Evaluation in Higher Education*, 44 (8), pp. 1253–1278.

Sridharan, B. Muttakin, M.B. and Mihret, D.G. (2018) 'Students' perceptions of peer assessment effectiveness: an explorative study', *Accounting Education*, 27 (3), pp. 259–285.

References

Bloom, B.S. (ed.) (1956) *Taxonomy of educational objectives: the classification of educational goals.* New York: David McKay.

Burger, R. (2017) 'Student perceptions of the fairness of grading procedures: a multilevel investigation of the role of the academic environment', *Higher Education: The International Journal of Higher Education Research*, 74 (2), pp. 301–320.

Carless, D. (2006) 'Differing perceptions in the feedback process', *Studies in Higher Education*, 31 (2), pp. 219–233.

Chalmers, C., Mowat, E. and Chapman, M. (2018) 'Marking and providing feedback face-to-face: staff and student perspectives', *Active Learning in Higher Education*, 19 (1), pp. 35–45.

Clifford, V., Adeunji, H., Haigh, M., Henderson, J., Spiro, J. and Hudson, J. (2011) *Report on Brookes student learning experience project: fostering interculturality and global perspectives at Brookes through dialogue with staff.* Oxford Centre for Staff Learning and Development: Oxford Brookes University.

Currant, N. (2021) *'My stomach churns': belonging and strategies for belonging for BME students in a white university.* EdD Thesis, Oxford: Oxford Brookes University.

Day, R. (1994) *How to write and publish a scientific paper.* Phoenix, AZ: Oryx Press.

Deeley, S.J., Fischbacher-Smith, M., Karadzhov, D. and Koristashevskaya, E. (2019) 'Exploring the "wicked" problem of student dissatisfaction with assessment and feedback in higher education', *Higher Education Pedagogies*, 4 (1), pp. 385–405.

Dewaele, J.M. (2016) 'Thirty shades of offensiveness: L1 and LX English users' understanding, perception and self-reported use of negative emotion-laden words', *Journal of Pragmatics*, 94, pp. 112–127.

Francis, R.A., Millington, J.D.A. and Cederlöf, G. (2019) 'Undergraduate student perceptions of assessment and feedback practice: fostering agency and dialogue', *Journal of Geography in Higher Education*, 43 (4), pp. 468–485.

Hyland, K. (1999) Academic attribution: fitation and the construction of disciplinary knowledge. *Applied Linguistics*, 20 (3), pp. 341–367.

Hyland, K. (2002) 'Authority and invisibility: authorial identity in academic writing'. *Journal of Pragmatics*, 34 (8), pp. 1091–1112.

Kaufman, J.H. and Schunn, C.D. (2011) 'Students' perceptions about peer assessment for writing: their origin and impact on revision work', *Instructional Science: An International Journal of the Learning Sciences*, 39 (3), pp. 387–406.

Lopez-Ozieblo, R. (2018) 'Disagreeing without a 'no': how teachers indicate disagreement in a Hong Kong classroom', *Journal of Pragmatics* 137, pp. 1–18.

Mulder, R., Baik, C., Naylor, R. and Pearce, J. (2014) 'How does student peer review influence perceptions, engagement and academic outcomes? A case study', *Assessment and Evaluation in Higher Education*, 39 (6), pp. 657–677.

Murphy, C. and Cornell, J. (2010) 'Student perceptions of feedback: seeking a coherent flow', *Practitioner Research in Higher Education*, 4 (1), pp. 41–51.

O'Donovan, B.N., den Outer, B., Price, M. and Lloyd, A. (2019) 'What makes good feedback good?', *Studies in Higher Education*, 46 (2), pp. 318–329.

Orsmond, P. and Merry, S. (2011) 'Feedback alignment: effective and ineffective links between tutors' and students' understanding of coursework feedback', *Assessment and Evaluation in Higher Education*, 36 (2) pp. 125–136.

Panadero, E. and Alqassab, M. (2019) 'An empirical review of anonymity effects in peer assessment, peer feedback, peer review, peer evaluation and peer grading', *Assessment and Evaluation in Higher Education*, 44 (8), pp. 1253–1278.

Ryan, T. and Henderson, M. (2018) 'Feeling feedback: students' emotional responses to educator feedback', *Assessment and Evaluation in Higher Education*, 43 (6), pp. 880–892.

Scott, D., Hughes, G., Evans, C., Burke, P.J., Walter, C. and Watson, D. (2013) *Learning transitions in higher education*. London: Palgrave Macmillan.

Scott, G.W. (2017) 'Active engagement with assessment and feedback can improve group-work outcomes and boost student confidence', *Higher Education Pedagogies*, 2 (1), pp. 1–13.

Song, G., Hoon, L.H. and Alvin, L.P. (2017) 'Students' response to feedback: an exploratory study', *RELC Journal: A Journal of Language Teaching and Research*, 48 (3), pp. 357–372.

Spencer, C. and Arbon, B. (1996) *Foundations of writing: developing research and academic writing skills*. Lincolnwood, Illinois: National Textbook Company.

Spiro, J. (2013) 'The reflective continuum: reflecting for change and student response to reflective tasks', *Brookes eJournal of Learning and Teaching*, 2013.

Spiro, J. (2014) 'Learning interconnectedness', *Higher Education Quarterly*, 68 (1), pp. 65–86.

Spiro, J., Henderson, J. and Clifford, V. (2012) 'Independent learning crossing cultures: learning cultures and shifting meanings', *Compare: A Journal of Comparative and International Education*, 42 (4), pp. 607–619.

Sridharan, B.Muttakin, M.B. and Mihret, D.G. (2018) 'Students' perceptions of peer assessment effectiveness: an explorative study', *Accounting Education*, 27 (3), pp. 259–285.

Williams, K., Wooliams, M. and Spiro, J. (2020) (2nd edition) *Reflective writing*. Basingstoke: Palgrave Macmillan.

Yucel, R., Bird, F.L. and Young, J. (2014) 'The road to self-assessment: exemplar marking before peer review develops first-year students' capacity to judge the quality of a scientific report', *Assessment and Evaluation in Higher Education*, 39 (8), pp. 971–986.

10 Navigating study cultures
From noticing to learning maps

Chapter 1 introduced the idea that noticing is one way of standing back from moments of surprise, discomfort or collision and interrogating the sources and causes of this discomfort: for example, why Katya felt so shocked when the lecturer referred to her personal life in an academic class (Chapter 2); why Cora was constantly in conflict with colleagues in her new appointment as a lecturer (Chapter 3); why Faisal constantly misunderstood what was expected of him in his assessed work (Chapter 8); why Winnie and Annabel burst into tears on receiving their first assessed grade (Chapter 9). These and many other stories in the book, point to the benefits of searching for the causes and sources widely and beyond the experience of the individual. We have found deeper sub-structures lying beneath the surface of events: for example, institutional values, national ideologies, assessment strategies, grading schemes, educator beliefs, learner identities and motivations. Our participants are diverse in multiple ways: their first language and culture, their subject discipline, where they have moved from and to, their stage in learning (undergraduate or postgraduate), whether they view higher education through a learner or teacher lens (or both). Yet, for the purposes of this book, they have one thing in common: they are encountering these critical moments for the first time and have travelled towards them from another place of learning. It is from this point of fresh experience that we are able to gather knowledge from them.

This final chapter asks what we can do with these critical moments to build learning maps for future learners and learning. It brings together recommendations from the participants themselves, themes which emerged from their experiences, and those which emerge too from the literature. All these offer ways of crossing borders with maps, tools and the voices of former travellers, arriving equipped to be a citizen and student of the world.

Crossing borders: from wicked problems to learning maps

> I have always liked to think that working in HE in the UK that I always put the needs of my students first and that their learning was the most important aspect of everything that I did. However, realizing that students in a different

DOI: 10.4324/9780429426261-10

country had different learning expectations and different learning needs opened my eyes to the way that I was approaching learning and teaching. It became apparent to me that in order to understand what was best for students I had to question my assumptions about learning environments, learning styles and the ways that I tried to encourage and enable student learning. (CSB, Alistair)

Alistair's encounter with his students revealed to him the relativity of his own beliefs. As with so many of the stories and vignettes in this book, *being uncomfortable* shines a light on unchallenged patterns of thinking (Strange and Gibson, 2017). Importantly, these moments of being unsettled open up problems which are "complex, lack clear boundaries, and attempts to solve them and have unforeseen consequences" (McCune et al., 2021, 1). McCune at al. (2021) call these "wicked problems". How should educators and learning institutions respond to being uncomfortable so it leads to the making rather than the breaking of learning? How can wicked problems be harnessed to provide learning maps for others?

As throughout this book, the recommendations in this chapter derive from learning diaries, field notes, interviews and focus groups between 2011 and 2021, and across four separate projects. These are:

- *Reflection in the Round* (RIR) with 38 student learning diaries and 10 annual focus groups of students on one-year postgraduate progammes between 2011 and 2020. In addition, teacher field notes track learning activities and learner responses during the same period. The project is published as Spiro (2013) and crystallised into teaching materials as Williams, Wooliams and Spiro (2020).
- *Fostering Interculturality* (FIC) with 16 participants, both staff and students, who identified as international, discussing their experience of crossing cultures in semi-structured interviews and focus groups. This project is published as Clifford et al. (2011) and Spiro et al. (2012).
- *Learning Interconnectedness* (LIC) with 50 international first degree students between 2010 and 2014 sharing weekly journals about their experiences of learning across cultures and languages. In addition, teacher field notes track cross-cultural learning activities and learner responses in the same period 2010–2014 (Spiro, 2014).
- *Crossing Study Borders* (CSB) with 24 staff and students who identified as having crossed borders in learning and teaching, interviewed between 2020 and 2021 and published here for the first time.

Participants in the *Crossing Study Borders* project were asked, with the benefit of hindsight, what advice would they now give to their former selves, to help smooth the transition to a new place of study? What messages would they now like to give to their institutions, their peers, teachers and managers? Their answers cover a wide spectrum, from whole person concerns such as preparing for independence, through to precise tips about managing deadlines and booking tutorials. These cluster broadly into seven main themes, which can be loosely sequenced from pre-arrival to mid-experience. In reporting these themes, we also consider their implications for the three main stakeholders in the higher education endeavour: learners, their teachers and their institutions – administrators, managers and leaders. The themes are presented in this chapter through insider voices, integrative analysis and learning maps shown in table form.

Theme 1: Prepare for things to be different

> *do as much preparation in advance as you can* (CSB, Otto)

Many of the participants in all four projects commented that they had not expected things to be different, and this had left them unprepared. Where the first language of study was the same, or where the subject discipline was the same, or where the geographical place was the same but the institution different, participants underestimated the differences they would encounter.

> There are systems – eg. 'global buddies' but I didn't sign up because I thought – my culture is pretty much the same – but it's actually the small 'c' things like what do you call your professor, how come the tasks are longer, what do your grades mean. My best resource has been other students. (CSB, Annabel)

Being unprepared for difference made these critical moments all the more difficult. Otto suggested that anticipating differences was helpful. Preparing for this included exploring not just information about academic programmes, but about the place and region, its history, politics, and cultural values, talking to those who had been there in advance, making contact with current and former students/teachers, learning their stories of surprise and cultural collision. His advice to those making the learning transition is:

> do as much preparation in advance, and not just academic preparation but try to get a detailed understanding of the educational, cultural and political differences in the location that you are going to. (CSB, Otto)

This first theme, preparing for differences, is shown in Table 10.1. This table provides practical, concrete ideas for the three stakeholder groups responding to this theme.

Theme 2: Ask questions and seek out answers

> *teasing out tacit knowledge*

Many of the participants described the importance of asking questions. *Feeling uncomfortable* and asking questions about this, often opened the doors to

Table 10.1 Learning map 1: Prepare for differences

	Recommendations
For students	Prepare before arrival: read all available information; browse institution's website, local website, and join student community groups. Plan your questions: not just about content of courses, but about the country, region, background to the institution, its former students and their subsequent lives. If you can, contact students currently or formerly in your new study institution.
For educators	Create ways for pre-arrival students to interact with current and former students. Invite graduating students to share their stories and learning journeys with future students.
For institutions	Include on your website links to non-academic information: life locally, tips for survival, things to know, bring, do and notice. Involve student voice in building and developing these links: their suggestions, recommendations and advice to newly arriving students. *Develop practical handbooks which are dynamic: where people can add their own discoveries and insights so it is a living document and comes from grass roots/the ground and not from people who think they know and are already established* (CSB, Sally).

knowledge, skills or strategies which no-one had thought to explain. Gerda comments on the shock of *tacit knowledge*, finding that what she needed to learn was not what had in fact been taught. The right questions opened up these pathways, which others took for granted. Each chapter in this book suggests the kind of questions which might reveal this tacit knowledge: for example, how formal or informal am I expected to be as a student? (Chapter 3); how is a seminar different from a lecture? (Chapter 6); what does a good assignment look like? (Chapter 8); how do I interpret my assignment feedback? (Chapter 9).

Yet there are conventions lurking under the surface of questions/answer dialogues, especially in an academic setting, which are rarely made explicit. Many studies of social interactions build on Grice's idea of cooperative conversation (1975), which categorises conversational conventions into four maxims (Murray, 2010). These four maxims, and associate implications for asking questions, are presented in Table 10.2.

As an adjacent skill, the capacity to find answers was also seen as critical, and students suggested several ways institutions could help them to do this. One idea was that institutions continually revise and expand their 'frequently asked questions' in the light of student feedback and seek dynamic ways of making the answers visible. Students valued answers being visible in several places: in course documentation, on noticeboards virtual or physical, signalled

Table 10.2 Learning map 2: Grice's cooperative principle and the pragmatics of asking questions (Grice, 1975; Murray, 2010)

Maxim	Explanation	Implications for asking questions
Quantity	Provide as much information as is needed but not too much or too little.	**For students** Be focused and precise about your questions. Background information and detailed story-telling are not needed. **For educators** Help students refine their questions to those that are answerable. Polite, focused and appropriate questioning may need to be explicitly taught. Adapt questions to elicit the level of response you wish for: short/closed answers are yielded by Yes/No, Right/Wrong questions. Expansive and developed answers are yielded by open-ended questions, often triggered by question forms such as Why? How do you know? Can you explain that?
Relation	Be relevant.	**For students** Stay with the question and subject that concerns you. Choose the questions that are important rather than a long list of others you might resolve yourself. **For educators** Higher level thinking is fostered by questions connected in a chain that develops a theme/topic, or that travel from eliciting information to contesting and deconstructing information.
Quality	Ask questions which you know to be justifiable and valid.	**For students** Ask questions where you have not been able to find answers elsewhere. Check the truth of background reasons such as "This was not in the handbook". **For educators** Help students to find their own answers and remind them of the places and sources where this can be done.
Manner	Be clear. Avoid obscurity and ambiguity. Be brief.	**For students** Focus your questions on the precise information you need (such as the sources of your 'discomfort'). Be aware of questioning ground rules. **For educators** If your own questions are not answered, rephrase them to factor out ambiguity, words which carry value judgement and may cause offence, or language which assumes prior knowledge of systems or subject discipline.

verbally in meetings, lectures and tutorials, with leaflets in the library (for example reminding them of citation conventions), through clear online links and in direct cohort messaging. In addition, participants felt they needed to be specifically taught to find out where to look for answers: for example, physically walking round buildings to identify tutor offices, careers offices or academic support centres with maps and guides; or guided through institutional websites to the sites of help centres and services. Educators, meanwhile, recommend their students do actively avail themselves of these multiple places where answers are to be found. They felt the question/answer dialogue was one of mutual responsibility, and educators were frustrated when answers were available, but students had not sought them out.

> Better to equip students to find the answers – talking to students about the differences/difficulties and setting up an FAQ.
> I think a lot of it is up to students to learn. Universities best really to make themselves available to ask questions. (CSB, Carmel)

However, there are an equal number of questions which will only raise their heads once something has gone wrong. Annabel appreciated that it was impossible for every eventuality to be covered and pre-taught.

> I like learning as I go. I think that's a good way to go. I don't know how I could know before I experience these things – to some these small things might be jarring. I don't think they really need to be taught before they are experienced. It is not possible to educate people about every difference – it's not a good use of time. (CSB, Annabel)

Several of the educators felt that these gaps were potentially helpful knowledge for their institutions; and just as learners needed to ask questions of their institutions, so the reverse should be happening; institutions needed to find more and multiple ways of gathering feedback from their learners. Luke writes:

> I really wish universities in general were genuinely able, as opposed to setting up a policy rather than saying the right words, to do much more bottom up working. So much still seems to be top down with all the attendant problems. (CSB, Luke)

Anticipating every kind of question or misunderstanding is unrealistic; yet knowing the kind of questions that arise when their learning culture is seen through fresh eyes is a valuable resource for institutions. These questions change over time; they may become more precise, or resolve themselves through experience, but formulating them in response to discomfort is an essential step towards answering them. Recommendations for teasing out tacit knowledge through questions and answers are presented in Table 10.3, for each of the stakeholder groups.

Table 10.3 Learning map 3: Questions and answers – teasing out tacit knowledge

Questions and answers	Recommendations
For students	Turn moments of discomfort into precise questions. Ask questions about content – *what*? but also about processes – *how*? and underlying reasons and values – *why*? Be proactive in finding answers to your questions.
For educators	Establish guidelines for acceptable question strategies: e.g. office hour times, questions in chat box of online sessions, one question each, five minutes at the end of class, online question-answer forum Include as an explicit part of teaching, the conventions for asking questions: what is polite, timely, appropriate and best practice. For example, how much question/answer time per student per lecturer is reasonable? When is it unreasonable? Provide explicit guidelines as to when and where questions can be answered. Be aware that student questions change at different stages of their learning: vary question opportunities depending on stage in their learning.
For institutions	Find multiple ways in which students can ask questions of the institution: feedback boxes around campus, end-of-course evaluations, dynamic 'frequently asked questions' site to which students can add new questions. Draw on student questions to identify *where*. *How* and *what* is needed to provide answers. Include as an explicit part of induction, where answers can be found to different kinds of question. Make services visible which meet a variety of different student needs at different stages in their learning: chaplaincy, counselling, buddying schemes, academic development centres, language centres, librarian support.

Theme 3: Notice what others are doing

　　learning through fresh eyes (CSB, Sally)

Another survival strategy many found helpful, was standing back from discomfort in order to notice what is happening in each situation. Chapter 1 introduced the idea of 'noticing' as an entry into a new culture and we have tracked this strategy through many of the stories in this book. Some of this noticing entailed what was physical and visible: for example, Sally, in Chapter 3, noticed that no-one in higher education came to college with a briefcase as this denoted a 'business-like' kind of professionalism that did not fit with lecturer identities. Some noticing was precisely linguistic; for example, Gerda in Chapters 2 and 8 found the language of writing alien and constraining; Katya felt the topics of conversation broke taboos for her; and Annabel found polite ways of addressing lecturers were very different in her new place of learning. Thus, much learning was dependent on recognising the finely tuned differences between one situation and another, without bringing to one the assumptions of the other. See our first references to this earlier in the book, such as Carbaugh (2013) and Philipsen (2010).

We have also discovered, through these stories, that 'noticing' happens with greater clarity through fresh eyes, when the situation is new. Sally (CSB) suggests that those seeing things anew and for the first time, have much to offer their receiving institution, and that this 'noticing' should be harnessed for the benefit of those coming next.

> Newly arrived staff from other professions bring fresh eyes to the landscape so this should be recognised and while they are still 'fresh' their insights should be what HE learns from. (CSB, Sally)

'Noticing' works most effectively when it is focused and precise, and when we know what to look for and the questions to ask. The many stories in this book allow us to draw up a 'noticing map' (Table 10.4), which can be applied to each learning event, as learners see with fresh eyes the first seminar, lecture or tutorial and notice what happens as a guide for the future.

Theme 4: Help-seeking and help-giving

> *They need to know it's OK to ask for help and who they can ask to help with what.* (CSB, Carmel)

Twelve out of 24 participants in the *Crossing Study Borders* project referred to help-seeking in various ways, as making a difference to success. Many felt they had not availed themselves of help and wished they had. We have seen the various reasons for not seeking help: systems for help-seeking being unclear or unfair, help being stigmatised, and fear of losing face. Much of the responsibility for normalising help-seeking lies with the institution. Carmel says:

> Saving face is very important. So it would be good to tell students who they can call and how eg. they can't call people at 1.0 in the morning.
> Also they need to be helped have confidence and permission to reach out, make clear they can do that if they need help. Perhaps teachers could be trained to realise that that would be very hard for some students, who won't be used to it and that might be a face-saving thing. So find ways to be approachable and be clear about what you want. (Carmel CSB)

Participants described some of the strategies which did normalise help and made it safe. Andrea was asked: "*What was best practice amongst the three institutions and cultures she had experienced?*" She replied:

Table 10.4 Learning map 4: A noticing map (from Spiro, 2013, p.175)

Notice	Noticing questions
How do people *talk* to one another?	What are the: • ways of being polite • ways of addressing one another • ways of agreeing and disagreeing • ways of joining in the conversation • ways of asking questions. Who talks and who is silent? Who initiates the conversations? Is interruption acceptable? Is it acceptable to disagree with the speaker/lecturer? Are there taboo subjects: topics no-one talks about? What happens when those topics are raised?
What kind of *text types* are read and written?	How do these texts structure information? What kind of vocabulary is expected (formal, informal, specialist)? Where should I position myself as author? Should I be visible or not? How much should I refer to the ideas, research and writing of others and how much to my own ideas? What are the disciplinary conventions for referencing and acknowledging these ideas?
How do people *behave* in the situation?	Am I expected to work independently or with others? Do people cooperate with one another, share and collaborate, or are they competitive? Am I expected to socialise with peers, or keep work/study/social life separate? Are people formal or informal: do they tell jokes, ask about personal life, stay on track or digress from the topic, use swear words? What is acceptable?
What do people seem to *know?*	Are people referring to people, places, events as if I am meant to know about these? (If I don't know, who can I ask?)

Individual support that we have at Oxford. So beneficial, creates a bond between tutor and student at the academic level. So interesting for us to see what makes them tick, what makes them interested. With larger groups you never get to see the individual, some you do see because they say or lot, or you have to coax them, but the really academically centred discussion I really enjoy with students in smaller groups. (CSB, Andrea)

Other helpful strategies were clear office hours posted on tutor doors, which gave permission to drop in for help; and booked tutorial slots offered at the start so the onus is not on the newly arrived student to take the initiative. Other students are also an important source of help. Mentoring or buddying between newly arrived and more senior students was an effective strategy, where it was systematically set up and newly arrived students trusted the process enough to participate. These were called variously: 'buddying', 'college sisters' and 'co-studenting'. Annabel, for example, described in Theme 1 above, the idea of 'global buddying'. She knew of the buddying scheme on arriving in a UK university, but assumed she would not need this as she was studying in her first language. An introduction to students who had benefited from being buddied would have made the difference; or the chance to opt in later as needs changed.

For higher education teachers, Sally describes the value of the mentor, as a colleague with more experience who supports one who is newly arrived. For colleague-to-colleague support, however, she advocates some kind of training to ensure all mentees have the same quality of support.

> people said they were 'lucky' if they got a good mentor, or a mentor at all – but it shouldn't really be just about luck. It would be good for people to have a mentor from their own background who is one or two stages further along. (CSB, Sally)

Alistair suggests the importance, as an academic moving into a new institution, of finding like-minded colleagues as potential co-researchers and collaborators (in the positive meaning of co-workers).

> Collaboration – identify as many collaborators as possible. Work with colleagues on the ground at the location you are visiting, particularly admin and technical staff. Try to establish academic collaborations that will extend beyond your visit.
>
> Discussion – linked to collaboration, but don't be frightened or ashamed to discuss anything from academic subjects, to pedagogic practice to pragmatics of living and working in a different environment.
>
> Share experience with others – when you return to your home institution be prepared to share your experiences with others and offer support and mentoring for colleagues who are going to go to different countries in the future. (CSB, Otto)

Whilst these ideas are about relationships, participants felt that the physical places where help could be found also made a difference. When the academic support centre moved from a closed room in the library *"that looked like a remedial centre to a table in the café that was just part of where we normally socialise"* (RIR Focus group), the status of help-seeking was changed instantly. The students were aware of its presence, its open-door policy and felt safe visiting it within the informal space of the cafeteria. Table 10.5

Table 10.5 Learning map 5: Help-seeking and help-giving

Help-seeking	Recommendations
For students	Find out where, how and from whom you can seek help. Be open to help from a range of people, including fellow students, tutors, counselling and wellbeing services, academic support centres. Check the conventions for seeking help (timing, forms of approach).
For educators	Offer clear times and places for help-giving. Initiate help-giving: be aware it may be hard for students to take the initiative. Be consistent in giving help to all students on an equal basis: don't assume it's easier for some kinds of student.
For institutions	Locate help-giving in social and safe places. Find varied and multiple ways of making help visible: e.g. physical and virtual noticeboards, programme handbooks, signage on doors. Pace help-giving for different stages in the learning cycle: induction, first encounters with subject discipline, first assessment, feedback, progression, approaching final stages, graduation and alumni opportunities.

presents help-seeking and help-giving recommendations grounded in what we have learned from insider voices and research.

Theme 5: Willingness to change

> *be ready and able to change quickly as different circumstances become apparent.*
> (CSB, Otto)

Whilst there are some kinds of change one might actively resist, many of the participants found changes they did commit to were sources of deep learning. Katya, for example, describes throughout these chapters her struggles to extract what she *must* change to succeed, and what she preferred *not* to change, as she adapted between three cultures. She did adapt her ways of writing academically to achieve success, but she struggled to decide whether or not to adopt politeness strategies, which seemed insincere. Aidan, whom we met in earlier chapters, described the way he had to relearn his idea of socialising when he moved to Japan. He was mortified to realise that gift-giving was expected when you visited a family, and to realise he had missed this important act of courtesy. He talks of the "*danger of sticking to habits you are used to*" and advised institutions to "*make it easier for them to mix with local students*" (CSB, Aidan).

Otto, as a visiting academic, describes the specific changes he made as he finely tuned his response to teaching computer studies in a South African university.

I loved being in a classroom environment where I was not only challenged by the students and their expectations, but also by having to adapt material to take into account the different cultural, political, legal and ethical environments.

I was completely invigorated about tackling the challenges and putting in place on-the-spot changes. I had to change the material that I covered in my module from a political point of view, both in terms of some of the legal and ethical material that I cover in the teaching of digital forensics, but also taking into account the political environment in South Africa. There were a few 'think on your feet' moments. (CSB, Otto)

'Thinking on your feet' and 'letting go of habitual ways of thinking' also suggest different timing. Otto responded 'on the spot' to taboos and sensitivities with the class in front of him. In contrast, Katya's process of change was slowly learnt and painful, and included a struggle with her own sense of self as a learner. She explains that only eventually did she realise how much she had learnt.

A useful framework for these different timings can be found in Schön's idea of the reflective practitioner (1983). He proposed reflections as preparation for action, as in our section above on preparedness for change; reflection that happens spontaneously *in* action and reflection *on* action looking back after the event. This model can be helpful to track the kind of change that is instantaneous, compared to change that is slowly learnt and painstakingly developed. In addition, Barkhuizen (2011) analyses teacher narratives in terms of where one can change the story and where one cannot. We saw Carmel, with her Saudi Arabian young women, struggling to change their culture of socialising and eating in class, realising there were limits to what she could do and resigning herself to doing the best within those limits. Thus, as we develop learning maps for change, we need to take account of spontaneous and slowly learnt change, desirable and undesirable change, and achievable change versus becoming resigned to limitations.

Some of the boxes in Table 10.6 are left open for you the reader to complete for yourself on the basis of your own needs, wishes, situation and experiences. The questions direct you to be aware of where you have agency and where you do not; and if not, who does have this agency for change.

Theme 6: Building independence

> Letting them know it's far more important to be independent than they are used to. (CSB, Carmel)
>
> Maybe it needs to made clear they have to do things off their own bat. (CSB, Aidan)

Many of the participants in all four projects reported that they were on their own, and required to be independent, more than they had expected. In some

Table 10.6 Learning map 6: Changing habits and Schon's moments of reflection (Schon, 1983)

	Learners	*Educators*	*Institutions*
Reflection for action: What might you need to do *before* an event to get the best from it?	What questions should you prepare in advance of a tutorial? What reading should you do in advance of a lecture?	Plan in advance clear ground rules so everyone in the class knows what they are expected to do: who is responsible for what and when.	Multiple aspects of event planning.
Reflection in action: What 'on the spot' responses have you made that helped you?		Recognise when a question opens up your own assumptions about what is known or not known. Respond to the assumptions behind the question (both yours and the learner's) as well as to the surface.	
Reflection on action: Reviewing after the event, what might you change for the next time?	Notice where you were unprepared for a class or session. Consider what you might need to do to be better prepared next time.	Create a cycle by which information from, and reflections on, one session feeds into planning of the next.	Encourage learner response to events, inductions and systems: invite questions, stories, insights. Draw on these insights to develop, clarify and adapt systems.

ways, they also admitted, it is hard to be prepared for this expectation through explanation alone. Annabel (CSB) is clear *"the learning has to come from experience"*. Yet we have seen that taking the initiative has challenges for the newcomer. How is it to be done? What is appropriate and what is not? Clear communication within the department helped, such as instructions about student responsibilities, and clear indications of how and when they could seek help. However, fostering independence clearly means leaving room for growth. Educators cannot legislate when and how learning will happen, nor which particular aspects will be most helpful. Katya, describing her own experience as both learner and teacher, comments:

> I believe it's okay for this process to be a little rough around the edges sometimes, because that's what life is and we should not patronise students, but should let them figure things out for themselves, with our support and gentle guidance. (CSB Katya)

We know there are certain qualities of mind which are helpful in coping with these 'rough edges'. 'Growth mindset' is identified in extensive studies as the quality which successful, even high-flying individuals have in common in business, in the professions, as well as in learning places (Dweck, 2016). Dweck describes its central premise as the belief that you can develop, "through hard work, good strategies, and input from others" (Dweck, 2016, 2). It is this self-belief which leads a learner to recover from setbacks and challenges, and to turn discomfort around so it becomes a source of learning. The opposite of this is the fixed mindset that makes a learner defensive and insecure. Dweck's research identifies blocks to growth mindset, such as being competitive, trying to appear smart, seeing setbacks as weakness, and being afraid to seek help when needed. The learning map in Table 10.7 derives from growth mindset research and invites the reader to think about their own relationship to growth and learning as the essential ingredients to becoming independent learners.

Theme 7: Intercultural as inclusive

> the global student

Another helpful realisation for many of the participants, was that they were not alone in their experience. Gerda, for example, found it a revelation that students studying in their first language found academic reading as hard to understand as she did. Lihua was amazed that some of the students who failed the same written assignment were home students studying in their first culture. In other words, it was helpful to realise the challenges of a new study experience were shared by others and did not belong exclusively to those with a 'different' language, culture or background. One participant characterises this discovery in her first message to institutions: "*stop thinking about students in two separate groups*" (CSB Pattie). To classify students as 'international' seemed not only divisive and unhelpful, but did not represent a useful reality. In the *Fostering Interculturality* project, staff identifying as international did not appreciate questions asking if they related better to international staff as opposed to home staff.

> Why would I? It doesn't make sense to me. I relate to colleagues because they share my interests, because we have the same sense of humour, because we are neighbours. Why would I care if they came from the same country or not? It just isn't a category that makes sense. (FIC)

Table 10.7 Learning map 7: Growth mindset and learning independence

Triggers (Dweck, 2016)	Learners	Educators	Institutions
Triggers to fixed mindset			
Receiving criticism	Respond to criticism as the opportunity to improve. Seek explanations where judgements are unclear.	Present criticism as constructive feedback. Use language that is developmental rather than judgmental.	Build in opportunities for learners to make mistakes and try again: for example, formative assessment.
Faring poorly beside others	Track your own progress between one task and the next, rather than by comparison with others.	Encourage students to learn from and share best work so grades are developmental. Give learners indications of their own personal progress.	Do not publish grades.
Competitive rewards		Celebrate successes rather than pitting students against one another.	Celebrate successes widely rather than selectively and on the basis of limited criteria.
Triggers to growth mindset			
Sharing information	Talk to students whose work is interesting or whose work you admire.	Publish best work with the permission of their authors.	
Collaboration	Share your own strengths and recognise the strengths of others.	Encourage students to learn from one another, e.g. syndicated reading circles; shared research projects; peer review of writing in progress.	
Seeking feedback	Ask for explanations if judgements are unclear. Use feedback as an opportunity to learn.	Make feedback precise, action-focused and constructive.	
Admitting errors	Consider errors as a way of knowing what not to do next time.	Discuss anonymised errors in class to model the fact that errors are part of the learning process.	

Alison (CSB), who had studied and worked in Russia, China and India, found a great deal more united these experiences than divided them. She noted that there were *"shared values across the globe"* even though the actual way of doing things might have surface differences, and even though students brought with them different knowledge and experience. They had similar desires to take control of their learning, to make a contribution short-term in their study sessions and long-term to their communities. Alison's experience is strongly supported by other studies of student experience, such as Littlewood (2000) or Rich (2005), who also found there were more similarities in approach between students from Asian and Western countries, than there were differences.

These studies, and the experiences of our participants, suggest that we need to rethink the idea of 'international' as a way of classifying either students or skills. There is no value in suggesting strategies based on where we come from specifically, or what our first language is in comparison to our study language. It is more generative and inclusive to think instead of 'intercultural competences', which help us navigate new situations and become citizens of the world. In Chapter 1 we looked at three different approaches to learning across cultural borders. The first was Byram's notion of 'savoirs'. These are five ways of knowing, which focus on what the learner should do, know or think to learn about a new culture (Byram, 1997). The second are frameworks for developing intercultural competence, which draw on the whole person and entail noticing both self and the new culture. Mader and Camerer (2010), for example, suggested eight components of intercultural competence, which include comparisons between home and host countries, and analysis of both surface and underlying philosophies. The third approach mentioned in Chapter 1 was social and pragmatic competence: analysing the semantics of human interactions to determine what is appropriate and typical, as in Kecskés (2013) and Wierzbicka (2003).

Each of these start from a slightly different place: the learner's doing and knowing, linguistic or non-linguistic interactions, or the self in relation to the culture. However, each of them problematise the idea of 'international' as submerging multiple differences into one kind of 'difference' by comparison with a host culture. The learning map in Table 10.8 suggests how these different perspectives can be drawn on to make the learner, the classroom and the institution places of intercultural exchange. The table also directs the reader to places in the book where they can find more information and ideas.

The learning maps have been constructed as a means to bring together the sources of discomfort in our learner stories, and tools for resolving them: by analysing, classifying, comparing, deconstructing, revisiting or simply noticing. The insider stories suggest questions and offer answers, but they also are a reminder that these answers are different for each situation and each individual. It is not cultures we interact with but people, situations and one another. This leaves many questions still to ask. Should we study specific kinds of students in specific places? When we read a good novel or short

Table 10.8 Learning map 8: Intercultural not international (Byram's savoirs, 1995 and Mader's intercultural abilities, 2010)

Byram's savoirs	Mader and Camerer's eight components of ICC	Learning maps and chapters in this book
Savoir etre: Learning attitudes	Ability to engage with otherness in a relationship of equality.	Learning map 7: Interacting with a growth mindset Chapter 4: Ways of learning
Savoir comprendre: Interpreting and relating skills	Knowledge of the types of cause and process of misunderstanding between interlocutors of different cultural origin.	Learning map 3: Questions and answers and teasing out tacit knowledge Chapter 9: Kinds of feedback
Savoir: Knowing	Knowledge about the processes and institutions of socialisation in one's own and in one's interlocutor's country.	Learning map 1: Preparing for differences by researching your new place of study Learning map 4: Noticing map
Savoir apprendre: Discovery or interaction skills	Ability to engage with politeness conventions and rites of verbal and non-verbal communication and interaction.	Learning map 2: Co-operative principles and asking questions Learning map 4: Noticing map
Savoir s'engager: Critical cultural awareness	Ability to mediate between conflicting interpretations of phenomena.	Chapter 5: Ways of knowing

story, the more specific the story in its human detail, the more closely we can relate to it. Can that be the same with research too, and is the gathering of stories something we should do more often as educators and researchers? As we see that these stories begin to share themes, questions and experiences, does that mean our insights become more specifically valuable or less so as we are tempted to make generalisations? In Chapter 4 we suggested readers think about autobiographies of two writers who were refugees as children and learnt and grew up between several cultures. What do their insider stories give us that research might miss out, or conversely, can research provide a context for their stories, which gives them even greater reach? We have suggested too, in Chapter 2, that we should take care to listen closely to voices that are not heard often enough, or become drowned out by louder and more visible ones. How can research help these voices to be heard, and build on them so they too become part of what we know and act on?

The stories we have shared through the chapters of this book suggest that there can be no straightforward route that will make the transition across learning borders seamless. Part of the learning is that it will not be, and that the nature of the challenges will be finely tuned to place and individual. One story does shine a light on others, but in the end does not replace the experience itself. Several of our insiders have admitted that no programme of study, set of guidelines, or roadmap can really cover all the surprises and setbacks they are likely to find on the way. However, what this book hopes to be is a companion on this journey, offering echoes and parallels, and different tools for safer navigation.

References

Barkhuizen, G. (2011) 'Narrative knowledging in Tesol', *TESOL Quarterly*, 45 (3), pp. 391–414.

Byram, M. (1997) *Teaching and assessing intercultural communicative competence.* Clevedon: Multilingual Matters.

Carbaugh, D. and van Over, B. (2013) 'Interpersonal pragmatics and cultural discourse', *Journal of Pragmatics*, 58, pp. 142–145.

Clifford, V., Adeunji, H., Haigh, M., Henderson, J., Spiro, J. and Hudson, J. (2011) *Report on Brookes Student Learning Experience Project: Fostering Interculturality and Global Perspectives at Brookes through Dialogue with Staff.* Oxford Centre for Staff Learning and Development: Oxford Brookes University.

Dweck, C. (2016) 'What having a "growth mindset" actually means', *Harvard Business Review*, 13 January2016 [online]. Available at: https://hbr.org/2016/01/what-having-a-growth-mindset-actually-means. (Accessed: 8 June 2021).

Grice, H.P. (1975) 'Logic and conversation' in Cole, P. and Morgan, J. (eds.) *Studies in Syntax and Semantics III: Speech Acts.* New York: Academic Press, pp. 183–198.

Kecskés, I. (2013) *Intercultural pragmatics.* Oxford: Oxford University Press.

Littlewood, W. (2000) 'Do Asian students really want to listen and obey?' *English Language Teaching Journal*, 54 (1), pp. 31–36.

Mader, J. and Camerer, R. (2010) 'International English and the training of intercultural communicative competence', *Intercultural Journal*, 9 (12), pp. 97–116.

McCune, V., Tauritz, R., Boyd, S., Cross, A., Higgins, P. and Scoles, J. (2021) 'Teaching wicked problems in higher education: ways of thinking and practising', *Teaching in Higher Education*, doi:10.1080/13562517.2021.1911986 Available at: www.tandfonline.com/action/showCitFormats?doi=10.1080%2F13562517.2021.1911986&area=0000000000000001 (Accessed: 26 June 2021).

Murray, N. (2010) 'Pragmatics, awareness raising and the co-operative principle', *English Language Teaching Journal*, 64, pp. 283–301.

Philipsen, G. (2010) 'Some thoughts on how to approach finding one's feet in unfamiliar cultural terrain', *Communication Monographs*, 77 (2), pp. 160–168.

Rich, S. (2005) 'Linguistically and culturally diverse students' perceptions of successful classroom practices in a UK graduate program', *Across the Disciplines,* 2*(Special Issue).* Available at:http://wac.colostate.edu/atd/lds/rich.cfm (Accessed: 20 October 2011).

Schon, D. (1983) *The reflective practitioner: how professionals think in action.* London: Temple-Smith.

Spiro, J. (2013) 'The reflective continuum: reflecting for change and student response to reflective tasks', *Brookes eJournal of Learning and Teaching*, 2013.

Spiro, J. (2014) 'Learning Interconnectedness: internationalisation through engagement with one another', *Higher Education Quarterly*, 68 (1), p65–84.

Spiro, J., Henderson, J. and Clifford, V. (2012) 'Independent learning crossing cultures: learning cultures and shifting meanings', *Compare: A Journal of Comparative and International Education*, 42 (4), pp. 607–619.

Strange, H. and Gibson, H.J. Frontiers (2017) 'An investigation of experiential and transformative learning in study abroad programs', *The Interdisciplinary Journal of Study Abroad*, 29 (1) pp. 85–100.

Wierzbicka, A. (2003) *Cross-cultural pragmatics: the semantics of human interaction.* 2nd edn. Berlin: Mouton de Gruyter (Mouton Textbook).

Williams. K., Wooliams, M. and Spiro, J. (2013) *Reflective writing.* Basingstoke: Palgrave Macmillan.

Index

Alphabetical

academic writing 62–63, 148
active learning 59, **118**
Adisa, T. 27–**30**
assessment literacy 183–187
assessment: case studies **153**; essays 146–157, **159**; exams 149–152; papers 145, 152, 154, **157, 159**; presentations 145, 153, 155; report writing 160; tutorials 151, 170, 183–185
assignment 145–148, 150, 153–155, 160
autonomy 69–71, 76–77

BAME 16, 22–29, 111
Becher, T. 95
belonging 9, 22, 26, 28–29, 37, 95, 124
Bloom, H. **159**, 175
Bloom's taxonomy 155–157, 175
Byram, M. 2, 10, 208–209

Camerer, R. 2, 208–209
campus: libraries 124, 128; student union 19, 124–126; classroom 124, 126, 128, 131–132
Carbaugh, D. 10, 27, 200
classroom 104, 106–107, 114, **118**; learner-centred 60–61
class discussion 9, 60, 142, 188
Clifford, V. 4, 12
Covid 7, 12, 76, 103, 104, 109, 116–117, 124
criteria 149–150, 171–172, 175–178, 183–184, 187
criticality 71–72, 84, 175
cultural codes 16, 23–24, 66
cultural competence see intercultural competence

cultural pragmatics 5, 10
Currant, N. 22–23, 28, 111, 184

discourse: spoken 104, 113–116, 118–119; written 158, 160–163, 174, 185–187
disciplinary knowledge 92, **98**,
Dweck, C. 73, 206, **207**

emotion 10, 26, **131**, 170, 182, 185–186
emotional intelligence 29–**30**
employability 70, 93
Evans, S. 52, 74, 116

face-saving 172, 200
fairness 155, 182–185
feedback: formative 152, 170–172, 185; on essays 170–171, 185; on exams 170–171; on papers 172, 175, 179, 183, 186; supervision 112
Finkelstein, M. 50, **51**
first encounter 2, 29, **30**, 170, 173, **203**
formality 45
forms of address 3, 45

grades 145, 150–154, 158, 170–171, 178 (about 86) see also marks
genre 96, 158, **159**, 163
graduate attributes 93–94
Grice, H.P. 10, 196–**197**
group work 3, 64, 72
growth mindset 73, 206–**207, 209**

habits 53, 58, 155, 203, **205**
Haigh, M. **30**, 31
hedging 23, 32, 44, 96
help-seeking 23, 200–203

hidden: challenges 67; codes 26–27; cultures 4, 27, 97, 147; knowledge 97; values 38, 45, 95
home-like spaces 132–133
hybrid learning 104
Hyland, K. 96, 160, **161**, 173–174, 186–187

identity 10, 124–125, 132–134; learner 26, 28–29; teacher 53
independence 67–71, 75–76, 117, 130, 132, 194, 204–**207**
induction 49, **199, 203, 205** see also first encounters
insider stories 5–9
intercultural competence 1–2, 9–10

learning: co-learning 115, compliance 67, 78, 85, 99 148–149; creativity 70–76, 84–85, 147–149
learning events:
lecture 103–119
libraries see campus
literacies 10, **98**, 145, 185–187

Mader, J. 208–**209**
marks 8, 39, 119, 151–153, 155, 169, 170, 172, 175, 177–178, 180–183; *see also* grades
mission statement 51–53, 67, 92–99, 126
Morrison, B. 52, 74, 116
Murray, R. 160, 196, **197**

narratives 6, 18, 64, 83, 124, 184, 204; *see also* vignettes
Nesi, H. 158–161
noticing 2, 194, 199–**201**, 208–**209**

Online learning 104–105, 124, 135–140; *see also* virtual learning
Osborn, M. 115

Philipsen, G. 15, 27, 32, 200
plagiarism 148, 165
portfolios 48, 70, **118**,
praxis 86–87, 93–95, **98**

Questions: Asking questions 195 – 197; Asking questions about assessment 157; Asking questions about text types 162 – 163

Reflection 158 – 159, 173, 205
Reflective writing See reflection
rubric 158–160, 171–173, 184

savoirs see Byram, M.
scholarship 41, 47, 51–53, 83, 86, **98**,
Schon, D. 204–**205**
Scott, D. 5, 11, 27, 64, 91, 185
self-esteem 28, 37, 39, 74, 116, 169, 182, 185
seminar 103, 105–106, 109–111, 113–114, **118**, 185, 196, 200
session 3, 108
silence 60, 107–108, 128
social spaces 63, 125, 127
socialising 18, 26, 30, 63–67, 125, 132, 203–204
soft skills 74, 84, 93
student groups 27–28
student union see campus
subject discipline 47, 51, 75, 81–83, 86, 94–97, 117, **118**, 135, 146–148, 173, 186, 193, 195, **197, 203**
supervision 103, 111–112

tacit knowledge 95, 146, 195–196, 198–**199, 209**
teaching culture 2, 37
text types 156–160, 163–164, 175, **201**
transferable skills 42, 86, 93–94
transformation 60, 78, 93
Trowler, P.R. 95
tutorial 74, 103, 109, 111–112, **118**, 119, 195, 198, 200–201, **205**

uncertainty 95–96

van Over, B. 10
vignettes 7–9, 11, 49, 71, 74, 79, 130, 134, 154–155, 163, 181, 186–187, 194; *see also* narratives
Virtual: communities 43; learning 104, 135, 138; placements 136; spaces 13, 104, 109, 111, 116–117, 124, 134–136

wellbeing 74, 116, 124–125, 132–134, **203**
Wenger, E. **163**
Wingate, U. 96, **159**

For Product Safety Concerns and Information please contact our EU representative GPSR@taylorandfrancis.com
Taylor & Francis Verlag GmbH, Kaufingerstraße 24, 80331 München, Germany

www.ingramcontent.com/pod-product-compliance
Lightning Source LLC
Chambersburg PA
CBHW051612230426
43668CB00013B/2075